REA's Test Prep Books Are The Best!

(a sample of the <u>hundreds of letters</u> REA receives each year)

" I did well because of your wonderful prep books... I just wanted to thank you for helping me prepare for these tests. "
Student, San Diego, CA

" My students report your chapters of review as the most valuable single resource they used for review and preparation. "
Teacher, American Fork, UT

" Your book was such a better value and was so much more complete than anything your competition has produced (and I have them all!) "
Teacher, Virginia Beach, VA

" Compared to the other books that my fellow students had, your book was the most helpful in helping me get a great score. "
Student, North Hollywood, CA

" Your book was responsible for my success on the exam, which helped me get into the college of my choice... I will look for REA the next time I need help. "
Student, Chesterfield, MO

" Just a short note to say thanks for the great support your book gave me in helping me pass the test... I'm on my way to a B.S. degree because of you! "
Student, Orlando, FL

" The gem of the book is the tests. They were indicative of the actual exam. The explanations of the answers are practically another review session. "
Student, Fresno, CA

(more on next page)

(continued from front page)

" I just wanted to thank you for helping me get a great score
on the AP U.S. History... Thank you for making great test preps! "
Student, Los Angeles, CA

" Your *Fundamentals of Engineering Exam* book was the absolute best
preparation I could have had for the exam, and it is one of the major
reasons I did so well and passed the FE on my first try. "
Student, Sweetwater, TN

" I used your book to prepare for the test and found that the advice and the
sample tests were highly relevant... Without using any other material, I earned
very high scores and will be going to the graduate school of my choice. "
Student, New Orleans, LA

" What I found in your book was a wealth of information sufficient to shore up
my basic skills in math and verbal... The section on analytical ability was
excellent. The practice tests were challenging and the answer explanations
most helpful. It certainly is the Best Test Prep for the GRE! "
Student, Pullman, WA

" I really appreciate the help from your excellent book. Please keep
up with your great work."
Student, Albuquerque, NM

" I used your *CLEP Introductory Sociology* book and rank it 99% — thank you! "
Student, Jerusalem, Israel

" The painstakingly detailed answers in the sample tests are the most helpful
part of this book. That's one of the great things about REA books. "
Student, Valley Stream, NY

(more on back page)

The Best Test Preparation for the

U.S. POSTAL EXAMS

Entrance Test Battery 470 & Rural Carrier Test 460

With Two CDs for the Audio Section of the Exams

Staff of Research & Education Association
Dr. M. Fogiel, Director

Research & Education Association
61 Ethel Road West
Piscataway, New Jersey 08854

The Best Test Preparation for the
U.S. POSTAL EXAMS
Entrance Test Battery 470 &
Rural Carrier Test 460
with Audio CDs for the Exams

Printed in the United States of America

Library of Congress Control Number 2003104226

International Standard Book Number 0-87891-080-8

Research & Education Association
61 Ethel Road West
Piscataway, New Jersey 08854

ABOUT RESEARCH & EDUCATION ASSOCIATION

Research & Education Association (REA) is an organization of educators, scientists, and engineers specializing in various academic fields. Founded in 1959 with the purpose of disseminating the most recently developed scientific information to groups in industry, government, high schools, and universities, REA has since become a successful and highly respected publisher of study aids, test preps, handbooks, and reference works.

REA's Test Preparation series includes study guides for all academic levels in almost all disciplines. Research & Education Association publishes test preps for students who have not yet completed high school, as well as high school students preparing to enter college. Students from countries around the world seeking to attend college in the United States will find the assistance they need in REA's publications. For college students seeking advanced degrees, REA publishes test preps for many major graduate school admission examinations in a wide variety of disciplines, including engineering, law, and medicine. Students at every level, in every field, with every ambition can find what they are looking for among REA's publications.

Unlike most test preparation books—which present only a few practice tests that bear little resemblance to the actual exams—REA's series presents tests that accurately depict the official exams in both degree of difficulty and types of questions. REA's practice tests are always based upon the most recently administered exams, and include every type of question that can be expected on the actual exams.

REA's publications and educational materials are highly regarded and continually receive an unprecedented amount of praise from professionals, instructors, librarians, parents, and students. Our authors are as diverse as the fields represented in the books we publish. They are well-known in their respective disciplines and serve on the faculties of prestigious high schools, colleges, and universities throughout the United States and Canada.

ACKNOWLEDGMENTS

We would like to thank Dr. Max Fogiel, President, for his overall guidance, which brought this publication to completion; Nicole Mimnaugh, Manager of New Book Development, for directing the editorial staff through each phase of the project; Larry B. Kling, Quality Control Manager, for supervising revisions; Lara DeMeo, Project Editor, for coordinating development of the book; Teresina Jonkoski, Editorial Assistant, for coordinating revisions for this edition; Robert Coover, Jen Kovacs, Kristin Massaro, Cara Lemantovich, Craig Yetsko, and Christine Zardecki for their editorial contributions; Robert Gelinas for narrating the Oral Examinations; Paul Sukovich of Suite 16 Studios, Piscataway, N.J., for recording the Oral Exam audio tapes; and Paula Musselman for typesetting the manuscript.

TABLE OF CONTENTS

Chapter 3: Strategies for Improving on "Address Checking" 61

Chapter 4: Strategies for Improving on "Memory for Addresses" 85

Chapter 1

Applying to the Postal Service

Chapter 1

APPLYING TO THE POSTAL SERVICE

CONSIDERING A CAREER WITH THE POSTAL SERVICE

Printer, publisher, author, inventor, diplomat, musician, scientist—Benjamin Franklin was many things. Among his most important and challenging jobs: serving as postmaster general for the 13 colonies that would become the United States of America. "To do this," Franklin would write in his autobiography, "a variety of improvements were necessary...." Upon his appointment by the Second Continental Congress in 1775, he set a course that made the postal system profitable and efficient. Faced with a new government that needed to communicate to its citizens, and businesses and individuals that needed a way to stay in touch with each other, he laid the foundation for a system that could move correspondence dependably from Point A to Point B and back.

Founded on Sept. 26, 1789, the Post Office Department became a permanent federal agency in 1792. Today's United States Postal Service—transformed into an independent establishment of the Executive Branch in 1971— has become one of the largest and most efficient entities of any kind in the world, delivering more than 200 billion pieces of mail annually. The Postal Service employs more than 800,000 people, who process and carry more mail to more people over a larger geographic area than in any other country. Retirements and expansion have created the need for tens of thousands of new employees in recent years. The USPS offers a secure career with good pay and opportunities for advancement, which makes working for the Postal Service a wise investment in your future.

If you're interested in job security, consider that the Postal Service must grow with the nation and is entwined in its very fabric. The U.S. Postal Service offers a solid array of benefits, including health and life insurance, a retirement plan, a savings/investment plan with employer contribution, a flexible spending account, flextime scheduling of core work hours, and annual and sick leave. Qualified applicants must pass a pre-employment drug screening to meet the requirement to be drug free. Applicants must also be U.S. citizens or have permanent resident alien status.

Opportunities for advancement abound. USPS policy directs that employee promotions be made solely on ability, without regard to race, sex, age, or political-party affiliation. On-the-job training and advancement courses are offered. Automation devices and computers are becoming indispensable in today's Postal Service. Consider that training on this type of high-tech equipment will serve you in any number of fields in which you might work later. While new technologies typically create the specter of job elimination, in the case of the Postal Service one needs to consider that the volume of mail has continued to increase. An ever-increasing population, along with the increase in direct-mail advertising that comes with an expanding economy, keeps the need for postal workers high. If you think that e-mail could threaten the postal business, remember that the Postal Service is itself a major e-mail service provider. In fact, after two and a quarter centuries, the Postal Service is as dedicated as ever to achieving the kind of innovation and efficiency championed— and achieved— by Ben Franklin.

DESCRIPTION OF POSITIONS

An employee of the Postal Service has the opportunity to transfer to other locations or bid for other positions. It is important to keep on top of advancements in the various positions. Because you will be making a career choice to enter the Postal Service, a lot of thought may be necessary when choosing the position for which you will be applying. Included here are brief descriptions of the major positions for which you may apply. It is a good idea to speak with a representative from the USPS before you choose this career path. Speak with family or friends employed by the USPS, your local carrier, the postmaster at your local office, or even a window clerk if there is a lull in the action at the window.

Carrier – City, Rural
Requirements: 470 Battery Test and Driving Test

The job of postal carrier may be the most recognized position in the Postal Service. Postal carriers find their jobs extremely rewarding, citing the relationship that they develop with their communities as one of the major pluses of the job. There are also many behind-the-scenes requirements of a mail carrier.

Carriers typically arrive early for their jobs, between 6 a.m. and 8 a.m. The mail must be sorted, racked, and tied before it can be loaded on the truck. Carriers must also check on changes of address, undeliverable mail, and special deliveries, such as COD, which involve customers on their route. If you work as a rural carrier you may sell stamps, carrier scales, and other mailing equipment, and take other services to those customers who cannot visit a town office.

The advantages of this job are many. Carriers can work at their own pace as long as the mail is delivered by a specific time. A relationship can be built between the carrier and the community. Carriers can serve as crime or emergency watchers, looking for mail left overnight or a suspiciously open door. They can also serve to aid lost pedestrians, especially children. If you like exercise in the outdoors, this position may be right for you. Expect a lot of exposure to the outdoors, in both good and bad weather.

Distribution Clerk
Requirements: 470 Battery Test and Eye Exam

Distribution clerks may work either at the front window or in the distribution center. Letters must be grouped into categories: letters, parcel post, and magazines and newspapers. The letters are either fed into stamp cancelling machines or are cancelled by hand. They are then taken to be sorted by destination: local area, nearby state, groups of distant states, or large individual cities. For instance, mail to New York or Chicago will be sorted into its own bin. If an automatic machine is being used, the clerk must enter codes which will instruct the machine to send the mail to the correct bin. Larger postal centers may have clerks working around the clock. Night workers usually receive a higher salary. It is necessary for a distribution clerk to have good eyesight. A candidate for this position will need to attain a good reading score on the eye exam to be considered. Corrective lenses are permitted.

Window clerks are responsible for helping customers who visit the post office. They may sell stamps, write money orders, register mail, weigh packages for correct postage, or check packages to make sure they are sturdy enough to be mailed.

Flat Sorting Machine Operator
Requirement: 470 Battery Test

Flat sorting machine operators must be able to handle a physically demanding job. They are responsible for handling large packages. They will be trained on automated machines to sort packages.

Mark-Up Clerk
Requirements: 470 Battery Test and Typing Test

A person in this position will be utilizing a CFS, or computerized forwarding system, which is among the newest technology on the scene. The clerk must use the computer to generate a database of the customers who have recently changed their addresses and the machine to make labels for the mail being rerouted for these customers.

Mail Handler
Requirements: 470 Battery Test and Fitness Test

Mail handlers have one of the most physically demanding jobs in the Postal Service. They are required to lift heavy items, up to 70 lbs. Work is done mainly in the dock area, loading and unloading mail. They may also work in the mail cancelling section, moving mail from one location to another. Mail handlers are trained on many pieces of equipment: forklifts, rewrapping machines, addressographs, and mimeographs. A physical test is required, consisting of being able to carry two 70 lb. bags to a truck, moving it to another area, unloading the truck, then returning it to its original position.

Mail Processor
Requirement: 470 Battery Test

Mail processors use a special automated machine called an OCR, or optical character reader. This machine reads the bar codes found on many labeled pieces of mail. Mail processors also collate, bundle, and then load the mail into the appropriate bins. Because mail processors have knowledge of the computerized equipment, they may help to troubleshoot for the equipment.

Rural Carrier Associate
Requirement: 460 Rural Carrier Associate Exam

Rural Carrier Associates are noncareer USPS employees. They either serve as a leave replacement in the absence of a regular rural carrier or provide extra service like selling stamps and other mailing equipment on auxiliary routes. After one year of service, an associate has bidding rights to USPS career vacancies as they occur.

APPLYING

Are You Eligible?

Before you begin the work necessary to apply to take the postal exam, you should read the following list. If you can answer "yes" to all of the questions, then you are eligible to take the test. If you answer "no" to a question, you should speak with a postal service representative before investing your time and effort.

- Are you a high school graduate or certified through local authorities to have terminated formal education for a valid reason?

- Will you be 18 years of age at the time of employment (not necessarily when you take the exam)?

- Are you a U.S. citizen or do you hold permanent resident alien status?

- Can you pass a routine physical including tests for hearing and sight and a urinalysis test that screens for illegal substances?

When to Apply

This may be the trickiest part of obtaining a Postal Service career. On average the 470 Battery Test is given only once every three years by any postal center. Some larger postal centers give the test more frequently. The 460 RCA Exam is given at least once a year. Some districts offer it several times a year, depending on the need for new employees. The tests are not given at the same time in every office so you will have to do some searching. First, you need to identify the area to which you would like to apply. You can do this by receiving information on office locations through your local post office. On the application you will be asked to choose three specific post offices. You need to find out when the next set of tests will be given for the area you have chosen to concentrate on. It will be necessary to call the personnel office or visit the postal bulletin board to check for registration announcements. You may also subscribe to a listing of government jobs, which will list registration dates. Some offices may post announcements over public service stations. You must be active in your search for registration periods. It is not unlikely that the office will accept registration for only one week. If you would consider commuting to a further location, you may find a test in another area that will be given sooner than the one in your area of initial interest. It is possible to transfer once you have established yourself in your job.

Some postal districts offer a different type of registration and testing system. OPTEX, Open Testing Exam System, uses a longer application period so you may have an easier time applying in one of these districts. To use this system, your name is put into a computer which then randomly draws names of applicants to sit for the exam as the need to hire arises. On the positive side, this system usually offers exams more frequently than the traditional testing pattern. However, you may spend some time waiting for your name to be drawn randomly from the list of applicants. It is a chance that some people take, hoping to be one of the lucky ones who have their name drawn early.

You may take this exam more than once. However, if you are taking the exam for the same position, you may not take the same version of the test that you previously took. You will need to wait until the Postal Service changes editions. Taking as many tests for as many positions as possible will benefit you by keeping your name readily available.

How to Fill Out an Application

Once you learn that they are accepting applications, go to the personnel department and pick one up. The application will have two parts for you to fill in. It is important to complete both sections carefully and accurately. Any application not completed correctly will be discarded. Keep the two sections together. Separated applications will also be discarded. The reverse side of the application contains the directions necessary to complete the application. It would benefit you to complete the application as quickly as possible and return it to the personnel department yourself so you need not worry about whether it will make it there in time for the deadline.

Once your application has been processed, you will receive half of the application form back in the mail. It is very important to keep this form, as it will serve as your ticket into the testing room. Along with your application card you will receive information as to where and when the exam will take place. Write this information down in a place you will not forget.

A sample answer sheet will accompany your registration card. It is important to fill this sheet out completely. There are some questions that will require information that may slip your mind come test day. Take this sheet with you to the test center. It will aid you in filling out the official answer sheet the day of the test.

Sample questions will also be sent to you. It is a good idea to complete these questions as you would the questions in this book. A little extra practice can't hurt. Look it over so you know what to expect.

THE DAY OF THE EXAM

Practicing for the postal exam should begin well in advance of the actual exam. Cramming the night before will not benefit you. In fact, it may serve to create stress, which can detract from your score. The night before the exam should be spent in a calm, relaxed fashion. Get plenty of sleep! Be sure to eat a good breakfast so a growling stomach will not cause anxiety or distraction.

When you arrive at the testing center, preferably with time to spare, be sure to have your admission card, sample answer sheet, a picture form of identification— such as a driver's license—and two No. 2 pencils. Consider dressing lightly; you may wish to carry a sweater or jacket, which can be doffed or donned to adjust for the temperature in the room. Whatever you wear, be sure it's comfortable. Leave your house early to allow time for any problems on the road. Latecomers will not be admitted to the test center!

Once you are seated in the exam room, you will be given an official answer sheet onto which you will copy the information that you put on your sample answer sheet. It is important to have your sample sheet with you because you will only be given 15 minutes to transfer the information. You will be asked to choose three specific locations in which you would like employment. It is therefore necessary to have researched this thoroughly beforehand.

You will also be asked to specify the positions for which you are applying. Again, you will have conducted research to find the best position suited to your abilities.

The examiner, along with monitors, will hand out the testing packet. Specific directions are given concerning when to complete certain steps in the testing process. Examiners are very strict on examinee compliance with these directions. You will have your test invalidated if you fail to follow the directions. Listen carefully!

FORMAT OF POSTAL EXAMS 460 AND 470

Late in 1993, the Postal Service changed the format of its testing program. Some tests became obsolete, others were rewritten. Though the 460 RCA Exam and the 470 Battery Test may seem like two different exams, they are identical.

The two tests carry different names because they are administered to two distinct candidate populations. The 460 RCA Exam is for applicants for the noncareer position of Rural Carrier Associate. However, since the RCA has similar responsibilities as a regular carrier and after one year of service has the opportunity to bid for USPS career vacancies, the Postal Service chooses to test RCA applicants in the same way as any other potential employee.

The formats of the 460 RCA Exam and the 470 Battery Test are completely alike. Therefore, all information given in this book is valid for either exam.

There are four parts to the 460 and 470 exams. Each section tests skills that the Postal Service requires in its employees. These qualities include a good memory, quick decision-making ability, and the ability to follow directions. The Postal Service prides itself on being able to deliver its mail quickly and accurately. Included in this section is a brief description of each part of the test along with a few sample questions.

Part One: Address Checking

In this section you will be asked to compare two lists of addresses, deciding if they are alike or different. If the addresses are alike you will darken oval "A"; if they are different you will darken oval "D." This section focuses on speed and accuracy. You will be given six minutes to compare 95 lines of addresses. You are not expected to complete this entire section. The object is to combine a fast enough pace with enough accuracy to get a high score. Here is an example of Part One.

1.	590 Bridge St.	590 Bridje St.	Ⓐ	Ⓓ
2.	3903 Hellington Ave.	3093 Hellington Ave.	Ⓐ	Ⓓ
3.	Central Ave. W.	Central Ave. W.	Ⓐ	Ⓓ
4.	Franklin NJ 08873	Franklin NJ 08837	Ⓐ	Ⓓ
5.	8639 Apt. 3	8936 Apt. 3	Ⓐ	Ⓓ

Answers: D, D, A, D, D

Part Two: Memory for Addresses

In this section you will be given time to memorize five boxes containing addresses and addressee names. You will then be asked to match a given address or name with the letter of the box in which it would be placed. You are given five minutes to complete 88 questions. Memorization and practice time will be given to you so you may prepare for this section sufficiently. Here are some examples.

There are 25 addresses located in these five boxes (A, B, C, D, E). Take five minutes to memorize as best you can the addresses in the boxes. Try looking at each box, covering it up, then repeating what you saw. After the five minutes are up, begin answering the questions. Be sure to cover the boxes. Match the address to the box in which you remember seeing the address.

A	B	C	D	E
4100-4799 Brindle	5100-5399 Brindle	3700-4099 Brindle	5400-5599 Brindle	4800-5099 Brindle
Dewey	Sampson	Bookster	Quinn	Dimartini
3700-4099 Foury	5400-5599 Foury	4800-5099 Foury	5100-5399 Foury	4100-4799 Foury
Langly	Class	Stevenson	Perillo	Onder
5100-5399 Packer	4800-5099 Packer	5400-5599 Packer	4100-4799 Packer	3700-4099 Packer

1. 3700-4099 Brindle   Ⓐ Ⓑ Ⓒ Ⓓ Ⓔ

2. Class   Ⓐ Ⓑ Ⓒ Ⓓ Ⓔ

3. 4100-4799 Brindle   Ⓐ Ⓑ Ⓒ Ⓓ Ⓔ

4. Bookster   Ⓐ Ⓑ Ⓒ Ⓓ Ⓔ

5. 5400-5599 Foury   Ⓐ Ⓑ Ⓒ Ⓓ Ⓔ

6. 4100-4799 Foury   Ⓐ Ⓑ Ⓒ Ⓓ Ⓔ

7. Stevenson   Ⓐ Ⓑ Ⓒ Ⓓ Ⓔ

8. 5100-5399 Packer   Ⓐ Ⓑ Ⓒ Ⓓ Ⓔ

9. Onder   Ⓐ Ⓑ Ⓒ Ⓓ Ⓔ

10. 4800-5099 Brindle   Ⓐ Ⓑ Ⓒ Ⓓ Ⓔ

Answers: C, B, A, C, B, E, C, A, E, E

Part Three: Number Series

Because many positions in the Postal Service require the use of machines, the Postal Service needs to know how you work with numbers. In "number series" you will be asked to look at a series of numbers and decide which two numbers will come next in the series. You will be given five answers to choose from. On the actual test you will be given 20 minutes to complete 24 problems. Try these.

1. 10   11   12   10   11   12   12   10 _____ _____

    (A) 10   11

    (B) 12   10

    (C) 11   10

    (D) 11   12

    (E) 10   12

2. 3   4   10   5   6   10   7   _____   _____
    (A)   10   8
    (B)   9   8
    (C)   8   14
    (D)   8   9
    (E)   8   10

3.   1   3   6   10   15   21   28   36   _____   _____
    (A)   40   48
    (B)   36   45
    (C)   38   52
    (D)   45   56
    (E)   45   55

4. 4   8   8   16   16   32   32   _____   _____
    (A)   32   64
    (B)   36   40
    (C)   64   64
    (D)   64   128
    (E)   64   82

5. 5   86   7   81   10   77   14   _____   _____
    (A)   16   80
    (B)   70   25
    (C)   79   13
    (D)   19   74
    (E)   74   19

Answers: D, E, E, C, E

Part Four: Following Oral Directions

During this portion of the exam, the examiner will read directions that you must follow by writing on a worksheet. After following the directions you will mark your answer on the answer sheet. For example, after the directions are complete, you have formed the combination 39D. You will be asked to darken the oval for row 39 oval (D). Because the directions are only read once, you must be a good listener. While completing this section you will jump around your answer sheet, filling in ovals in a nonsequential pattern. Here is an example of what you will do.

1. Ⓐ Ⓑ Ⓒ Ⓓ Ⓔ

2. Ⓐ Ⓑ Ⓒ Ⓓ ●   2E is the answer arrived at for the fourth question.

3. Ⓐ Ⓑ Ⓒ Ⓓ Ⓔ

4. Ⓐ Ⓑ Ⓒ Ⓓ Ⓔ

5. ● Ⓑ Ⓒ Ⓓ Ⓔ   5A is the answer for the sixth question.

6. Ⓐ Ⓑ Ⓒ Ⓓ Ⓔ

7. Ⓐ Ⓑ Ⓒ Ⓓ Ⓔ

8. Ⓐ Ⓑ Ⓒ Ⓓ Ⓔ

9. Ⓐ Ⓑ Ⓒ Ⓓ Ⓔ

10. Ⓐ Ⓑ Ⓒ Ⓓ ●   10E is the answer for the fifth question.

11. Ⓐ Ⓑ Ⓒ Ⓓ Ⓔ

12. Ⓐ Ⓑ Ⓒ ● Ⓔ   12D is the answer arrived at for the first question.

13. Ⓐ Ⓑ Ⓒ Ⓓ Ⓔ

14. Ⓐ Ⓑ Ⓒ Ⓓ Ⓔ

15. ● Ⓑ Ⓒ Ⓓ Ⓔ   15A is the answer arrived at for the third question.

16. Ⓐ Ⓑ Ⓒ Ⓓ Ⓔ

17. Ⓐ Ⓑ Ⓒ Ⓓ Ⓔ

18. Ⓐ Ⓑ Ⓒ Ⓓ Ⓔ

19. Ⓐ Ⓑ Ⓒ Ⓓ Ⓔ

20. Ⓐ Ⓑ ● Ⓓ Ⓔ   20C is the answer arrived at for the second question.

21. Ⓐ Ⓑ Ⓒ Ⓓ Ⓔ ⎫
                        ⎬   Certain numbers may never be used as an answer and, therefore, will remain blank.
22. Ⓐ Ⓑ Ⓒ Ⓓ Ⓔ ⎭

AFTER THE TEST

When the test is completed, your answer sheet will be sent to a center where a machine will grade your test paper automatically. This is why filling in the ovals correctly is crucial. After the paper is scored you will be given a score. The formula for this scoring is kept top secret. As you proceed through this book you will be scoring your tests, coming up with a raw score. The Postal Service finds your raw score in this same fashion then adjusts it with the confidential formula. Allow four to eight weeks to receive your scores. The passing score is 70. If you score below 70, you will receive a notice stating that your score was not high enough to pass. You will need to try the test again at a later date if you wish to continue the process. If you achieve a passing score you will receive your score along with the location to which your name will be sent.

Once your scores have been sent to the location you specify, you are put on what is called a register of eligibles. This list contains names of those people who are eligible for employment by the Postal Service. Where your name is placed on the list depends on your score. The higher you score, the higher your name will appear on the list. As positions become available and people are called for employment, names are removed. When your name is chosen from the top of the list, you will receive an application for employment. This application must be completed and returned to the post office at which you are being hired. You will be notified of dates and times for an interview and physical.

Names remain on the register of eligibles for a period of two years. If after two years your name has not come up for employment, you may extend your eligibility for another year. Three years is the maximum time a name can spend on an eligibles list. If you wish to have your eligibility extended an extra year, you must put your request in writing to the postmaster between the 18th and 24th month. It is important to remember to put this request in writing. Once two years have elapsed, your name will be stricken from the register unless you notify the post office otherwise.

The last item concerning scoring is the five-to-ten-point preference given to veterans. If a veteran meets certain requirements for serving his or her country, it is assumed he or she should receive preferential treatment. His or her name will be placed five to ten points higher than his or her original score if it is above the 70-point passing mark. This person is placed before all others who receive that same grade. Here is a list of requirements for receiving the veteran's benefit. If you feel you may be eligible for this benefit, you must complete the section on the official answer sheet concerning veterans. You will be asked for proof of this veteran status.

Five extra points are awarded if the applicant served in active duty:

- during a war

- between April 28, 1952, and July 1, 1955

- on any campaign or expedition during which a campaign badge was authorized

- for more than 180 consecutive days any part of which occurred after January 31, 1955, and before October 15, 1976

- in southeast Asia on or after August 2, 1990, and if awarded a Southeast Asia Service Medal

Ten points are added if:

- you were disabled while on active duty or received a Purple Heart Award

- you are a wife of a disabled veteran if the veteran is physically disqualified due to service-connected disabilities to return to his usual occupation

- you are a widow of a serviceman who died on active duty (only if not remarried)

- you are the mother of a deceased or disabled veteran son or daughter, if you are widowed, divorced, or separated or if your present husband is permanently and totally disabled

Chapter 2

Assessing Your Skills

Chapter 2

ASSESSING YOUR SKILLS

PRETEST SUGGESTIONS

This chapter will be used to gauge your ability to take the postal exam as prepared as you are now. It is important to know what you could score on this exam before you begin studying. By doing this you will be able to chart your progress, and if you follow this guide carefully you will make progress. Your first lesson deals with completing the preliminary test answer sheet correctly.

In Chapter 1 you were introduced to the four question types. All of the question types require you to fill in an oval on your answer sheet. Believe it or not there are actually correct and incorrect ways to fill in an oval. The trick is learning to fill the oval in as quickly as possible. Remember, time is a key factor in this test. You do not want to waste time filling in ovals.

Begin all of the exams with a properly prepared pencil. You must bring two #2 pencils into the exam room with you. Prepare your pencil points a day or two before the exam. You can prepare your pencil point in one of two ways. The point should not be pin-point sharp. A dull point is good. This will give you more lead surface on the paper. This means that it will take less movement of the pencil to fill in the oval. Work your pencil point to a dull slant. You may also chisel a 45 degree slant on your pencil point. Work at perfecting this point. The time spent doing this will pay off in the long run. Remember to prepare two pencils with the slanted point.

Because a machine reads your answer sheet, it is important to answer the questions in a manner the machine can read. The oval you choose should be filled in as completely as possible with no lead going over the edge. The machine may understand stray marks as two filled in ovals. This will result in a wrong answer, since only one answer is allowed per line. The following are incorrectly completed answers and a correctly completed answer. Be sure your ovals look like the correct choice.

INCORRECT

CORRECT

Once you understand the correct way to complete your answer choice, you need to perfect filling in the ovals to maximize your time. Because your pencil has a slanted 45 degree angle point, you will be able to cover the oval with a lead mark in one or two swipes of the pencil on the paper. Your arm and hand should not be moving. Small, precise movements by the fingers save you time and energy. Covering the oval in one swipe may not be easy at first. You must remember to cover it completely enough so the computer can read it. Therefore, practice sheets have been provided for you. On the exam you will use an answer sheet that contains from two ovals, for Part One, to five ovals, for Part Two. The practice sheet contains five ovals so you can practice while visualizing any part. The objective here is to become comfortable filling in the blanks with one or two quick swipes of your pencil. This exercise should be taken very seriously. You can actually save time by speeding up your filling-in technique.

Now you are ready to take the preliminary test. The directions for each section have been provided for you as part of the exam. Focus on this preliminary exam as you would on the actual test so you can get a true reading of your strengths and of areas in which you need improvement. Sit at a table where there is ample lighting. Be sure that there are no distracting noises and no possibility of interruption before you have finished the entire preliminary exam. The "Following Oral Directions" section of the test is provided for you on a compact disc. If you do not have access to a compact disc player, transcripts have been included in the Detailed Explanations of Answers. You can have someone read the transcripts to you.

After you have finished the exam, check your answers with the answers provided following the test. Mark your scores on the chart provided. An explanation of the chart follows the exam. Remember to fill in the answer blanks correctly. Warning! Do not panic if you find this test difficult or confusing. Upon completing this book you will feel confident in your ability to pass the real exam with a high score. Techniques to help you begin in Chapter 3. When you have your testing location and atmosphere set and you have a #2 pencil prepared correctly, you can begin the preliminary exam.

DIAGNOSTIC TEST

Address Checking

(Answer sheets appear in the back of this book.)

TIME: 6 Minutes
95 Questions

DIRECTIONS: In this section you will be asked to compare two lists of addresses, deciding if they are alike or different. If the addresses are alike, you will mark oval "A" on your answer sheet; if they are different, you will mark oval "D" on your answer sheet.

1. 372 Hickory Drive   374 Hickory Street
2. 38 Howard Street   38 Howard Street
3. 2112 First St. Apt. 3D   2112 First St. Apt. 3
4. 2009 Interstate 9   2009 Interstate 9
5. 500 Sunnydale Drive   5000 Sunnydale Drive
6. 99 Thistle Lake   99 Thistle Lane
7. 48B First Ave NW   48B First Ave N
8. 75 Route 516   75 Route 516
9. 8001 Hwy. No. 29   9001 Hwy. No. 29
10. 8 Winding Lake Drive   8 Winding Lake Rd
11. 3 Houston Drive   3 Horston Drive
12. 48 Calada Way   48 Kalada Way
13. 38 Lenape Drive   37 Lenape Drive
14. 17 South Flatbush Road   17 South Flatbush Road
15. 205 Washington Avenue   205 Washington Avenue
16. 66 Homestead Lane   66 Homestead Ct.

17.	145 Sullivan Street	143 Sullivan Street
18.	44-B Marting Ct.	44-D Marting Ct.
19.	1014 Lakefront Terr.	1014 Lakefront Ave.
20.	5 Dartmouth Ave. Apt. 3B	5 Dartmouth Ave. Apt. 3B
21.	76 Apple Farm Road	76 Apple Farm Drive
22.	99 Senior Street Apt. 1	99 Senior Street Apt. 1A
23.	35 Division Street	35 Dividing Street
24.	89 S. Altamonte Dr.	89 S. Altamonte Ave
25.	77 Rock Lake	77-C Rock Lake
26.	78 (E) Third Apt. 3B	77 (E) Third Apt..3B
27.	90021 Denver Court	90021 Denver Court
28.	716 Lloyd Dr.	766 Lloyd Dr.
29.	2 Sand Hill Road	20 Sand Hill Road
30.	9 Westfield Road	9 Westfield Road
31.	80 Elkridge Way West	80 Elkridge Way West
32.	1776 Steward St.	1776 Steward St.
33.	71 Quailbrook Ct.	71 Quailbrook Ct.
34.	66 Bethany Rd. West	66 Bethany Rd.
35.	2121 Holyhock Ave.	2112 Holyhock Ave.
36.	989-C N. Falling Hill	989-C N. Falling Hill
37.	55 Prior Terr.	55 Prior Terr.
38.	86 Woodside Rd.	86 Wood Side Rd.
39.	40 Gogol Way	40 Gogel Way
40.	5-H Sycamore Lane	5-I Sycamore Lane
41.	619 Highway 51	619 Highway 51
42.	520 Hudson St. W.	520 Hudson St. W
43.	37 Route 47 South	37 Route 47 North

44.	20129 South Brush	20130 South Brush
45.	820 Winding Brook Way	820 Windy Brook Way
46.	318 W. 14th St.	318 W. 14th St.
47.	5 Jorgenson Lane	5 Jorgensen Lane
48.	69 Johnson Way	69 Johnson Way
49.	10 189th St. W.	10 18th St. W.
50.	52 (E) 96 Street	52 W. 96 Street
51.	5 Route 6115	5 Route 5116
52.	First & Willow	First & Willow
53.	91/2 Danbury	91 Danbury
54.	99 Max Avenue	99 Max Avenue
55.	36 Maya Ct.	36 Mayan Ct.
56.	87 Thirteenth St.	87 Thirtieth St.
57.	7 Vinton Circle	9 Vinton Circle
58.	40 LaGrande Avenue	40 LaGrande Avenue
59.	6889 South Ave.	6898 South Ave.
60.	92 Manatou Way	92 Manatee Way
61.	6887 Route 1783	6887 Route 1783
62.	65 Jupiter Way	65 Juniper Way
63.	91 Horatio St.	91 Horatio St.
64.	1001 Walter St.	10001 Walter St.
65.	29 Mineo Circle	29 Minerva Circle
66.	8D Charles St. W.	8D Charles St. W.
67.	317A Route 28 South	317 Route 28 South
68.	39 Chancellor Court	39 Chancellor Court
69.	87 Tumbleweed Drive	87 Tumbleweed Drive
70.	89 Post Mill Road	89 Post Mill Road

71.	91 Seguso Pl.	910 Seguso Pl.
72.	1017 Johnson Drive	1017 Johnston Drive
73.	4511 Adelaide Ct. Apt. 1D	4511 Adelaide Ct. Apt. 1D
74.	560 Biennial Way	560 Biennial Way
75.	289 Thistle St.	289 Thistle St.
76.	47 Snug Harbor Avenue	47 Snug Harbor Avenue
77.	120-R2 Sanford Street	120-R2 Sanford Street
78.	94 Brooke St.	94 Brook St.
79.	29 Rice Avenue	291 Rice Avenue
80.	732 Campus Drive	732 Campus Drive
81.	54 State Hwy. No. 31	54 State Hwy. No. 31
82.	7121 Glenside Rd.	7121 Glenside Rd.
83.	44C Lamberts Mill	44C Lamberts Mill
84.	61 Elm Street	61 Elm Street
85.	93 Packards Glen	93A Packards Glen
86.	6 Louis Avenue	6 Louise Avenue
87.	48-3000 Gardentree Rd.	48-300 Gardentree Rd.
88.	777 Central	777D Central
89.	68 Austen Avenue W.	68 Austin Avenue W.
90.	5001-A Dover Glen	5001-A2 Dover Glen
91.	298 Sommerville West	298 Sommerville West
92.	20 Dochester Drive	201 Dochester Drive
93.	45 Douthette Ln.	45 Douthette Ln.
94.	23 Brock Avenue W.	23 W. Brock Avenue
95.	5C Brink St.	5C Brink St.

DIAGNOSTIC TEST

Memory for Addresses

(Answer sheets appear in the back of this book.)

TIME: Study 5 Minutes, Work 5 Minutes
88 Questions

DIRECTIONS: Below are five boxes labeled A,B,C,D, and E. Each box contains five addresses. You will be given five minutes to memorize the addresses in the boxes and their locations. After five minutes are up, you will have an additional five minutes to answer the following 88 questions and mark on the answer sheet the letter of the box in which the address belongs. You will not be able to refer back to the boxes once you begin answering the questions.

A	B	C	D	E
3400-8999 Sullivan	7600-9299 Sullivan	4700-8299 Sullivan	1800-5699 Sullivan	6300-6799 Sullivan
Kramer	Parkinson	de la Cruz	Perry	Houston
4700-8299 Jain	1800-5699 Jain	3400-8999 Jain	6300-6799 Jain	7600-9299 Jain
Chen	Fuxwreiter	Tymon	Georges	Gamble
6300-6799 Miller	3400-8999 Miller	7600-9299 Miller	4700-8299 Miller	1800-5699 Miller

1. 6300-6799 Jain
2. Tymon
3. Chen
4. 3400-8999 Sullivan
5. 4700-8299 Jain
6. Houston
7. 7600-9299 Sullivan
8. 1800-5699 Jain
9. Gamble
10. 1800-5699 Miller
11. 4700-8299 Sullivan
12. Kramer
13. 1800-5699 Sullivan
14. 3400-8999 Sullivan
15. Perry
16. 7600-9299 Jain
17. 6300-6799 Sullivan
18. Fuxwreiter
19. 6300-6799 Miller
20. 7600-9299 Miller
21. 1800-5699 Jain
22. de la Cruz
23. Parkinson
24. 3400-8999 Jain
25. Georges
26. 4700-8299 Miller
27. 3400-8999 Sullivan

28. Houston
29. Parkinson
30. 6300-6799 Jain
31. 1800-5699 Sullivan
32. de la Cruz
33. 7600-9299 Sullivan
34. 6300-6799 Miller
35. Chen
36. 1800-5699 Miller
37. Perry
38. Tymon
39. 6300-6799 Miller
40. Kramer
41. 4700-8299 Sullivan
42. Gamble
43. Fuxwreiter
44. 4700-8299 Jain
45. de la Cruz
46. 7600-9299 Miller
47. Houston
48. 6300-6799 Jain
49. 3400-8999 Sullivan
50. 6300-6799 Miller
51. 3400-8999 Jain
52. 1800-5699 Sullivan
53. Parkinson
54. Fuxwreiter

55. Chen

56. Georges

57. 3400-8999 Miller

58. 7600-9299 Jain

59. Kramer

60. 4700-8299 Jain

61. 6300-6799 Sullivan

62. 4700-8299 Sullivan

63. Parkinson

64. 4700-8299 Miller

65. Houston

66. Gamble

67. 6300-6799 Jain

68. 6300-6799 Miller

69. Fuxwreiter

70. Perry

71. 7600-9299 Jain

72. 1800-5699 Miller

73. 1800-5699 Jain

74. de la Cruz

75. 3400-8999 Sullivan

76. 4700-8299 Miller

77. 6300-6799 Sullivan

78. Parkinson

79. 3400-8999 Miller

80. Tymon

81. Georges

82. Gamble

83. 4700-8299 Jain

84. 3400-8999 Jain

85. Houston

86. Kramer

87. Fuxwreiter

88. 1800-5699 Sullivan

DIAGNOSTIC TEST

Number Series

(Answer sheets appear in the back of this book.)

TIME: 20 Minutes
24 Questions

DIRECTIONS: For each question, there is a series of numbers that follow some definite order. Look at the series of numbers and decide which two numbers will come next in the series. You will be given five answers to choose from.

1. 20 1 40 3 60 5 80 7 _____ _____
   (A) 100, 9
   (B) 60, 3
   (C) 80, 7
   (D) 100, 13
   (E) 20, 1

2. 0 0 4 0 0 8 0 0 _____ _____
   (A) 0, 10
   (B) 0, 12
   (C) 12, 0
   (D) 0, 0
   (E) 14, 0

3. 1 3 4 7 11 18 29 47 _____ _____
   (A) 47, 76
   (B) 76, 123
   (C) 123, 76

(D) 47, 123

(E) 48, 76

4.   1   2   3   6   4   5   6   15   _____   _____

(A) 19, 1

(B) 8, 23

(C) 7, 32

(D) 21, 7

(E) 7, 8

5.   98   1   77   2   65   3   54   4   _____   _____

(A) 4, 45

(B) 3, 32

(C) 43, 5

(D) 45, 4

(E) 54, 4

6.   1   2   3   12   13   14   23   24   _____   _____

(A) 32, 18

(B) 26, 36

(C) 25, 26

(D) 26, 38

(E) 36, 26

7.   14   28   13   26   12   24   11   22   _____   _____

(A) 11, 10

(B) 20, 10

(C) 22, 44

(D) 10, 20

(E) 40, 10

8. 1   3   5   7   11 13 17 19 _____   _____

    (A) 23, 30

    (B) 25, 27

    (C) 23, 29

    (D) 25, 29

    (E) 23, 31

9. 1   1   7   6   14 12 21 18 _____   _____

    (A) 28, 24

    (B) 20, 27

    (C) 28, 36

    (D) 25, 29

    (E) 24, 28

10. 2   2   4   8   8   16 32 32 _____   _____

    (A) 64, 66

    (B) 64, 64

    (C) 64, 128

    (D) 64, 100

    (E) 128, 254

11. 1   2   4   4   9   8   16 16 _____   _____

    (A) 16, 32

    (B) 25, 36

    (C) 36, 25

    (D) 25, 32

    (E) 24, 32

12. 0   3   8   6   16 9   24 12 _____   _____

    (A) 15, 18

    (B) 49, 35

    (C) 32, 15

    (D) 18, 32.

    (E) 28, 18

13. 22 1 22 8 22 16 22 24 _____ _____

    (A) 22, 32

    (B) 32, 32

    (C) 22, 22

    (D) 22, 24

    (E) 22, 40

14. 2 5 10 13 26 29 58 61 _____ _____

    (A) 64, 128

    (B) 122, 125

    (C) 64, 122

    (D) 125, 64

    (E) 124, 124

15. 5 6 8 9 11 12 14 15 _____ _____

    (A) 19, 20

    (B) 17, 19

    (C) 19, 18

    (D) 18, 19

    (E) 17, 18

16. 3 2 1 4 3 2 5 4 _____ _____

    (A) 3, 6

    (B) 3, 2

    (C) 6, 5

    (D) 4, 4

    (E) 2, 1

17.   2000   4   2020   8   2040   12   2060   16   _____   _____
   (A) 2018, 20
   (B) 2060, 16
   (C) 2080, 20
   (D) 2040, 12
   (E) 2000, 24

18.   5   12   26   54   110   222   446   894   1790   _____   _____
   (A) 8000, 8002
   (B) 3580, 7162
   (C) 3582, 7164
   (D) 3588, 7162
   (E) 3582, 7166

19.   2   4   8   10   14   16   20   22   _____   _____
   (A) 24, 26
   (B) 26, 30
   (C) 26, 28
   (D) 28, 30
   (E) 28, 32

20.   1   1   2   6   6   12   36   36   _____   _____
   (A) 72, 216
   (B) 72, 72
   (C) 72, 144
   (D) 144, 216
   (E) 144, 144

21.   12   6   14   7   16   8   18   9   _____   _____
   (A) 20, 8
   (B) 20, 10

    (C) 22, 11

    (D) 20, 22

    (E) 8, 22

22.   22   23   24   26   28   30   33   36   _____   _____

    (A) 37, 45

    (B) 39, 43

    (C) 28, 29

    (D) 41, 43

    (E) 23, 25

23.   1000   27   960   27   920   27   880   27   _____   _____

    (A) 900, 27

    (B) 860, 27

    (C) 800, 27

    (D) 860, 840

    (E) 840, 27

24.   11   3   22   6   33   9   44   12   _____   _____

    (A) 44, 14

    (B) 55, 14

    (C) 15, 9

    (D) 48, 12

    (E) 55, 15

DIAGNOSTIC TEST

Following Oral Directions - Worksheet

(Answer sheets appear in the back of this book.)

TIME: Instructions will be read at approximately 80 words per minute.

DIRECTIONS: Follow the instructions that are read to you. They will not be repeated during the examination. You are to mark your worksheets according to the instructions that are read to you. After each set of instructions, you will be given time to record your answer on your answer sheet. You should have only one space darkened for each number. If you go to darken a space for a number and you have already darkened another space, either erase the first mark and darken the space for your new choice **or** let the original mark remain.

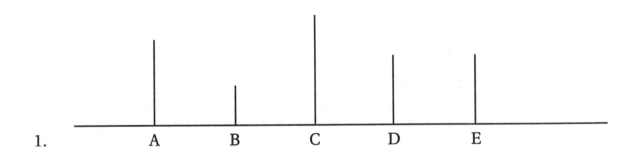

1.   A   B   C   D   E

2. Monday   Tuesday   Wednesday   Thursday   Friday
    45___   60___   5___   16___   31___

3. 220 Taylor Road
    9 Maxwell Street
    11 Dombrowski Way
    560 Taylor Road
    71 Avery Court, Apt. B

4. [21] (B) /55\ [1] (21)

5. NEVADA   CALIFORNIA   NEW YORK   FLORIDA   MAINE

6. 902   105   631   518

7.
| ELM ST.
55 | DORIS AVE.
72 | SANDERS CT.
13 |

8. PARK   PERRY   PATEL   PREET

9. 5   10   15   20   25

10. ⬡ ▭ ○ △

DIAGNOSTIC TEST

ANSWER KEY

Address Checking

1. (D)	15. (A)	29. (D)	43. (D)	57. (D)	71. (D)	85. (D)
2. (A)	16. (D)	30. (A)	44. (D)	58. (A)	72. (D)	86. (D)
3. (D)	17. (D)	31. (A)	45. (D)	59. (D)	73. (A)	87. (D)
4. (A)	18. (D)	32. (A)	46. (A)	60. (D)	74. (A)	88. (D)
5. (D)	19. (D)	33. (A)	47. (D)	61. (A)	75. (A)	89. (D)
6. (D)	20. (A)	34. (D)	48. (A)	62. (D)	76. (A)	90. (D)
7. (D)	21. (D)	35. (D)	49. (D)	63. (A)	77. (A)	91. (A)
8. (A)	22. (D)	36. (A)	50. (D)	64. (D)	78. (D)	92. (D)
9. (D)	23. (D)	37. (A)	51. (D)	65. (D)	79. (D)	93. (A)
10. (D)	24. (D)	38. (D)	52. (A)	66. (A)	80. (A)	94. (D)
11. (D)	25. (D)	39. (D)	53. (D)	67. (D)	81. (A)	95. (A)
12. (D)	26. (D)	40. (D)	54. (A)	68. (A)	82. (A)	
13. (D)	27. (A)	41. (A)	55. (D)	69. (A)	83. (A)	
14. (A)	28. (D)	42. (D)	56. (D)	70. (A)	84. (A)	

Memory for Addresses

1. (D)	14. (A)	27. (A)	40. (A)	53. (B)	66. (E)	79. (B)
2. (C)	15. (D)	28. (E)	41. (C)	54. (B)	67. (D)	80. (C)
3. (A)	16. (E)	29. (B)	42. (E)	55. (A)	68. (A)	81. (D)
4. (A)	17. (E)	30. (D)	43. (B)	56. (D)	69. (B)	82. (E)
5. (A)	18. (B)	31. (D)	44. (A)	57. (B)	70. (D)	83. (A)
6. (E)	19. (A)	32. (C)	45. (C)	58. (E)	71. (E)	84. (C)
7. (B)	20. (C)	33. (B)	46. (C)	59. (A)	72. (E)	85. (E)
8. (B)	21. (B)	34. (A)	47. (E)	60. (A)	73. (B)	86. (A)
9. (E)	22. (C)	35. (A)	48. (D)	61. (E)	74. (C)	87. (B)
10. (E)	23. (B)	36. (E)	49. (A)	62. (C)	75. (A)	88. (D)
11. (C)	24. (C)	37. (D)	50. (A)	63. (B)	76. (D)	
12. (A)	25. (D)	38. (C)	51. (C)	64. (D)	77. (E)	
13. (D)	26. (D)	39. (A)	52. (D)	65. (E)	78. (B)	

Note: There is an answer key only for the "Memory for Addresses" section.

Number Series

1.	(A)	13.	(A)
2.	(C)	14.	(B)
3.	(B)	15.	(E)
4.	(E)	16.	(A)
5.	(C)	17.	(C)
6.	(C)	18.	(E)
7.	(D)	19.	(C)
8.	(C)	20.	(A)
9.	(A)	21.	(B)
10.	(C)	22.	(B)
11.	(D)	23.	(E)
12.	(C)	24.	(E)

Following Oral Directions

(Please see "Detailed Explanations of Answers.")

DETAILED EXPLANATIONS
OF ANSWERS

Diagnostic Test

Address Checking

1. 372 Hickory Drive   374 Hickory Street
2. alike
3. 2112 First St. Apt. **3D**   2112 First St. Apt. **3**
4. alike
5. **500** Sunnydale Drive   **5000** Sunnydale Drive
6. 99 Thistle **Lake**   99 Thistle **Lane**
7. 48B First Ave **NW**   48B First Ave **N**
8. alike
9. **8**001 Hwy. No. 29   **9**001 Hwy. No. 29
10. 8 Winding Lake **Drive**   8 Winding Lake **Rd**
11. 3 Hou**s**ton Drive   3 Hor**s**ton Drive
12. 48 **C**alada Way   48 **K**alada Way
13. **38** Lenape Drive   **37** Lenape Drive
14. alike
15. alike
16. 66 Homestead **Lane**   66 Homestead **Ct.**
17. 1**45** Sullivan Street   1**43** Sullivan Street
18. 44-**B** Marting Ct.   44-**D** Marting Ct.
19. 1014 Lakefront **Terr.**   1014 Lakefront **Ave.**
20. alike

21. 76 Apple Farm **Road**   76 Apple Farm **Drive**
22. 99 Senior Street Apt. 1   99 Senior Street Apt. 1**A**
23. 35 Divis**ion** Street   35 Divid**ing** Street
24. 89 S. Altamonte **Dr.**   89 S. Altamonte **Ave.**
25. 77 Rock Lake   77-**C** Rock Lake
26. **78** E. Third Apt. 3B   77 E. Third Apt. 3B
27. alike
28. 7**1**6 Lloyd Dr.   7**6**6 Lloyd Dr.
29. 2 Sand Hill Road   2**0** Sand Hill Road
30. alike
31. alike
32. alike
33. alike
34. 66 Bethany Rd. **West**   66 Bethany Rd.
35. 21**21** Holyhock Ave.   21**12** Holyhock Ave.
36. alike
37. alike
38. 86 **Woodside** Rd.   86 **Wood Side** Rd.
39. 40 Gog**o**l Way   40 Gog**e**l Way
40. 5-**H** Sycamore Lane   5-**I** Sycamore Lane
41. alike
42. 520 Hudson St. **W.**   520 Hudson St. W
43. 37 Route 47 **South**   37 Route 47 **North**
44. 201**29** South Brush   201**30** South Brush
45. 820 Wind**ing** Brook Way   820 Wind**y** Brook Way
46. alike
47. 5 Jorgen**so**n Lane   5 Jorgen**se**n Lane

48. alike
49. 10 189th St. W.   10 18th St. W.
50. 52 **E.** 96 Street   52 **W.** 96 Street
51. 5 Route **6115**   5 Route **5116**
52. alike
53. 91/2 Danbury   91 Danbury
54. alike
55. 36 Maya Ct.   36 Mayan Ct.
56. 87 Thirteenth St.   87 Thirtieth St.
57. **7** Vinton Circle   **9** Vinton Circle
58. alike
59. **6889** South Ave.   **6898** South Ave.
60. 92 Mana**tou** Way   92 Mana**tee** Way
61. alike
62. 65 Ju**pit**er Way   65 Ju**nip**er Way
63. alike
64. 1001 Walter St.   10001 Walter St.
65. 29 Mine**o** Circle   29 Mine**rva** Circle
66. alike
67. 317**A** Route 28 South   317 Route 28 South
68. alike
69. alike
70. alike
71. 91 Seguso Pl.   91**0** Seguso Pl.
72. 1017 Johnson Drive   1017 Johnston Drive
73. alike
74. alike

75. alike

76. alike

77. alike

78. 94 Brooke St.   94 Brook St.

79. 29 Rice Avenue   291 Rice Avenue

80. alike

81. alike

82. alike

83. alike

84. alike

85. 93 Packards Glen   93A Packards Glen

86. 6 Louis Avenue   6 Louise Avenue

87. 48-3000 Gardentree Rd. 48-300 Gardentree Rd.

88. 777 Central   777D Central

89. 68 Austen Avenue W.   68 Austin Avenue W.

90. 5001-A Dover Glen   5001-A2 Dover Glen

91. alike

92. 20 Dochester Drive   201 Dochester Drive

93. alike

94. 23 Brock Avenue **W.**   23 **W.** Brock Avenue

95. alike

Number Series

1. **(A)** There are two alternating series. In the first series, the pattern begins with 20 and increases by 20. The second series begins with 1 and increases by 2. The correct answer is (A) 100, 9.

2. **(C)** In this series, the number 0 is repeated twice and then followed by a number increasing by 4. The correct answer is (C) 12, 0.

3. **(B)** Beginning with the numbers 1 and 3, this series is created by adding the last two numbers in the series to form the next number. The correct answer is (B) 76, 123.

4. **(E)** This series is created by listing three numbers increasing by 1, and then adding these three numbers together to get the next number. Then the consecutive pattern continues again for another three numbers, then those numbers are added together to get the next. The correct answer is (E) 7, 8.

5. **(C)** There are two alternating patterns in this series. The first, beginning with 98, decreases by 11. The second, beginning with 1, increases by one. The correct answer is (C) 43, 5.

6. **(C)** In this series, the numbers increase by 1, by 1, and then by 9. The correct answer is (C) 25, 26.

7. **(D)** In this series, the first number is multiplied by 2 to form the next number. Then the first number decreases by 1 to get the third number. Then the pattern repeats. The correct answer is (D) 10, 20.

8. **(C)** This series is comprised of prime numbers listed in consecutive order. The correct answer is (C) 23, 29.

9. **(A)** There are two alternating series. The first lists powers of 7. The second lists the powers of 6. The correct answer is (A) 28, 24.

10. **(C)** In this series, beginning with the number 2, a number is repeated twice, and then multiplied by 2 to get the next number. Then this number is multiplied by 2 to get the first number of the next cycle. The correct answer is (C) 64, 128.

11. **(D)** There are two alternating patterns here. The first pattern consecutively lists perfect squares. The second pattern lists the powers of 2. The correct answer is (D) 25, 32.

12. **(C)** There are two alternating patterns here. The first pattern, beginning with 0, increases by 8. The second pattern begins with and increases by 3. The correct answer is (C) 32, 15.

13. **(A)** This series lists the multiples of 8 with each number separated by the number 22. The correct answer is (A) 22, 32.

14. **(B)** In this series, beginning with 2, 3 is added to get the next number. Then that number is multiplied by 2 to get the next number. This pattern is then repeated. The correct answer is (B) 122, 125.

15. **(E)** Beginning with 5, 1 is added to the number, and then 2 is added to the number. The correct answer is (E) 17, 18.

16. **(A)** The series is made of three numbers decreasing by 1. The first number of each pattern of three begins with the number 3 and increases by 1. The correct answer is (A) 3, 6.

17. **(C)** There are two alternating series in this sample. The first series, beginning with the number 2000, increases by 20. The second series, beginning with 4, increases by 4. The correct answer is (C) 2080, 20.

18. **(E)** This series, beginning with 5, is formed by multiplying the number by 2 and then adding 2 to this number to form the next number. The correct answer is (E) 3582, 7166.

19. **(C)** Beginning with 2, this series is formed by adding 2 to get the next number. Then 4 is added to get the next number. The correct answer is (C) 26, 28.

20. **(A)** Beginning with 1, this series is formed by multiplying by 1 to get the next number, then by 2 to get the next number, then by 3 to get the next number. The pattern then repeats. The correct answer is (A) 72, 216.

21. **(B)** This series, beginning with 12, is formed by dividing the first number by 2 to get the second number. The next number is then formed by adding 2 to the first number. The correct answer is (B) 20, 10.

22. **(B)** This series is made by increasing each number by 1 for three numbers, then by 2 for three numbers, then by 3 for three numbers, and so on. The correct answer is (B) 39, 43.

23. **(E)** A series of numbers beginning with 1000 and decreasing by 40 is interrupted by the repeating number 27. The correct answer is (E) 840, 27.

24. **(E)** There are two alternating series. Multiples of 11 are interrupted by multiples of 3. The correct answer is (E) 55, 15.

Following Oral Directions

This is how your worksheet should look:

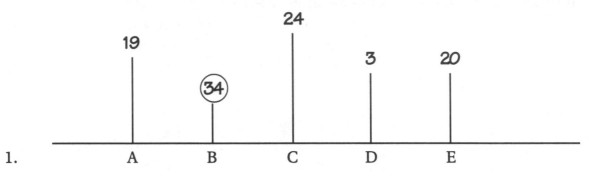

1.   A   B   C   D   E

2. Monday   Tuesday   Wednesday   Thursday   Friday
    45 _C_   60 _D_   5 _A_   16 ___   31 _B_

3. 220 Taylor Road
    9 Maxwell Street
    11 Dombrowski Way
    560 Taylor Road
    71 Avery Court, Apt. B

4. [21]   (B)   △55 _A_   [1]   (21)

5. NEVADA   (C)ALIFORNIA   NEW YORK _D_   FLORIDA   MAINE _A_

6. 902   105   (63)1 _D_   5(18)

7. [(E)LM ST. 55]   [(D)ORIS AVE. 72]   [(S)ANDERS CT. 13]

8. PARK   PERRY   PATEL   PREET

9. (5)   10   (15)   20   (25)

10. ⬡A   ▭   (D)   △

In this section, please note that the solution to each problem is preceded by the actual instructions read by the examiner.

Examine sample one. (Pause 2-3 seconds) Write the number 24 above the longest line. (Pause 2-3 seconds) Then write the number 34 above the shortest line. (Pause 2-3 seconds) Then write the numbers 19, 3, and 20, in that order, above the remaining lines. (Pause 2-3 seconds) Go to the number written above the line next to A and darken that number/letter combination. (Pause 5 seconds)

ANSWER: You should have written the number 19 above the line next to A which is B. Darken that number/letter combination— 34 B.

Examine sample one again. (Pause 2-3 seconds) Find the number written above the line next to the fourth letter of the alphabet. If this number is odd, then go to line 25 and darken the space for C as in "cat." (Pause 2-3 seconds) Otherwise, circle the number/letter combination for the shortest line in the sample. (Pause 2-3 seconds) Now find the number 3 on the answer sheet and darken the space for E as in "elephant." (Pause 5 seconds)

ANSWER: You should have written the number 20 above E (the line next to D). Since this number is even, circle the number/letter combination for the shortest line in the sample (34 B). Now find the number 3 on your answer sheet and darken the oval for E.

Examine sample two. (Pause 2-3 seconds) These numbers represent the number of magazines delivered by one carrier during one workweek. If the most magazines were delivered on Friday, go to number 53 on the answer sheet and darken the circle for B as in "boy." (Pause 2-3 seconds) Now write the letter A as in "apple" next to the smallest number of magazines. Write the letter D as in "dog" next to the day with the greatest number of magazines. Then go to the number listed for Thursday on the answer sheet and darken the space for E as in "elephant." (Pause 5 seconds)

ANSWER: The most magazines were not delivered on Friday—they were delivered on Tuesday (60). You should have written the letter D next to 60. You should have written A next to 5 (the smallest number of magazines). Then go to the number listed for Thursday (16) on your answer sheet and darken the space for E.

Examine sample two again. (Pause 2-3 seconds) Write the letter B as in "boy" next to the number of magazines delivered on Friday. Write the letter C as in "cat" next to the number that is greater than the number of magazines delivered on Friday but less than the number of magazines delivered on Tuesday. Then darken the number/letter combination listed for Wednesday. (Pause 2-3 seconds) Then go to the number listed that does not have a letter next to it on the answer sheet and darken the space for B as in "boy." (Pause 5 seconds)

ANSWER: You should have written the letter B next to the number of magazines delivered on Friday (31). Write the letter C next to 45, the number that is greater than the number of magazines delivered on Friday but less than the number of magazines delivered on Tuesday. Then darken the number/letter combination listed for Wednesday-5 A. Then go to the number listed that does not have a letter next to it (16) on your answer sheet and darken the oval for B.

Examine sample three. (Pause 2-3 seconds) These are five addresses on the same postal route. Find the number of the house listed on Maxwell Street on the answer sheet and darken the circle for C as in "cat." (Pause 2-3 seconds) Then find the number listed as an apartment on the answer sheet and darken the oval for D as in "dog." (Pause 2-3 seconds) If any of the addresses listed are on the same street, go to number 31 on the answer sheet and darken the oval for A as in "apple." (Pause 5 seconds)

ANSWER: Find the number 9 (the number of the house listed on Maxwell Street) on the answer sheet and darken the oval for C. Then find the number listed as an apartment (71) on the answer sheet and darken the oval for D. Since 200 Taylor Road and 560 Taylor Road are on the same street, go to number 31 on your answer sheet and darken the oval for A.

Examine sample three again. (Pause 2-3 seconds) Find the street with the most letters. On the answer sheet, go to the number listed at this address and darken the oval for E as in "elephant." (Pause 2-3 seconds) Find the street that is first alphabetically. Go to the number of the address at this street on the answer sheet, and darken the space for the first letter of this street. (Pause 5 seconds)

ANSWER: The street that has the most letters is "Dombrowski Way". Go to the number listed at this address (11) and darken the oval for E. Since "Avery" is the street that is first alphabetically, go to the number of this address (71) on your answer sheet and darken the oval for A. Since 71 D is already darkened, you have two choices. You can erase 71 D and darken the oval for A or you can not erase 71 D and not darken the oval for 71 A.

Examine sample four. (Pause 2-3 seconds) Go to number 14 on the answer sheet and darken the oval for the letter that is listed in this sample. (Pause 2-3 seconds) If any of the numbers in this sample are listed in both a box and in a circle, write the letter A as in "apple" under the triangle. Darken this new number/letter combination on the answer sheet. (Pause 2-3 seconds) Now find the number on the answer sheet that is listed twice in the sample and darken the space for the second letter of the alphabet. (Pause 5 seconds)

ANSWER: Go to the number 14 on your answer sheet and darken the oval for B, since it is the only letter listed in this sample. Since 21 is listed in both a box and a circle, write the letter A under the triangle. Since 55 is the number in the triangle, darken this number/letter combination (55 A) on your answer sheet. Now find the number on the answer sheet that is listed twice in the sample (21) and darken the space for B (the second letter of the alphabet).

Examine sample four again. (Pause 2-3 seconds) Find the smallest number in the sample on the answer sheet and darken the oval for E as in "elephant." (Pause 2-3 seconds) Then go to number 54 on the answer sheet and darken the space for the letter that is listed in the circle. (Pause 2-3 seconds) Then go to number 45 on the answer sheet and darken the space for B as in "boy." (Pause 5 seconds)

ANSWER: Find the smallest number in the sample (1) on the answer sheet and darken the oval for E. Then go to number 54 on your answer sheet and darken the space for the letter that is in the circle (B). Then go to number 45 on your answer sheet and darken the oval for B.

Examine sample five. (Pause 2-3 seconds) Find the state listed with the smallest number of letters. Write the letter A as in "apple" next to it. If the third state listed is to the south of the fourth state listed, go to number 29 on the answer sheet and darken the letter for E as in "elephant." (Pause 2-3 seconds) If this is not true, go to number 23 on the answer sheet and darken the same letter. (Pause 2-3 seconds) Now write the letter C as in "cat" next to the first state listed. (Pause 5 seconds)

ANSWER: The state listed with the smallest number of letters is Maine so write the letter A next to it. Since the third state listed (New York) is not south of the fourth state listed (Florida), go to number 23 on your answer sheet and darken the oval for E. Write the letter C next to the first state listed (Nevada).

Examine sample five again. (Pause 2-3 seconds) Write the letter D as in "dog" next to the state name that has two words in it. If the state next to the letter A as in "apple" is north of the state next to the letter D as in "dog," go to number 29 on the answer sheet and darken the oval for the letter next to NE-VADA. (Pause 2-3 seconds) Now find the state that comes first alphabetically, and circle the first letter in this name. Then go to number 61 on the answer sheet and darken the oval for the letter that was just circled. (Pause 5 seconds)

ANSWER: Write the letter D next to the state name that has two words in it (New York). Since the state next to the letter A (Maine) is north of the state next to the letter D (New York), go to number 29 on your answer sheet and darken the oval for C (the letter next to Nevada). Now find the state that comes first alphabetically (California) and circle the first letter in this name (C). Then go to number 61 and darken the oval for C.

Examine sample six. (Pause 2-3 seconds) Find the second largest-number listed and write the letter D as in "dog" under it. Circle the first two digits in this number. Find the number that you just circled on the answer sheet and darken the oval for the letter that is written underneath it. (Pause 2-3 seconds) If the last number listed is less than the second number listed, go to number 42 on the answer sheet and darken the oval for A as in "apple." Otherwise, go to the same number on the answer sheet and darken the oval for B as in "boy." (Pause 5 seconds)

ANSWER: Find the second largest number listed (631) and write the letter D under it. Circle the first two digits (63) and find this number on your answer sheet and darken the oval for D. Since the last number listed (518) is not less than the second number listed (105), go to number 42 on your answer sheet and darken the oval for B.

Examine sample six again. (Pause 2-3 seconds) Find the second even number listed. Circle the last two digits of this number. Go to the number you just circled on the answer sheet and darken the space for E as in "elephant." (Pause 2-3 seconds) If the smallest odd number is listed before the largest odd number, go to number 39 on the answer sheet and darken the space for B as in "boy." Otherwise, go to number 2 on the answer sheet and darken the same space. (Pause 5 seconds)

ANSWER: Find the second even number listed (518) and circle the last two digits of this number (18). Go to 18 on your answer sheet and darken the oval for E. Since the smallest odd number (105) is listed before the largest odd number (631), go to number 39 on your answer sheet and darken the oval for B.

Examine sample seven. (Pause 2-3 seconds) Inside each box is the name of a street on a certain postal route, followed by the number of addresses on that particular route. If the number of addresses on Doris Ave. is less than the number of addresses on Elm St., go to number 24 on the answer sheet and darken the oval for A as in "apple." If this is not true, go to the number of addresses on Sanders Ct. and darken the same oval. (Pause 5 seconds)

ANSWER: Since the number of addresses on Doris Ave. (72) is more than the number of addresses on Elm St. (55), go to number 13 (the number of addresses on Sanders Ct.) and darken the oval for A.

Examine sample seven again. (Pause 2-3 seconds) Circle the first letter of each street name. Find the street with the most addresses. If this street has more addresses than the other streets combined, go to the number listed in the box and darken the space for the letter that is circled in this box. Otherwise, go to number 65 on the answer sheet and darken the space for the letter that is circled in the first box. (Pause 5 seconds)

ANSWER: Find the street with the most addresses (Doris Ave.). Since Doris Ave. has more addresses (75) than the other streets combined (55 + 13 = 68), go to the number in the box on your answer sheet and darken the space for the letter that is circled in the box—72 D.

Examine sample eight. (Pause 2-3 seconds) This sample lists the names of some of the customers on a certain postal route. If the second name is where it would be if the names were arranged in alphabetical order, go to number 7 on the answer sheet and darken the oval for B as in "boy." If this is not true, go to number 12 on the answer sheet and darken the same oval. (Pause 5 seconds)

ANSWER: Since the second name (Perry) is not listed where it should be if the names were listed alphabetically (it would be third), go to number 12 on your answer sheet and darken the oval for B.

Examine sample eight again. (Pause 2-3 seconds) Find the name with the lowest number of letters. Divide the number of letters in this name by 2. Go to this number on the answer sheet and darken the space for A as in "apple." (Pause 2-3 seconds) Then go to number 47 on the answer sheet and darken the space for C as in "cat." (Pause 2-3 seconds) If the third or fourth names listed have a letter repeated, go to number 49 on the answer sheet and darken the space for D as in "dog." (Pause 5 seconds)

ANSWER: The name with the lowest number of letters is Park (4 letters). Divide the number of letters by 2 (4/2=2). Go to number 2 on your answer sheet and darken the oval for A. Then go to number 47 on the answer sheet and darken the oval for C. Since the fourth name has a letter repeated ("e"), go to number 49 on your answer sheet and darken the oval for D.

Examine sample nine. (Pause 2-3 seconds) Circle all of the odd numbers. If the last number circled is more than the sum of the uncircled numbers, go to number 52 on the answer sheet and darken the oval for E as in "elephant." If this is not true, go to numbers 58 and 75 on the answer sheet and darken the same oval for each. (Pause 5 seconds)

ANSWER: Circle all of the odd numbers (5, 15, and 25). Since the last number circled (25) is less than the sum of the uncircled numbers (10+20=30), go to numbers 58 and 75 on your answer sheet and darken the ovals for E.

Examine sample nine again. (Pause 2-3 seconds) If the third number listed is the sum of the first two numbers, go to number 60 on the answer sheet and darken the oval for B as in "boy." (Pause 2-3 seconds) If the first number listed is the difference between the fourth and fifth numbers, go to number 64 on the answer sheet and darken the oval for C as in "cat." (Pause 2-3 seconds) If the second number is the difference between the fourth and first numbers, go to number 81 on the answer sheet and darken the oval for E as in "elephant." (Pause 5 seconds)

ANSWER: Since the third number listed (15) is the sum of the first two numbers (5+10=15), go to number 60 on your answer sheet and darken the oval for B. Since the first number listed (5) is the difference between the fourth and fifth numbers (25-20=5), go to number 64 on your answer sheet and darken the oval for C.

Examine sample ten. (Pause 2-3 seconds) Write the letter A as in "apple" in the shape with the most sides and the letter D as in "dog" in the shape with no sides. If the difference between the number of sides on the shapes that do not have letters in them is one, then go to number 77 on the answer sheet and darken the space for B as in "boy." (Pause 5 seconds)

ANSWER: Write the letter A in the first shape (the shape with the most sides—6) and the letter D in the third shape (the shapes with no sides—the circle). Since the difference between the number of sides on the shapes that do not have letters is one (4-3=1), go to number 77 on your answer sheet and darken the oval for B.

Examine sample 10 again. (Pause 2-3 seconds) On the answer sheet, find the number that is the same as the largest number of sides in this sample. Darken the oval for the letter that is written in this shape. (Pause 2-3 seconds) Add the number of sides for all of the shapes together. Add 15 to this number. Find this number on the answer sheet and darken the oval for B as in "boy." (Pause 2-3 seconds)

ANSWER: On your answer sheet, find number 6 (the number that is the same as the largest number of sides in this sample) and darken the oval for A (the letter that is written in the shape). Add the number of sides for all of the shapes together (6+4+0+3=13). Add 15 to this number (13+15=28). Find this number on your answer sheet (28) and darken the oval for B.

POSTAL EXAM
Diagnostic Test - Following Oral Directions
ANSWER KEY

#	Answer		#	Answer		#	Answer
1.	E		34.	B		68.	—
2.	A		35.	—		69.	—
3.	E		36.	—		70.	—
4.	—		37.	—		71.	A, D
5.	A		38.	—		72.	D
6.	A		39.	B		73.	—
7.	—		40.	—		74.	—
8.	—		41.	—		75.	E
9.	C		42.	—		76.	—
10.	—		43.	—		77.	B
11.	E		44.	—		78.	—
12.	B		45.	B		79.	—
13.	A		46.	—		80.	—
14.	B		47.	C		81.	—
15.	—		48.	—		82.	—
16.	B, E		49.	D		83.	—
17.	—		50.	—		84.	—
18.	E		51.	—		85.	—
19.	—		52.	—		86.	—
20.	—		53.	—		87.	—
21.	B		54.	B		88.	—
22.	—		55.	A		89.	—
23.	E		56.	—		90.	—
24.	—		57.	—		90.	—
25.	—		58.	E		91.	—
26.	—		59.	—		92.	—
27.	—		60.	B		93.	—
28.	B		61.	C		94.	—
29.	C		62.	—		95.	—
30.	—		63.	D			
31.	A		64.	C			
32.	—		65.	—			
33.	—		66.	—			

PROGRESS CHART

The following chart has been provided so you may keep track of your progress as you complete the practice exams. Upon completing the review sections of this book, you will begin taking the practice exams. As you score those exams, you will fill your scores into the appropriate spaces on the chart. By doing this you will see documented proof of your progress and any areas for which you may need to reread the review chapters.

These progress report forms allow you to track your progress and help you to target your weaker areas. The forms also guide you through scoring your practice tests, since each section has a different method of scoring.

While the tests only score the questions that you answer, it is also a good idea to track how many questions in each section you are able to answer. Keeping an eye on this number allows you see to which areas you feel more confident in, and can help track your progress.

The rankings provided should serve as loose guidelines. Recording your rank gives you a quick way of analyzing your progress.

Progress Report 1: Address Checking

Rank:	50 and higher	Excellent
	30 - 49	Fair
	29 and below	Needs to improve

- Score = No. correct–No. incorrect
- Do not include unanswered questions

	Diagnostic Test	Practice Test 1	Practice Test 2	Practice Test 3	Practice Test 4	Practice Test 5	Practice Test 6
Date	____	____	____	____	____	____	____
No. completed	____	____	____	____	____	____	____
No. correct	____	____	____	____	____	____	____
– No. incorrect	____	____	____	____	____	____	____
Score:							
Rank:							

Progress Report 2: Memory for Addresses

Rank:	45 and higher	Excellent
	24 - 44	Fair
	23 and below	Needs to improve

- Score = No. correct – ¼ No. incorrect
- Do not include unanswered questions

	Diagnostic Test	Practice Test 1	Practice Test 2	Practice Test 3	Practice Test 4	Practice Test 5	Practice Test 6
Date	____	____	____	____	____	____	____
No. completed	____	____	____	____	____	____	____
No. incorrect	____	____	____	____	____	____	____
¼ • No. incorrect	____	____	____	____	____	____	____
No. correct	____	____	____	____	____	____	____
– ¼ • No. incorrect	____	____	____	____	____	____	____

Score:

Rank:

Progress Report 3: Number Series

Rank:	16 and higher	Excellent
	11 - 15	Fair
	10 and below	Needs to improve

- Score = No. correct
- Do not include wrong or unanswered questions

	Diagnostic Test	Practice Test 1	Practice Test 2	Practice Test 3	Practice Test 4	Practice Test 5	Practice Test 6
Date	____	____	____	____	____	____	____
No. completed	____	____	____	____	____	____	____
No. incorrect	____	____	____	____	____	____	____
No. correct	____	____	____	____	____	____	____

Score:

Rank:

Progress Report 4: Following Oral Directions

Rank:	26 and higher	Excellent
	25 and below	Needs to improve

- Score = No. correct
- Do not include wrong or unanswered questions

	Diagnostic Test	Practice Test 1	Practice Test 2	Practice Test 3	Practice Test 4	Practice Test 5	Practice Test 6
Date	____	____	____	____	____	____	____
No. completed	____	____	____	____	____	____	____
No. incorrect	____	____	____	____	____	____	____
No. correct	____	____	____	____	____	____	____

Score:
Rank:

Chapter 3

Strategies for Improving on "Address Checking"

Chapter 3

STRATEGIES FOR IMPROVING ON "ADDRESS CHECKING"

"Address Checking" is the first part of this four-part exam. The test-makers are starting you off with a bang. You do not really have to work faster than a speeding bullet but you will have to work very fast, four seconds for each line. This chapter will help you to build skills needed to work at a quick yet accurate pace so you may score high on this portion of the exam. Take your time reviewing this chapter. The more time you devote to perfecting these techniques, the higher you can score on the exam.

GENERAL TEST STRATEGIES

As you learned in Chapter 1, "Address Checking" requires you to read and then compare two lines of addresses. Your best strategy for this part of the exam would be to forget most rules you have learned governing multiple-choice test taking.

Guessing

On this portion of the postal exam you should not guess! Please remember this since the strategy on guessing will be different for the subsequent tests. Scoring procedures for this section take the number you have correct minus the number you have incorrect. The lines that you do not answer do not count as a score. Even though your odds are pretty good to guess the correct answer, it is not beneficial to your score to try. Stick with the ones you have put effort into answering and the odds are that your correct answers will be enough to get a good score. This is the only section where it does not help to guess.

Reading

For this portion of the exam it is a good idea to change your reading style. Many people have found the traditional way of reading—sounding out unknown words, possibly rereading misunderstood words, or reading at a rate good for comprehension—will not help you earn a high score. Instead of reading the addresses, master looking at them. You do not need to remember the address, so do not waste time trying to decipher strange street or city names. Look at their spelling and move on to the next. Precious time is wasted trying to sound out a name. Who cares? You only care if it is spelled similarly or differently.

Complete Accuracy

While you were in school the teachers probably told you to always go for a perfect paper. A score of 100 was always the most desirable. Another strategy is to believe that getting every problem right is not always going to get you a higher score. Let's say I am taking this exam. I work carefully on each line, so carefully that I only get three wrong. However, I only finish 30 problems. This gives me a score of 27 (number correct minus number incorrect). My study partner works a bit faster, making six mistakes. He, however, is able to complete 40 problems. This means his score would be a 34, higher than mine even though he got more incorrect answers. Slow and steady will not win this race! Expect to get a few wrong answers.

Attitude

A good attitude will supersede many shortcomings. If you review these strategies and techniques and believe that you can work fast and accurately, you probably will. Imagine yourself sitting in the exam room working quickly and accurately. On test day, as you are taking the exam, fit yourself into that picture.

TECHNIQUES FOR IMPROVING YOUR SKILLS

Setup

Every extra second counts so follow these instructions carefully. Place your answer sheet at the edge of your test booklet, so the pages line up perfectly. This will save time having to look across the desk to mark down answers. There will also be less time and distance to cause you to skip a line whether on the test book or on your answer sheet. Working with the papers at a 90 degree angle in front of you may be uncomfortable at first. This is why you must practice this technique.

Hands

Your hands are going to be your best friends. They will keep you on track as long as you do not let them wander. Hands naturally move slightly when a person moves his or her eyes or head to do another activity, say marking an answer on the answer sheet. It is of the utmost importance that you practice keeping your hands and head still, only moving your eyes.

Your hands should be placed in front of you in a relaxed manner. Having your elbows at your sides with your wrists tense will not help. Place your left hand on the test booklet. The pinky finger should be on column A and the pointer finger should be on column D. As you move from line to line, simply slide your fingers down the page. Your arm never needs to move, simply your fingers. By doing this you will save time having to look for your next line and avoid skipping over a line or looking at one twice. If after practicing you find this too difficult, try using a pencil as a straight edge. Rulers and the like are not permitted in the exam room, but since you are allowed to have an extra pencil, why not use it to its greatest potential? Line the pencil up under or over the line you are working on. Move the pencil down as you go. Again, this technique will save time because you will not have to check to see where your next line is. Practicing this technique will make it seem more natural come test day.

Do not forget the other hand. Your right hand should be placed lightly on the answer sheet. It should always be waiting at the number of the line you are comparing. By having your pencil marking the line, you will not have to waste seconds looking for the line. There is also less chance of skipping a line or marking two answers on the same line. Remember to hold your pencil lightly and merely place it next to the number. This will keep your paper free of stray marks and your muscles more relaxed. This is no time for a cramp. Set your hands up while the examiner is going over the instructions. Get two pieces of lined paper and a pencil. Make two columns on the one sheet to represent a test page. Place your fingers where they should go. Mark a column of numbers on the other page, representing answer lines. Practice moving your hands down a row as you pretend to look from paper to paper. When you feel comfortable holding your hands in these positions, try using the blank answer sheet provided instead of the lined paper. Remember to fill in the ovals with one quick swipe of the pencil. You are provided with answer rows running horizontally and vertically so you may practice with both setups. As you progress you should be able to fill in 95 ovals in approximately one minute's time.

A note to left-handers: there is a chance the answer sheet will be attached to the test booklet, making it necessary to fill in the answer with your right hand. Practice will help alleviate discomfort in using your right hand to fill in the ovals. When you drop off your admission form, ask about the setup your post office uses for materials.

Eyes

The eyes have it. Eyes have a natural distance that they travel across a piece of written material. The eye looks at the written words in segments, with your muscles moving the eye from segment to segment. The length of each segment is called eye span. You want to increase your eye span to the optimum length so you can see more in each segment your eye moves. The more you see in each segment, the quicker you can compare each column.

Here is an example of a short eye span. The lines separate the row to show each segment the eye sees.

/ 273 / Heathrow Dr. / Burdy, / IA /

To save time and energy, a better eye span would be as follows.

/ 273 Heathrow Dr. / Burdy, IA /

Once an eye span of this length has been acquired, see if you can see the whole line in just one sweep of the eye.

/ 273 Heathrow Dr. Burdy, IA /

Few people have an eye span this large, and acquiring one takes practice. There are some tricks and techniques to widen your eye span. Practice these slowly and over time.

What you see: When you look at a group of words or letters, begin by looking toward the middle of the group. Let your peripheral vision see the beginning and ending letters. To practice catching more in one sweep, you will need index cards or small strips of paper. In the middle of each card place a black dot, large enough for your eye to catch it as you look at the card. Underneath each dot write a line of words or numbers, being sure to center it around the black dot. Have a variety of line lengths, one-, two-, or three-word phrases, working your way to longer lines. Include many complete addresses: 489 Hobbey Way South. Choose four or five cards of a length you feel comfortable with. Place them in a line or column in front of you. Practice reading the cards by focusing on the black dot, using your peripheral vision to take in the sides. A few examples have been modeled here for you.

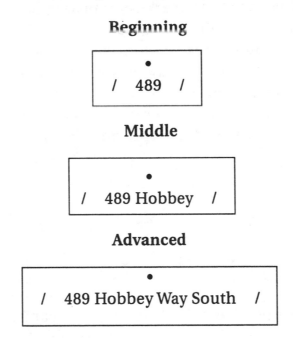

We are not saying to only look at the middle numbers or words on the exam. These exercises are to widen your eye span. Working on peripheral vision is meant to increase your field of sight, which will help your speed on the exam. Later on in this chapter you will learn how to read all written work correctly.

Rhythm

Have you ever found yourself setting up a rhythm while you work? While painting a wall you may dip the brush, wipe it off, stroke three times, dip the brush, wipe it off, stroke three times...Your movements become efficiently ingrained in your head. A similar rhythm should be established while answering the Address Checking portion of the exam.

If you want to make a high score, you should compare two lines every four seconds. This is not a lot of time. To make sure that you truly are comparing two lines every four seconds, find a rhythm of moving to a new line every four seconds. With a watch, time out the desired number of seconds you need to compare each line. At this point you have a few options.

If you have been working on developing your eye span and feel comfortable sweeping the line in one movement, set your rhythm as follows: For each column take one second to sweep, take one second to look at your answer key, and take another second to mark your answer, being sure to look at the next line of comparisons. Count to yourself 1, 2, 3, 4 as you progress. Each step has a number. If you set up a rhythm, you can then work at fitting the act of comparing into the rhythm you have established. Remember, not everyone is expected to complete all of the comparisons, so if you need to take more time do so, only be sure that you are completing enough correctly to give you a high score. An example has been provided to illustrate appropriate eye movements.

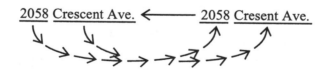

Here is another option that is also fast and accurate. Begin your rhythm by looking at the numbers of the address in column A. Then quickly shift to the place where your index finger is pointing to in column B. You haven't forgotten to use your hands, have you? After you compare both numbers, you need to decide if they are alike or different. If they are different, you are done with this comparison. Follow across to where your pencil is waiting and, in one swoop, fill in oval D for "different." If the numbers are the same, look at the abbreviations in column B. If there are no abbreviations, you may proceed to look at the street or city name in column B. Then proceed to column A where you will compare the names. Now make your decision. Follow to where your pencil is and mark your answer, returning your eyes to the new addresses waiting for you by your finger. By moving left, right, right, left you save precious seconds moving your eyes back and forth. If you are already there, stay there. Practice this until it feels natural. Practice on the lines provided. Use a piece of paper to cover the eye paths drawn for you. After you compare the lines, making sure you stick to the rhythm, remove the paper to see if you followed the suggested path. If not, try it again later, this time looking for the most efficient way to move your eyes.

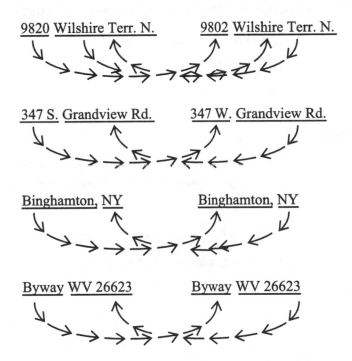

Correct Looking

In the previous material it was suggested that rather than read the addresses you simply look at them. There is a technique to be sure you are not wasting time trying to sound out funny words or make sense of strange abbreviations. Read the words or numbers exactly as they are printed. Here are some examples:

104	One oh four
Dr.	Dee Ahr
NJ	En Jay

This will save you from overlooking a simple change. The brain functions by filling in missing parts. If you did not make yourself conscious of a letter change in a state abbreviation, your brain will probably overlook it and fill in what it feels is correct.

Sound out each syllable when you look at street addresses. By doing this you make yourself conscious of smaller chunks, and make it easier to pick out a wrong letter in the middle of a word. For instance, "Cornwall" would be seen as "Corn-wall." Practice saying these addresses as suggested.

9024, 384, 1002, 3920, 5578, 29, 1582

St., Ct., Ave., Pl., S., W., N., NE., Terr.

IA, CA, NY, AL, WY, WA

Common Changes

Studies have shown these are common changes in addresses. Be aware of these changes so you can expect them. Your eyes may make changes for you even if they are not on paper.

Letter reversals: b/d, a/o, a/e, m/w, n/m, p/e, q/d, u/n, u/v

Parts of names: Walker, Walk, Waller, Walken, Wilken

Number reversals: 478, 487, 748, 847, 784, 874

To practice recognizing these changes, prepare index cards with a number, name, or letter on one side and on the back either the same figure or a slight variation. Quickly turn the card over, not looking at it for more than a second or two. State whether it is the same or different. If you want to brush up on your stroking technique, use a blank answer sheet to fill in A or D.

Here are some drills to help you differentiate between number and name reversals.

Complete the chart as you progress. Mark the number space in which you saw the word. If you did not see the exact word repeated, mark a zero. You may want to repeat this exercise periodically to keep fresh.

1. Boyton	Boyon	Boyton	Boytun	Boyten	Bayton	_____
2. Leary	Learry	Laary	Leavy	Leary	Lerry	_____
3. Sporten	Spoten	Sportan	Sgorten	Sporten	Sgortan	_____
4. Kline	Klinn	Klime	Klina	Klima	Kliwe	_____
5. Gelinas	Galinas	Gellnas	Gelinas	Gelinns	Gilenas	_____
6. Griego	Qriego	Griego	Griago	Griega	Qrigo	_____
7. Avacedo	Avacebo	Awacedo	Avacado	Avaceda	Avacedo	_____
8. Kessler	Kezzler	Kessler	Kassler	Kesslr	Kesselr	_____
9. Lipton	Lidton	Libton	Lijton	Lipten	Lipton	_____
10. Dobde	Dodbe	Dobda	Dobdo	Dodbo	Dobde	_____

Answers: 2, 4, 4, 0, 3, 2, 5, 2, 5, 5

1. 489	849	489	494	498	499	_____
2. 2904	2900	2940	2904	2094	2099	_____
3. 5918	5918	5198	5988	5919	5198	_____
4. 6643	6443	6634	6644	6646	6643	_____
5. 1001	1000	1010	1100	1001	1011	_____
6. 2189	2891	2981	2189	2991	2198	_____
7. 7791	7991	7191	7197	7719	7791	_____
8. 3357	3557	3551	3531	3775	3357	_____
9. 11010	10110	01101	11010	00110	10101	_____
10. 696	969	696	669	969	996	_____

Answers: 2, 3, 1, 5, 4, 3, 5, 5, 3, 2

Looking Back

Do not fall into the trap of looking back to check your work. Many people feel the urgent need to look over the addresses one last time. If you had all day this would be fine, but remember you only have a few seconds for each one. Once you have made your initial sweeps, make your choice with no strings attached. For those of us who like to be meticulous, this may be difficult. Here are two exercises to break you of the habit of looking back.

Take a piece of paper folded lengthwise to form a rectangle. Use this to cover up the written text above the line you are working on. Use your left hand to move the paper down as you go. Obviously this won't work if you are correctly marking your lines with your fingers. Until you no longer feel the need to look back, forsake holding your spot with your fingers. Let the paper mark your spot. As you become more comfortable sticking with your original answer, you can wean yourself away from using the paper cover.

If you tend to look back only at column A when you should be looking at column B, use an index card to cover the column. This can be moved easily to allow you to scan the next line when needed but cover up the column once you have scanned the appropriate information.

Three practice exercises follow. Each exercise gets a bit harder. Ninety-five comparisons have been given so you can become familiar with the length of the exam section. Review the techniques described in the previous pages. Continue to work on and use these techniques as you complete these exercises. Practice makes them seem like second nature.

(Continue with three practice comparisons each with 95 comparisons. The first should be only numbers, the second numbers and streets, and the third a combination including states and zip codes.)

Drill: Address Checking with Numbers Only

1.	3215	3125	Ⓐ	Ⓓ
2.	4001	4001	Ⓐ	Ⓓ
3.	5931	5931	Ⓐ	Ⓓ
4.	32187	32178	Ⓐ	Ⓓ
5.	08842	08842	Ⓐ	Ⓓ
6.	74123	74123	Ⓐ	Ⓓ
7.	67	67	Ⓐ	Ⓓ
8.	2331	2332	Ⓐ	Ⓓ
9.	07512	07512	Ⓐ	Ⓓ
10.	110	1100	Ⓐ	Ⓓ
11.	51620	51620	Ⓐ	Ⓓ
12.	43102	43101	Ⓐ	Ⓓ

13. 98714	97814	Ⓐ	Ⓓ
14. 4233	4322	Ⓐ	Ⓓ
15. 37430	37431	Ⓐ	Ⓓ
16. 10112	11012	Ⓐ	Ⓓ
17. 40213	40213	Ⓐ	Ⓓ
18. 9893	9893	Ⓐ	Ⓓ
19. 31021	31021	Ⓐ	Ⓓ
20. 59710	57910	Ⓐ	Ⓓ
21. 7529	7259	Ⓐ	Ⓓ
22. 2941	294	Ⓐ	Ⓓ
23. 00145	00143	Ⓐ	Ⓓ
24. 3102	3120	Ⓐ	Ⓓ
25. 157	167	Ⓐ	Ⓓ
26. 20014	20015	Ⓐ	Ⓓ
27. 23419	23459	Ⓐ	Ⓓ
28. 485	486	Ⓐ	Ⓓ
29. 10529	10929	Ⓐ	Ⓓ
30. 14209	14209	Ⓐ	Ⓓ
31. 3391	3191	Ⓐ	Ⓓ
32. 52018	52018	Ⓐ	Ⓓ
33. 36210	36210	Ⓐ	Ⓓ
34. 98213	98213	Ⓐ	Ⓓ
35. 42189	42189	Ⓐ	Ⓓ
36. 0227	02272	Ⓐ	Ⓓ
37. 6003	6008	Ⓐ	Ⓓ
38. 973	373	Ⓐ	Ⓓ
39. 12203	12203	Ⓐ	Ⓓ
40. 49513	49518	Ⓐ	Ⓓ
41. 42038	42038	Ⓐ	Ⓓ
42. 78421	78421	Ⓐ	Ⓓ
43. 57892	57392	Ⓐ	Ⓓ
44. 32095	32005	Ⓐ	Ⓓ
45. 43215	42315	Ⓐ	Ⓓ
46. 90542	90452	Ⓐ	Ⓓ
47. 86832	86632	Ⓐ	Ⓓ
48. 95031	95031	Ⓐ	Ⓓ
49. 13922	13222	Ⓐ	Ⓓ

50. 208	208		Ⓐ	Ⓓ
51. 4096	4069		Ⓐ	Ⓓ
52. 4409-2348	4409-2348		Ⓐ	Ⓓ
53. 4864	4854		Ⓐ	Ⓓ
54. 37034	37035		Ⓐ	Ⓓ
55. 376	374		Ⓐ	Ⓓ
56. 84563	84566		Ⓐ	Ⓓ
57. 4862	4862		Ⓐ	Ⓓ
58. 694	694		Ⓐ	Ⓓ
59. 64920	64820		Ⓐ	Ⓓ
60. 482	482		Ⓐ	Ⓓ
61. 49135	49135		Ⓐ	Ⓓ
62. 79013	97013		Ⓐ	Ⓓ
63. 9465	9465		Ⓐ	Ⓓ
64. 48210	48210		Ⓐ	Ⓓ
65. 2384	2334		Ⓐ	Ⓓ
66. 593	593		Ⓐ	Ⓓ
67. 872	872		Ⓐ	Ⓓ
68. 76	76		Ⓐ	Ⓓ
69. 3947-6492	3947-6942		Ⓐ	Ⓓ
70. 5934	5934		Ⓐ	Ⓓ
71. 49892	49892		Ⓐ	Ⓓ
72. 4823	4328		Ⓐ	Ⓓ
73. 38107	38107		Ⓐ	Ⓓ
74. 53267	53267		Ⓐ	Ⓓ
75. 28103	24103		Ⓐ	Ⓓ
76. 794	794		Ⓐ	Ⓓ
77. 8524	8224		Ⓐ	Ⓓ
78. 4695	46950		Ⓐ	Ⓓ
79. 05681	05681		Ⓐ	Ⓓ
80. 582	582		Ⓐ	Ⓓ
81. 493	493		Ⓐ	Ⓓ
82. 71905	7190		Ⓐ	Ⓓ
83. 46824	46824		Ⓐ	Ⓓ
84. 31824	31824		Ⓐ	Ⓓ
85. 39640	3964		Ⓐ	Ⓓ
86. 9462	94621		Ⓐ	Ⓓ
87. 38	381		Ⓐ	Ⓓ

88.	46722	46742		Ⓐ	Ⓓ
89.	3664	3646		Ⓐ	Ⓓ
90.	548770	584770		Ⓐ	Ⓓ
91.	463	4631		Ⓐ	Ⓓ
92.	4568	4568		Ⓐ	Ⓓ
93.	734	0734		Ⓐ	Ⓓ
94.	46823	46823		Ⓐ	Ⓓ
95.	95237	95237		Ⓐ	Ⓓ

Answers to Drill: Address Checking with Numbers Only

1. (D)	20. (D)	39. (A)	58. (A)	77. (D)
2. (A)	21. (D)	40. (D)	59. (D)	78. (D)
3. (A)	22. (D)	41. (A)	60. (A)	79. (A)
4. (D)	23. (D)	42. (A)	61. (A)	80. (A)
5. (A)	24. (D)	43. (D)	62. (D)	81. (A)
6. (A)	25. (D)	44. (D)	63. (A)	82. (D)
7. (A)	26. (D)	45. (D)	64. (A)	83. (A)
8. (D)	27. (D)	46. (D)	65. (D)	84. (A)
9. (A)	28. (D)	47. (D)	66. (A)	85. (D)
10. (D)	29. (D)	48. (A)	67. (A)	86. (D)
11. (A)	30. (A)	49. (D)	68. (A)	87. (D)
12. (D)	31. (D)	50. (A)	69. (A)	88. (D)
13. (D)	32. (A)	51. (D)	70. (A)	89. (D)
14. (D)	33. (A)	52. (A)	71. (A)	90. (D)
15. (D)	34. (A)	53. (D)	72. (D)	91. (D)
16. (D)	35. (A)	54. (D)	73. (A)	92. (A)
17. (A)	36. (D)	55. (D)	74. (A)	93. (D)
18. (A)	37. (D)	56. (D)	75. (D)	94. (A)
19. (A)	38. (D)	57. (A)	76. (A)	95. (A)

Drill: Address Checking with Numbers and Street Names

1. 2112 Hilltop Road	1221 Hilltop Road	Ⓐ	Ⓓ
2. 34 Blossom Trail Road	34 Blossom Trail Avenue	Ⓐ	Ⓓ
3. 450 Chester Ct.	45 Chester Ct.	Ⓐ	Ⓓ
4. 30 Saddle River Dr.	30 Saddle River Dr.	Ⓐ	Ⓓ
5. 89 W. Fifteenth Ave. (E)	89 W. Fiftieth Ave. (E)	Ⓐ	Ⓓ
6. First & Main	First & Main	Ⓐ	Ⓓ
7. 234 Thousand Oaks	234 Thousand Oaks	Ⓐ	Ⓓ
8. 26 Apt. 5I Tenth Ave.	26 Apt. 5K Tenth Ave.	Ⓐ	Ⓓ
9. 10012 Square Mill Run	10012 Square Mill Run	Ⓐ	Ⓓ
10. 450 Hudson Apt. 52	450 Hudson Apt. S2	Ⓐ	Ⓓ
11. 49 JFK Blvd.	49 JFK Blvd.	Ⓐ	Ⓓ
12. 764 Shadowbrook	764 Shadowbrook	Ⓐ	Ⓓ
13. 420 Lafayette	420 Lafayette	Ⓐ	Ⓓ
14. 99 Harvard Street Apt. 3	99 Harvard Street Apt. 3	Ⓐ	Ⓓ

15.	8200 Tulane Street	820 Tulane Street	Ⓐ Ⓓ
16.	2193 Georges Avenue	2193 George Avenue	Ⓐ Ⓓ
17.	83 Washington Blvd.	83 Washington St.	Ⓐ Ⓓ
18.	732 Hunter's Mill	732 Hunter's Mill Run	Ⓐ Ⓓ
19.	84 Freeman Street	841 Freeman Street	Ⓐ Ⓓ
20.	30 Langford Drive	30 Lanford Drive	Ⓐ Ⓓ
21.	586 Broadway	586 W. Broadway	Ⓐ Ⓓ
22.	42 Green Street	42 Greene Street	Ⓐ Ⓓ
23.	71 Prince Avenue	71 Prince Avenue	Ⓐ Ⓓ
24.	485 Mark Drive	485 Mark Drive	Ⓐ Ⓓ
25.	55 Ludlow Street Apt. 3D	55 Ludlow Street Apt. 3D	Ⓐ Ⓓ
26.	91 Sonoma Place	91 Somona Place	Ⓐ Ⓓ
27.	66 Freeland Ave.	66 Frieland Ave.	Ⓐ Ⓓ
28.	18 Lori Drive	18 Lorry Drive	Ⓐ Ⓓ
29.	72 Beaumont Place	72 Beaumonte Place	Ⓐ Ⓓ
30.	35 Plainsville Road	35 Plainsview Road	Ⓐ Ⓓ
31.	27 Mountainview Drive	27 Mountainside Drive	Ⓐ Ⓓ
32.	87 Longley Terr.	87 Longley Terr.	Ⓐ Ⓓ
33.	49 Martin Blvd.	49 Martin Blvd.	Ⓐ Ⓓ
34.	62 Demot Lane	62 Demott Lane	Ⓐ Ⓓ
35.	23 Amwell Drive East	23 Amwell Drive East	Ⓐ Ⓓ
36.	75 (E) Broad Street	75 W. Broad Street	Ⓐ Ⓓ
37.	9067 Lyde Avenue	9076 Lyde Avenue	Ⓐ Ⓓ
38.	8213 Vert Road	8213 Vert Road	Ⓐ Ⓓ
39.	78 Franklin Blvd.	78 Franklin Blvd.	Ⓐ Ⓓ
40.	63 Rock Lake Circle	63 Rock Lake Circle	Ⓐ Ⓓ
41.	42 Fort Wayne Drive	42 Fort Wayne Drive	Ⓐ Ⓓ
42.	PO Box 4063	PO Box 4063	Ⓐ Ⓓ
43.	76 Longfellow Drive	76 Longefellow Drive	Ⓐ Ⓓ
44.	928 Beford Street	928 Medford Street	Ⓐ Ⓓ
45.	729 Deal Place	729 Deal Place	Ⓐ Ⓓ
46.	937 Black Terr.	937 Black Terr.	Ⓐ Ⓓ
47.	7650 Deland St.	7650 Dealand St.	Ⓐ Ⓓ
48.	8420 Seventh Ave.	8420 Seventh St.	Ⓐ Ⓓ
49.	8983 MacGregor Pl.	8983 McGregor Pl.	Ⓐ Ⓓ
50.	451 Highland Dr.	451 Highland Dr.	Ⓐ Ⓓ
51.	6243 US Hwy. No.1	6243 US Hwy. No.1	Ⓐ Ⓓ

52.	7459 Durham Avenue	745 Durham Avenue	Ⓐ	Ⓓ
53.	834 Edwards Blvd.	834 Edward Blvd.	Ⓐ	Ⓓ
54.	7840 King Pl.	7840 King Pl.	Ⓐ	Ⓓ
55.	67 Prospect Ave. Apt. 3	67 Prospect Ave. Apt. 3F	Ⓐ	Ⓓ
56.	985 Foxwood Road	885 Foxwood Road	Ⓐ	Ⓓ
57.	33 Causeway	333 Causeway	Ⓐ	Ⓓ
58.	401 N. Main St. Apt. 5H	401 S. Main St. Apt. 5H	Ⓐ	Ⓓ
59.	S Park & Adams	S Park & Adam	Ⓐ	Ⓓ
60.	7789 Morris Ave.	7789 Morris Ave.	Ⓐ	Ⓓ
61.	889 Handy St.	8889 Handy St.	Ⓐ	Ⓓ
62.	789 Parsonage Rd.	789 Parsonage Rd.	Ⓐ	Ⓓ
63.	76 Redmond St.	76 Readmond St.	Ⓐ	Ⓓ
64.	74921 Amboy Blvd.	74921 Amboy Blvd.	Ⓐ	Ⓓ
65.	797 Hamliton Drive	797 Hamilton Drive	Ⓐ	Ⓓ
66.	US Hwy. No. 18	US Hwy. No. 18	Ⓐ	Ⓓ
67.	831 Morgan Rd.	831 Morgan Rd.	Ⓐ	Ⓓ
68.	4447 Dayton Drive	4477 Dayton Drive	Ⓐ	Ⓓ
69.	9421 Ryan Road Apt. 2	9412 Ryan Road Apt. 2	Ⓐ	Ⓓ
70.	49 Mill Run Road	493 Mill Run Road	Ⓐ	Ⓓ
71.	1510 Stelton Street	1015 Stelton Street	Ⓐ	Ⓓ
72.	225 Madison Ave.	225 Madison Ave.	Ⓐ	Ⓓ
73.	11 Alvin Court	11 Alvin Court	Ⓐ	Ⓓ
74.	888 Railroad Drive	88 Railroad Drive	Ⓐ	Ⓓ
75.	667 French Street	667 French Street	Ⓐ	Ⓓ
76.	6775 Woodside Rd.	6775 Woodside Rd.	Ⓐ	Ⓓ
77.	597 Nassau St.	597 Nassau St.	Ⓐ	Ⓓ
78.	7546 Route 518	7456 Route 518	Ⓐ	Ⓓ
79.	56 Myrtle Drive	56 Myrtle Drive	Ⓐ	Ⓓ
80.	662 Ford Ave.	662 Fords Ave.	Ⓐ	Ⓓ
81.	2263 Baldwin Drive	226S Baldwin Drive	Ⓐ	Ⓓ
82.	20 Rose St.	20 Rose St.	Ⓐ	Ⓓ
83.	6646 Ray St.	6664 Ray St.	Ⓐ	Ⓓ
84.	8872 Duchamp Drive	8872 Duchamp Drive	Ⓐ	Ⓓ
85.	2135 Route 1	2135 Route 1	Ⓐ	Ⓓ
86.	84 North Avenue	845 North Avenue	Ⓐ	Ⓓ
87.	Main & Water	Main & Water	Ⓐ	Ⓓ
88.	775 Pfieffer Blvd.	771 Pfieffer Blvd.	Ⓐ	Ⓓ
89.	6732 Lawrence St.	6732 Lawrence St.	Ⓐ	Ⓓ

90.	34 White Oak Lane	34 White Oak Lane	Ⓐ	Ⓓ
91.	6 Patrick Blvd.	6 Patrick Blvd.	Ⓐ	Ⓓ
92.	US Hwy. No. 13 S.	US Hwy. No. 130	Ⓐ	Ⓓ
93.	84 Cotter Drive	48 Cotter Drive	Ⓐ	Ⓓ
94.	370 Ridge Road	307 Ridge Road	Ⓐ	Ⓓ
95.	541 E. Hazlewood Dr.	541 W. Hazlewood Dr.	Ⓐ	Ⓓ

Answers to Drill: Address Checking with Numbers and Street Names

1. (D)	20. (D)	39. (A)	58. (D)	77. (A)
2. (D)	21. (D)	40. (A)	59. (D)	78. (D)
3. (D)	22. (D)	41. (A)	60. (A)	79. (A)
4. (A)	23. (A)	42. (A)	61. (D)	80. (D)
5. (D)	24. (A)	43. (D)	62. (A)	81. (D)
6. (A)	25. (A)	44. (D)	63. (D)	82. (A)
7. (A)	26. (D)	45. (A)	64. (A)	83. (D)
8. (D)	27. (D)	46. (A)	65. (D)	84. (A)
9. (A)	28. (D)	47. (D)	66. (A)	85. (A)
10. (A)	29. (D)	48. (D)	67. (A)	86. (D)
11. (A)	30. (D)	49. (A)	68. (D)	87. (A)
12. (A)	31. (D)	50. (A)	69. (D)	88. (D)
13. (A)	32. (A)	51. (A)	70. (D)	89. (A)
14. (A)	33. (A)	52. (D)	71. (D)	90. (A)
15. (D)	34. (D)	53. (D)	72. (A)	91. (A)
16. (D)	35. (A)	54. (A)	73. (A)	92. (D)
17. (D)	36. (D)	55. (D)	74. (D)	93. (D)
18. (D)	37. (D)	56. (D)	75. (A)	94. (D)
19. (D)	38. (A)	57. (D)	76. (A)	95. (D)

Drill: Full Address Checking

1. 776 Circle Ave.	776 Circle Ave.	Ⓐ	Ⓓ
2. 111 Paulison Road	1111 Paulison Road	Ⓐ	Ⓓ
3. 80 Mattison Ave.	80 Mattison Ave.	Ⓐ	Ⓓ
4. 37 Minnisink Drive	37 Minnisink Drive	Ⓐ	Ⓓ
5. New York, NY	New York, NJ	Ⓐ	Ⓓ
6. 1020 Circe Ave.	1020 Circle Ave.	Ⓐ	Ⓓ
7. 349 Pier Lane Apt. 34	3490 Pier Lane Apt. 34	Ⓐ	Ⓓ
8. 27 Ellison Drive	27 Ellison Drive	Ⓐ	Ⓓ
9. 55 Fairview Drive	55 Fairlawn Drive	Ⓐ	Ⓓ
10. 114 Beach Parkway	114 Beach Parkway	Ⓐ	Ⓓ
11. 426 Fern Terr.	426 Fern Drive	Ⓐ	Ⓓ
12. 1001 Bethl Road W.	101 Bethl Road W.	Ⓐ	Ⓓ
13. Mtn. View, CA 94040	Mtn. View, CA 95040	Ⓐ	Ⓓ
14. 26 Lackawanna Ave.	26 Lackawanna Ave.	Ⓐ	Ⓓ

15. 251 Belmont	251 Belmont Apt. 1	Ⓐ	Ⓓ
16. 38 Sunset Drive	38 Sunset Drive	Ⓐ	Ⓓ
17. 4428 Manchester Road	4248 Manchester Road	Ⓐ	Ⓓ
18. 748 Barclay Court	748 Barclay Court	Ⓐ	Ⓓ
19. 134 Hamburg Drive	134 Hapsburg Drive	Ⓐ	Ⓓ
20. 71 Wooley Ave.	71 Woodley Ave.	Ⓐ	Ⓓ
21. 8 Burlington Drive	8 Burlington Drive	Ⓐ	Ⓓ
22. 34 Grand St.	34 Grand St.	Ⓐ	Ⓓ
23. 4226 Brookside Dr.	426 Brookside Dr.	Ⓐ	Ⓓ
24. 1030 Doremus La.	1030 Dormus Lane	Ⓐ	Ⓓ
25. 33 E. Second St.	33 W. Second St.	Ⓐ	Ⓓ
26. Clifton, NJ 07012	Clifton, NJ 07012	Ⓐ	Ⓓ
27. 17 Pequannock Dr.	17 Pequannock Dr.	Ⓐ	Ⓓ
28. 896 Lee Avenue	896 Leigh Avenue	Ⓐ	Ⓓ
29. 34 Robertson Drive	34 Robertsen Drive	Ⓐ	Ⓓ
30. 79 Elizabeth Pl.	79 Elizabeth Pl	Ⓐ	Ⓓ
31. 22 Little Falls Rd.	22 Little Falls Rd.	Ⓐ	Ⓓ
32. 36 Berry Drive	46 Berry Drive	Ⓐ	Ⓓ
33. 1173 Goffle St.	11173 Goffle St. W.	Ⓐ	Ⓓ
34. 3050 State Hwy. No. 280	3050 State Hwy. No. 280	Ⓐ	Ⓓ
35. 117 Westervelt Ave.	117 Westerbelt Ave	Ⓐ	Ⓓ
36. Chelsea, MA 02150	Chelsea, MD 02150	Ⓐ	Ⓓ
37. 59 Elmwood Park Apt. 2	59 Elmwood Park Apt. 2	Ⓐ	Ⓓ
38. 7801 Burlington Drive	7801 Burlington Drive	Ⓐ	Ⓓ
39. 4021 N Haledon St.	4021 S Haledon St.	Ⓐ	Ⓓ
40. 44501 Union Ave.	44501 Union Ave.	Ⓐ	Ⓓ
41. 159 Paterson Ave.	195 Paterson Ave.	Ⓐ	Ⓓ
42. 5 Lorelei Drive Apt. 55	5 Lorelei Drive Apt 5S	Ⓐ	Ⓓ
43. 77 E. Garden Pl.	77 W. Garden Pl.	Ⓐ	Ⓓ
44. Glendale, AZ 85306	Glendale, AZ 85306	Ⓐ	Ⓓ
45. 100 Busse Ln.	100 Bussel Ln.	Ⓐ	Ⓓ
46. 17 Iowa Avenue	170 Iowa Avenue	Ⓐ	Ⓓ
47. 65 S Kinellon Ave.	65 S Kinelon Ave.	Ⓐ	Ⓓ
48. 157 Valley Road	167 Valley Road	Ⓐ	Ⓓ
49. 7901 Ackerman Ct.	7901 Ackerman Ct.	Ⓐ	Ⓓ
50. 264 US Hwy. No. 46	2644 US Hwy. No. 46	Ⓐ	Ⓓ
51. 88 Forest Road S.	888 Forest Road S.	Ⓐ	Ⓓ

			A	D
52.	Brooklyn, NY 11211	Brooklyn, NY 11231	Ⓐ	Ⓓ
53.	831 Kajiawara Drive	831 Kajiawara Drive	Ⓐ	Ⓓ
54.	505 Court St.	5005 Court St.	Ⓐ	Ⓓ
55.	63 H Street Apt. 4A	631 H Street Apt. 4A	Ⓐ	Ⓓ
56.	151 Bergenline Ave.	15 Bergenline Ave.	Ⓐ	Ⓓ
57.	47 McBride Drive	47 McBride Drive	Ⓐ	Ⓓ
58.	110 Kipp Avenue	1110 Kipp Avenue	Ⓐ	Ⓓ
59.	77-1 Alabama Drive	77-1 Alabama Drive	Ⓐ	Ⓓ
60.	274 Haledon Avenue	274 Haldon Avenue	Ⓐ	Ⓓ
61.	1240 Tonnelle Avenue S	1240 Tonnelle Avenue S	Ⓐ	Ⓓ
62.	Houston, TX 77019	Houston, TX 77019	Ⓐ	Ⓓ
63.	669 Park Slope Blvd.	699 Park Slope Blvd.	Ⓐ	Ⓓ
64.	475 Crooks Ave.	475 Cook Ave.	Ⓐ	Ⓓ
65.	250 Berdan Ave. Apt. 55	250 Berdan Ave. Apt. 5D	Ⓐ	Ⓓ
66.	14-33 Plaza Blvd.	14-33 Plaza Blvd.	Ⓐ	Ⓓ
67.	216 Ellis Blvd.	216 Eli Blvd.	Ⓐ	Ⓓ
68.	E-2110 State Hwy. No. 6	W-2210 State Hwy. No 6	Ⓐ	Ⓓ
69.	400 Bushes Lane	4000 Bushes Lane	Ⓐ	Ⓓ
70.	410 Fifth Ave. Apt. 22	410 Fifth Ave. Apt. 22	Ⓐ	Ⓓ
71.	155 Willowbrook Terr.	155 Willowbrook Terr.	Ⓐ	Ⓓ
72.	55 Colfax Drive	55 Colfax Drive	Ⓐ	Ⓓ
73.	932 Piaget Ave.	932 Piage Ave.	Ⓐ	Ⓓ
74.	1112 Peakness Avenue	112 Peakness Avenue	Ⓐ	Ⓓ
75.	8 Doig Rd.	8 Dog Rd.	Ⓐ	Ⓓ
76.	Bowling Green, OH 43402	Bowling Green, OK 43402	Ⓐ	Ⓓ
77.	22 Sandcastle Drive	223 Sandcastle Drive	Ⓐ	Ⓓ
78.	1121 Key Street	1121 Key Street	Ⓐ	Ⓓ
79.	8833 Church Street	8833 Church Street	Ⓐ	Ⓓ
80.	15 Summit Ave.	15 Summit Ave.	Ⓐ	Ⓓ
81.	77 Essex Road	770 Essex Road	Ⓐ	Ⓓ
82.	4 Bramar Drive	4 Braemar Drive	Ⓐ	Ⓓ
83.	Elkridge, MD 21227	Elkridge, MD 21227	Ⓐ	Ⓓ
84.	122 Parish Drive Apt. 44	122 Parish Drive Apt. 12	Ⓐ	Ⓓ
85.	US Hwy. No. 16 & US Hwy. No. 34	US Hwy. No. 16 & US. Hwy. No. 33	Ⓐ	Ⓓ
86.	88 Broad Avenue	88 Broadview	Ⓐ	Ⓓ
87.	San Francisco, CA 94110	San Francisco, CA 94111	Ⓐ	Ⓓ
88.	1 Station Road	11 Station Road	Ⓐ	Ⓓ

89. Boulder, CO 80306	Boulder, CO 80306	Ⓐ	Ⓓ
90. 6643 Notch Ct.	7743 Notch Ct.	Ⓐ	Ⓓ
91. Carboro, NC 27510	Carrboro, NC 27510	Ⓐ	Ⓓ
92. 221 Emery Dr.	221 Emery Ave.	Ⓐ	Ⓓ
93. 5458 Alps Drive	5485 Alps Drive	Ⓐ	Ⓓ
94. 20 Onyx Terr.	20 Onyx Terr.	Ⓐ	Ⓓ
95. Orlando, FL 32801	Orlando, FL 32802	Ⓐ	Ⓓ

Answers to Drill: Full Address Checking

1. (A)	20. (D)	39. (D)	58. (D)	77. (D)
2. (D)	21. (A)	40. (A)	59. (A)	78. (A)
3. (A)	22. (A)	41. (D)	60. (D)	79. (A)
4. (A)	23. (D)	42. (D)	61. (A)	80. (A)
5. (D)	24. (D)	43. (D)	62. (A)	81. (D)
6. (D)	25. (D)	44. (A)	63. (D)	82. (D)
7. (D)	26. (A)	45. (D)	64. (D)	83. (A)
8. (A)	27. (A)	46. (D)	65. (D)	84. (D)
9. (D)	28. (D)	47. (D)	66. (A)	85. (D)
10. (A)	29. (D)	48. (D)	67. (D)	86. (D)
11. (D)	30. (A)	49. (A)	68. (D)	87. (D)
12. (D)	31. (A)	50. (D)	69. (D)	88. (D)
13. (D)	32. (D)	51. (D)	70. (A)	89. (A)
14. (A)	33. (D)	52. (D)	71. (A)	90. (D)
15. (D)	34. (A)	53. (A)	72. (A)	91. (D)
16. (A)	35. (D)	54. (D)	73. (D)	92. (D)
17. (D)	36. (A)	55. (D)	74. (D)	93. (D)
18. (A)	37. (A)	56. (D)	75. (D)	94. (A)
19. (D)	38. (A)	57. (A)	76. (D)	95. (D)

Chapter 4

Strategies for Improving on "Memory for Addresses"

Chapter 4

STRATEGIES FOR IMPROVING ON "MEMORY FOR ADDRESSES"

The second section of the postal exam is one that will test your memory. You will be given five minutes to use your memory to match 88 names and number addresses to an appropriate box. This may seem like an intimidating section, but with the techniques you will develop in this chapter, you can score high.

GENERAL TEST STRATEGIES

Guessing

While completing part one of the postal exam, "Address Checking," it is suggested that you do not guess because guessing can hurt your score. In part two, "Memory for Addresses," guessing does not hurt your score. It is therefore suggested that you guess on those problems for which you are not sure of the correct answer. Because there are five answer choices, you have a one in five or 20 percent chance of getting the answer correct. You will probably be able to discount one or two choices as not correct by the information you remember, making your chances of guessing the correct answer even better.

Shortening Information to Memorize

You will be given five boxes to memorize. It is not, however, necessary to memorize all of the five boxes. If you spend the allotted time memorizing four of the boxes so that you are sure you know the information contained in each, you need not memorize the remaining box. You never actually need to look at the fifth box. When you come across a name or number and name combination that you do not recognize, you will know that it belongs to the box which you did not memorize. Simply mark the answer for that box. This may seem a bit of a risk for some people because it seems that you are neglecting the information. This strategy is proven to maximize your time.

Using Every Minute

Prior to beginning this portion of the exam, you will be given five minutes to memorize the names and addresses in the five boxes, four of which you will worry about. After this memorization period, you will have three minutes to complete sample questions. Some people may find it helpful to complete these questions, gearing up for the ones that actually count. Most examinees use this time best by continuing the memorization process. These three minutes can serve you well in finalizing your memorization process. Because there is time allotted for the examiner to check that all students clearly understand the directions, you may find you have a few more minutes to continue memorizing, especially if there are questions from the test-takers.

TECHNIQUES FOR REMEMBERING NAME ADDRESSES

Name addresses, also referred to as direct addresses, appear two in each box. This means that you need only memorize eight names, two in each of the four boxes you have chosen to use. Below are several ways to help you memorize the names in the boxes. Practice using each one before you decide on a method. Some may take longer to master than others, but you may find you have better results using them.

Shortening

Very rarely will two names be spelled similarly. Use this to your advantage. Shorten each name to just the first syllable. By doing this you are cutting down on the information stored in your short-term memory. It is proven that the brain can store more when the information is put into chunks. The first syllable of the name can serve as a chunk. Look at how the following names have been transformed into one chunk each.

Florence	<u>Flor</u>
Higgins	<u>Hig</u>
Auerbach	<u>Auer</u>
Martino	<u>Mart</u>
Sutton	<u>Sut</u>

Now try shortening the following names. This will become a quick and easy process for you on the exam.

Surma	_____
Viggiano	_____
Packer	_____
Feldman	_____
Arnett	_____
Kislack	_____
Coleman	_____
Bandura	_____
Kauffman	_____
Newton	_____

Personal Connections

Many people remember information best when it can be given a personal meaning. Using personal items to visualize the names will help you. To do this, take a name and match it with something meaningful to you. It could be a person you know or something you enjoy doing. For instance, one name might be Bach. If you happen to know of or enjoy classical music, you will be able to associate the name Bach with the famous composer.

Imagery

Visualizing has proven effective in remembering information. If you can place the two names from the box into a meaningful picture, it will be easier to remember the names. This technique works best when you can place both names in the same visualization. Let's say one box contains the names Westwood and Charley.

Westwood: west, trees, westward, directions

Charley: a man's name, perfume, candy

Now put the two ideas into a sentence which you can visualize in your head. It might be: Charley headed west.

It is also important to remember the box in which the names were located. These names were in box D. Now make up words that begin with the letter D that you can visualize in the sentence. How about Charley headed due west? This is one sentence that you will have to remember. It may help to picture a person driving a bright orange car with pink polka dots heading west? The more outrageous the picture the easier it is to remember. Try forming imaginative sentences using the following word combinations.

First Letters

If you find that none of the names have the same first letter, you may use the first letter of each name to form associations. To begin, take the first letter from each word working horizontally across each box. The next row of names will serve as the second visualization. Suppose you see the following boxes.

A	B	C	D	E
Hoffman	Cole	Klein	Richards	Yeats
Miller	Baker	Gilbert	Dickerson	Smith

The first letters of the names in the first row are HCKRY. Now you need to use these letters to form an association. You may think of the word "hickory." Perhaps you can imagine yourself eating a large plateful of hickory-smoked sausage. Because the letters must stay in the order in which they are read from box A to E, you know that the name that starts with an H is in box A. You need not remember the name that starts with an H, just the letter it begins with.

This technique may also be used vertically if you feel there is some sort of connection to be made. An example has been done for you.

A	B	C	D	E
H	C	K	R	Y
I	A	A	E	E
M	B	G	D	S

Loci or Places

Some people find it easier to use a written set of directions while others would rather go by sight memory. Sight memory can be used to memorize the names contained in the boxes. A specific place is devoted to a specific name. To use sight memory, the name must first be given some sort of association. Take for instance the previous names of Westwood and Charley. Westwood can be remembered as the direction of west and Charley can be remembered as a man. Where the names are placed in the picture is important.

The picture that you choose should be very familiar to you, perhaps something you see every day. For this association an office hallway will be used. The place associated with box A should be first, followed by the place for box B, and so on. The names in box A can be found behind the first door, that of an office. We would say that Charley looked out the window to see the sun setting in the west.

The two names are now associated with the first room in the office. Because the path down the office hallway will never change, it is not necessary to associate the names with a letter. The first space is going to be A and the last thing seen in the office hallway will be for box E. Remember to make the association personal so that it is easier to remember quickly and easily.

Below is a list of names in five boxes. Form associations for each name using any of the above techniques. Then cover up the boxes and try matching the names to the original boxes.

A	B	C	D	E
Hoffman	Salagj	Pentz	Gage	Cogan
Rock	Kearsing	Latham	Soke	Concodora

TECHNIQUES FOR REMEMBERING NUMBERED ADDRESSES

You will be required to memorize eight sets of number addresses. Technically, you will be presented with 12 sets of numbers but remember that you will only have to memorize the numbers for four boxes. There are five ranges of numbers, which are repeated for three different streets. That means that there are 15 different possibilities you will need to remember.

Chunking

While working on memorizing names for addresses, you were introduced to chunking syllables of names. This will work for the numbers as well. All numbers are four characters ending in either 00 or 99. This makes memorizing the numbers easier. You will only have to memorize the first two numbers of each range. You may want to combine the first two numbers of each range in each box to form four numbers of six characters. Remember, we are eliminating one box. You may also want to match numbers across boxes. For instance, put the numbers for the first street in box A with the numbers for the first street in box B. You will need to choose the technique that best fits your style.

Below are examples of how you would memorize the first two numbers for each box, then chunk them for easier memorizing.

Association

You may find a personal association with a chunk of numbers. If you can find meaning in combinations of numbers, you may want to form pictures to associate with the characters. For instance, the first and second lines of numbers, when chunked, make the number 2010. The third line has the number 39. You may say "In the year 2010, I will be 39 years old." Some associations may be made by dates in history, such as 1492 with Christopher Columbus.

Number Codes

It may take some time to master this form of memorization, but it is proven to be effective. Take time to practice this technique and you will find success with it.

You will need to memorize a letter code for each number from 0 to 9. The letters are assigned by their relationship to the numbers, whether the letter starts with that sound, looks like that letter when written, or has the letter as a middle sound in the word. Memorize the following list.

1	=	W
2	=	T
3	=	R
4	=	F
5	=	P
6	=	S
7	=	V
8	=	B
9	=	N
0	=	Z

In this technique you will again take the first two numbers of the number address range. Change the numbers to letters. Following are examples of how this would be done.

56	=	PS
23	=	TR
71	=	VW
98	=	NB
14	=	WF

Now you will need to make associations. The number 56 would be PS, which could be made into "pass" by adding the vowel. Vowels may be added between the two consonants. Now match the word with the box in which it is found. This number was found in box A, so a relationship with an "a" word needs to be set up. Perhaps "pass around" would make sense for you. The number 89 would be BN, which could be associated with the word "bin." If this is in box B, you could say ""bread bin." The number 89 is found in box (B)

Drill:

DIRECTIONS: *Next to each number, write the letter combination with which it corresponds. Then, practice making word associations in the lines next to the letter combinations you have written.*

1. 72 _____ _____
2. 53 _____ _____
3. 88 _____ _____
4. 16 _____ _____
5. 92 _____ _____
6. 18 _____ _____
7. 24 _____ _____
8. 36 _____ _____
9. 45 _____ _____
10. 70 _____ _____

Answers

1. 72	=	VT	6. 18	=	WB
2. 53	=	PR	7. 24	=	TF
3. 88	=	BB	8. 36	=	RS
4. 16	=	WS	9. 45	=	FP
5. 92	=	NT	10. 70	=	VZ

Chapter 5

Strategies for Improving on "Number Series"

Chapter 5

STRATEGIES FOR IMPROVING ON "NUMBER SERIES"

Part three, "Number Series," contains 24 questions in which you are given a series of numbers and you need to find a pattern so you can determine the next two numbers in the series. Because this section requires some thought, you are given 20 minutes to finish, which is a bit more time than in the two previous sections. This part of the exam is used to show the Postal Service how well you might work with the new mechanized sorting, marking, and routing technology. It comes from the old distribution clerk exam.

Although this section may appear to deal with complicated mathematical ideas, the questions basically rely on the four basic operations: addition, subtraction, multiplication, and division. If you practice looking for patterns, there is a good chance you can score a perfect mark on this section.

GENERAL TEST STRATEGIES

Guessing

In this section, guessing will not penalize you the way it would in the "Address Checking" section. However, if you practice the techniques in this chapter and develop a rhythm, you should not have to guess very often. There should be time for you to go back to any problems you may have skipped.

Filling in Answers

You can use the fact that you have time to scrutinize the answers to your advantage. If you become stuck on a series and have time remaining, start filling in the answer choices into the series. By looking at the way the answer choices relate to the beginning of the series, you may see a relationship. Sometimes relationships will jump out at you if you can visualize the entire series. Remember, one of the answers must be correct.

Keep with Your Rhythm

By now you should be aware of the advantage of developing a rhythm on timed tests; it will be important for determining the amount of time you can allot to each number series. If, during the exam, you find yourself out of the rhythm, you may be spending too much time on difficult series. Once you give a series a good try, skip it and do the next one. Be sure to resume answering on the correct line.

TECHNIQUES TO IMPROVE SKILLS

Simple Number Series

The pattern to a simple number series should jump right out at you. It takes but a few seconds to look at the list and choose the correct answer. These series may be made by adding one to each consecutive number or by multiplying each consecutive number by three. Here are some examples of simple number series. Expect to find an array of operations as patterns for the number series on the exam.

1. 2 3 4 5 6 7 .... (adding one)

2. 34 30 26 22 18 ... (subtracting four)

3. 3 9 12 15 18 ... (multiplying by three)   It begins by multiplying then adding.

4. 81 72 63 54 45 ... (dividing by nine)   This is subtracting nine. Yes, but others may see it as products of the nine times table. Both are fine.

Complex Number Series

Unfortunately, in many of the number series that you will see on the exam, the pattern will not be as apparent as in the four examples above. By making yourself aware of the possible types of complex number series that can be devised, you will be able to decipher almost any rule presented to you. Study the typical patterns presented below. They represent rules that are frequently used on the exam.

Simple Series with a Repeating Number

1 2 3 1 4 5 1 6 ... (This is a simple pattern adding one, with a number one repeating after every two numbers in the adding series.)

Alternating Operations

7 9 6 8 5 7 ... (This is a series of plus two then minus three.)

3 18 6 36 12 ... (This pattern is times six then divide by three.)

2 4 4 8 8 16 ... (This pattern is times two with that number repeating.)

Repeating Numbers and Operations

5 12 12 5 14 14 5 16 ... (This pattern contains a repeating number, 5, with a series of plus zero then plus two.)

Two Alternating Series

5 86 7 81 10 77 14 ... (This series has one series of adding progressively by one starting with two then subtracting by one starting with five.)

Reversals of Numbers

91 19 82 28 73 ... (This pattern contains reversals of the digits in the tens and ones position.)

Cycles

4 40 44 5 50 55 6 ... (This pattern contains a progressive cycle of three numbers: a ones digit, ones digit times ten, and ones digit times eleven.)

INCREASING MATHEMATICAL SKILLS

In order to increase the speed with which you find patterns, it may be necessary to practice simple math operations. Work at performing simple addition and subtraction quickly. It may be necessary to review the multiplication tables. It is assumed that you will be able to perform the four basic mathematical operations: addition, subtraction, multiplication, and division.

Addition

Because the numbers are presented in a horizontal fashion, it may be necessary to mentally change the numbers to a vertical problem. For instance, you may have to add 17 and 18 to find a pattern. Begin by lining the ones digits one on top of the other. Once you have added the ones digits, you will add the tens digits. Do not forget to include any number that has been carried over. In other words, if the number in the ones column is greater than ten, you will need to carry the extra number into the tens column.

$$17 + 18 =$$

$$
\begin{array}{r}
17 \\
+18 \\
\hline
35
\end{array}
$$

Subtraction

Subtraction problems should be addressed in about the same manner. Begin by lining up the ones digits. Subtract these numbers first proceeding with each column to the left. If a column does not contain enough to subtract properly, you will need to borrow a group from the column on the left.

$$
\begin{array}{r}
32 \\
-11 \\
\hline
21
\end{array}
\qquad
\begin{array}{r}
{}^{2}\!\!\!\!{}^{12} \\
\cancel{32} \\
-16 \\
\hline
16
\end{array}
\qquad
\begin{array}{r}
{}^{6}\!\!\!\!{}^{18} \\
\cancel{78} \\
-39 \\
\hline
39
\end{array}
$$

Multiplication and Division

The multiplication chart has been provided so you may brush up on your facts. It may be necessary to study this so you can multiply with speed. Find one factor on the left side then the remaining factor on the top. Place your fingers on each number. If you move one right and one down, they will meet at the answer to the problem. Division is simply multiplication backwards. If you take the quotient and find the number you are dividing by on one of the sides, the answer is going to be the number on the other side.

	1	2	3	4	5	6	7	8	9	10
1	1	2	3	4	5	6	7	8	9	10
2	2	4	6	8	10	12	14	16	18	20
3	3	6	9	12	15	18	21	24	27	30
4	4	8	12	16	20	24	28	32	36	40
5	5	10	15	20	25	30	35	40	45	50
6	6	12	18	24	30	36	42	48	54	60
7	7	14	21	28	35	42	49	56	63	70
8	8	16	24	32	40	48	56	64	72	80
9	9	18	27	36	45	54	63	72	81	90
10	10	20	30	40	50	60	70	80	90	100

Drill: Practice Using Jumps of Simple Operations

1.	+2	4	6	8	10	12	14	16	18
2.	+4	___	___	___	___	___	___	___	___
3.	−9	___	___	___	___	___	___	___	___
4.	−5	___	___	___	___	___	___	___	___
5.	×7	___	___	___	___	___	___	___	___
6.	×4	___	___	___	___	___	___	___	___
7.	÷6	___	___	___	___	___	___	___	___
8.	÷8	___	___	___	___	___	___	___	___
9.	−7	___	___	___	___	___	___	___	___
10.	×3	___	___	___	___	___	___	___	___

11. +6 ___ ___ ___ ___ ___ ___ ___ ___

12. +5 ___ ___ ___ ___ ___ ___ ___ ___

13. +2 ___ ___ ___ ___ ___ ___ ___ ___

14. −4 ___ ___ ___ ___ ___ ___ ___ ___

15. ×6 ___ ___ ___ ___ ___ ___ ___ ___

16. +7 ___ ___ ___ ___ ___ ___ ___ ___

17. +4 ___ ___ ___ ___ ___ ___ ___ ___

18. −3 ___ ___ ___ ___ ___ ___ ___ ___

19. ×9 ___ ___ ___ ___ ___ ___ ___ ___

20. ×8 ___ ___ ___ ___ ___ ___ ___ ___

Chapter 6

Strategies for Improving on "Following Oral Directions"

Chapter 6

STRATEGIES FOR IMPROVING ON "FOLLOWING ORAL DIRECTIONS"

SPECIAL DIRECTIONS FOR THIS SECTION

"Following Oral Directions" is the final phase of the postal exam. It is also unconventional. The test is derived from the old Mail Handlers Exam. It is designed to tell the Postal Service how well you listen. Supervisors are looking for people who will require minimum reminders of job procedures. This test will give them an idea of how you will respond to directions on the job. Up until this point, the exam has been systematic; you progressed at your own pace marking answers down the columns as you went. This section is quite different! This is not a hard test, but because it is different from most you have seen, it may take some getting used to. On the following pages you will be presented with techniques to make you a better listener for this section of the exam and in your everyday life!

GENERAL TEST STRATEGIES

Surroundings count! Where you sit, whom you sit by, and what you are wearing may all affect your score. First, make sure that you are wearing comfortable clothing that will not momentarily distract you from the directions. Distractions may be extra long sleeves, bracelets, or tassels. Second, be sure you are sitting where you can hear. Because all of the test questions are given orally, you must be able to hear the examiner speaking. This is of the utmost importance, so if you cannot hear the examiner, politely ask that your seat be moved closer to the examiner or a loudspeaker. There is a chance the directions will be read to you from an audio cassette. Be sure that the tape player is sufficiently loud. The examiner should be made aware if the tape is not loud enough for all to hear. If you know you have trouble hearing, request a special seat before the testing date. You will be given a few practice questions before the real test begins. This is the time to make sure you can hear sufficiently. Be wary of people sitting around you. You may need to block out these people.

Although you may guess on this part of the test, please do so cautiously. The directions state that there may only be one answer on a line. If you guess blindly you may throw off a correct answer down the line. If you find you need to guess at an answer, you may want to place a very small, light "x" next to the left-hand side of the number on the answer sheet. If you want to put another answer there at a future time and you are sure that you heard those directions clearly, you may want to quickly change that answer. Be sure to erase any "x" you mark immediately after the examiner finishes. Stray marks may interfere with the grading process. Placing your answer in the correct location, as well as what to do if you find two seemingly correct answers for the same spot, will be discussed later.

TECHNIQUES FOR IMPROVING YOUR LISTENING SKILLS

Setting Yourself Up

You must take full advantage of the practice session. The examiner will read a sample of the test items. You will be listening to the volume and tone of the speaker. Become aware of the pitch and accent of the words. Becoming familiar with the pattern of speech now will make listening on the real exam easier. Acquainting yourself with the speed of the questions is also important. Remember, it is slow enough for you to answer the questions as long as you are paying attention.

Relax Yourself

No one is out to trick you on this test. Visualize yourself listening well, as if you were a soldier listening to his or her commanding officer. This would be a good time to try a relaxation technique. Here is a list of techniques you may try:

- Put down your pencil, stretch your fingers out and apart, and wiggle them. Try twirling your wrists at the same time. This will relax the muscles in your hands and wrists.

- If your back and neck are stiff, raise your shoulders while forming circular motions both backwards and forwards. Roll your head slowly from left to right, then back again, being careful not to roll your head to the back (where you might cause neck strain, which you don't need now)!

- Sit in your chair very straight with your eyes closed. Take a deep breath to the count of five. Hold it briefly then exhale slowly feeling any apprehension leaving you. Do this a few times.

- Sometimes simply sitting quietly, imagining yourself listening well, will relax you.

Practice any personal relaxation techniques that work well for you so that on the day of the test you will feel comfortable doing them.

Answer the Questions Correctly

Every question will begin with a similar line, "Look at the line..." or something very close to it. You already know those words are coming, so you can take those few moments to ready yourself for what comes next. Be prepared to look at the line the examiner is on. During these brief moments and the two-second pause after them, you should be scanning the given line. Scanning is a technique that may take some practice.

To scan correctly, begin by looking at the left side of the line. Move your eyes to the right, noticing characteristics about what you see. Are there shapes, numbers, a combination? Are the shapes and numbers large or small? You do not have to memorize exactly what you see, but you should finish the scan with a general idea of what is on the line. Take the following example.

The examiner reads, "Look at line 23. (pause) Place an X on the largest number, then ..." When the examiner began saying, "Look ...," you scanned the line and saw this:

You should have seen that there were two small squares and one large square, each with numbers in the middle. The first two numbers were single-digit numbers, while the last number had many more digits. You were NOT memorizing the numbers, just the setup of the line.

The next trick is to completely accept what the examiner is telling you. If he/she tells you to put an "x" on a certain shape or letter, you put that mark on your worksheet on the item you choose. This is called responding actively to the examiner. As the examiner is reading you should be making marks on your paper. Be sure to keep listening while you are doing this. Here is an example of an examinee who actively listened.

The examiner said, "Circle the largest shape

and put Z above the shape."

"Now, on your answer sheet, darken the space for the combination that is in the shape you just wrote in."

With your non-writing hand you should be pointing to the line that you are working on. Your fingers can keep track of any items that are important. For instance, if the examiner said, "The second to last box has a two in it …," you should have put your finger on the second to last box.

Working with the Examiner

It is important that you keep pace with the examiner. You should be thinking along with the instructions. If you find that you have missed a part of the direction or are confused, put that part of the direction out of your mind and continue with the examiner. Hopefully, you can still answer the question correctly by hearing the rest of the directions. If you spend too much time on any given aspect, there is a chance you will miss the next set of directions. You will then chance answering incorrectly on two questions. You can afford to miss the first, if you do not jeopardize the one following it. If you do miss an important part of the directions, do not panic. Set your mind to be a better listener on the next set. One missed answer will not put your entire score in jeopardy.

Marking Your Answer

This is a bigger chore than you may think. Up until now the questions have followed a numerical order. In this part of the test the examiner is going to ask you to mark your answer sheet in random order. For instance, you may be instructed to look at line one of your worksheet but mark your answer on line 57 space D of your answer sheet. For line two of your worksheet you may be asked to mark your answer in line 73 of your answer sheet.

You will not have an answer for every line on your answer sheet, in fact you will have many blanks, so do not be alarmed. You must be careful, however, to mark only one answer choice per line. If you go to mark a choice and find an answer already there, you must either erase the first mark and darken the space for your new choice or let the original mark remain. **Note: For questions that have two possible answers, the answer key will provide you with both correct choices.**

Do not be surprised if the examiner asks you to look at a line on your worksheet more than once. It is possible to be asked to use a line two, three, or even more times. You will be asked to put all of those answers on different lines on your answer sheet. You may want to practice skipping around on an answer sheet. Knowing that you can find a certain line quickly then get back to your worksheet will help keep you calmer the day of the exam.

SUGGESTIONS FOR HANDLING DIRECTIONS

"If ... then ..." or "If ... otherwise ..."

These two types of questions need to be handled carefully. Two-step problems need to be heard completely before you decide on an answer. It is important to use active listening but do not commit yourself to an answer before you hear the entire question. The following question has two parts to it; see if you can decide why you must listen to the entire direction.

"Look at line 38 on your worksheet. There are four small barrels. Each barrel has a number. If the number on the first one is less than 17, put an A after the number; otherwise, put a D after the number on the last barrel." If you had stopped after the first part, you would not have heard what to do if the first number is more than 17.

Two small but important words are "and" and "or." When the word "and" comes between two phrases, it means that both phrases must be true in order for you to complete the command or answer "yes." "If seven plus two equals nine and four is an even number, then write a C" is an example of a correct "and" statement. If seven plus two did not equal nine, it would be false even if the second part were true. Here is an example of a false "and" statement. "If the circle has corners and there is a number 17 in the circle, write A next to it. Because a circle does not have corners, this statement cannot be accepted as true. You will need to be listening for what to do in the "otherwise" statement that will follow.

"Or" statements are a bit different. In order for an "or" statement to be considered true, only one of its parts needs to be true. If the above statement contained "or," it would be true because the circle did have a number 17 inside of it.

Your score can be higher if you focus on a few important words whose definitions are critical to finding the right answer. There are location words that will help you identify items. They are "between," "including," "before," and "after." There are also words that combine information. These are the tricky ones so review what each means. They are "and," "or," "only," "all," "each," "only," "if... then..." and "if... otherwise..."

Extra Information

In the previous example, the directions asked you to look at the small barrels. It is important to focus only on important information when you are answering these questions. The fact that these were small barrels is irrelevant. As long as the shapes are all the same, the exact name is irrelevant. Pick out the irrelevant information in this sample direction.

"Look at line 5 again on your worksheet. You see bowls for pouring a pet's food in. Put an x over the one that has an even number in it. Write a C next to the number to the left of the one you "x"-ed out. Mark your answer in the space for the number/letter combination that you just made."

Counting from Left to Right

It is assumed on this part of the test that you will always count ordinal spaces from left to right. This means that if the directions state, "the second number," they describe the number in the second spot from the left-hand side of the line. Of course, if the directions specifically state a different direction, that direction is used. From which side would you start counting in these examples?

"Line 30 contains some shapes and numbers. Find the third number. If it is less than the number of days in the shortest month..." (Left)

"Look at line 15 on your worksheet. Mark a B to the right of the second number from the right." (Right)

More Than and Less Than

These words can give you trouble if you do not fully understand them. You, however, will not be fooled. When you are asked to find a number between two numbers, those numbers are never included. For instance, if you were asked to write the numbers between 40 and 45, you would need to write 41, 42, 43, and 44. The numbers 40 and 45 would not be taken into consideration.

Writing on Your Worksheet

You are allowed to write on your worksheet. In fact if you are doing active listening as was suggested, there should be marks on the lines. Remember, you may need to reuse certain lines, so keep your markings light and neat. Writing in the margins is also permissible. If you are asked to pick a number out of a list, write the list lightly and neatly in the margins of your worksheet. There is no need to memorize the list. This will only give more of a chance of error, and it may take too much time to recall and think about every number.

Looking Quickly

In the beginning of the chapter, you read about the importance of good scanning. Once the directions are being read, however, you must switch to good looking. Scanning will no longer cut it. Good looking means you must be able to look at a line quickly and know exactly what you saw. This may seem tough at first, considering there is little wait time, but it can be done quickly and easily, especially if you practice. Here are some practice ideas.

- Have a friend make sample lines for you on strips of white paper. The combinations should be of varying lengths. Use ones with three or four initially, increasing the number of items on the strip as you improve. The strips should be approximately the same dimensions as those on the practice test. You should place the pile face down then flip over one strip. Look at the strip for two seconds then turn it over. If your friend is still there, tell him/her as much of what you saw as you can remember. If your friend is not there, draw on another piece of paper what you saw.

- Create practice cards that can be used similar to a memory game. Draw items on individual cards. Shuffle the cards, turning over three or four. Look at the ones turned over for two seconds then look away. Draw or tell a friend what you saw.

- Take a quick look at something around you that you are not familiar with. The color of cars sitting next to you at a light would work well. Look away and tell someone or yourself what you saw. Attempt to be as specific as you can. This is a good way to increase your general memory skills. It will also increase your observation skills.

- Ask a friend to make up sample directions and worksheet lines. He/she can use the usual wording from the actual test so you can better familiarize yourself with them. You can practice filling in the answer sheet as you do this activity. As you are practicing these directions try to figure out if there are any specific types of questions that you have trouble completing. Are they the ones that contain arithmetic and ordinal numbers, or are they "if ... otherwise ..." directions? It would be a good idea to practice that type of question more often.

Check Your Understanding

Here is a sample set of directions. On the left side you will find the directions broken down into steps. On the right side will be the active steps or thoughts you should be having as you go along. Try covering the right side of the paper with a piece of paper. Write your steps and answer on that sheet. When you uncover the right side, check to see if you included all of the steps.

"Look at line 5 on your worksheet."

You should be scanning the line for characteristics. Your finger should be at line 5.

"Put a line under the third circle."

With a finger find the third circle and underline it.

$\underline{10}$

"Add four to the number in the circle."

Cross out the number and write down the answer to the addition problem.

$\underline{\cancel{10}}$ 14

"Write the letter D next to the new number."

Write a D.

$\underline{\cancel{10}}$ 14D

"Now on your answer sheet, darken the space for the number/letter combination."

Find line 14 on your answer sheet and shade in the oval D.   14. Ⓐ Ⓑ Ⓒ ● Ⓔ

Remember, you can do very well on this part of the test simply by having an open mind to accepting all of the directions and being a good listener and looker. Practice the skills mentioned and you will be headed toward a high score!

Postal Examination

Test 1

TEST 1

Address Checking

(Answer sheets appear in the back of this book.)

TIME: 6 Minutes
95 Questions

DIRECTIONS: In this section you will be asked to compare two lists of addresses, deciding if they are alike or different. If the addresses are alike, you will mark oval "A" on your answer sheet; if they are different, you will mark oval "D" on your answer sheet.

1. 29 Hamburg Ave.   29 Hamburg Ave.
2. 240 So. Prince Blvd.   240 So. Prince Blvd.
3. 22a Varrick St.   22a Varik St.
4. 2501 W. Huston Lane   2501 W. Huston Ave.
5. 2c November Rd.   2c November Rd.
6. 460 Highway 66   461 Highway 66
7. 35 No. 5th Ave.   35 So. 5th Ave.
8. 412A Spring Lane   412A Spring Lane
9. 2121 Broadway   2121 Broad Way
10. 232d Blake Ave.   232d Blake Ave.
11. 247 Church Blvd.   247 Church Rd.
12. 29 Roanoke Lane   29 Roanoke Lane
13. 4113E No. Campus Rd.   4113N No. Campus Rd.
14. 14 Florence Court   41 Florence Court
15. 46D Grandview Place   46B Grandview Place
16. 46 Liberty Drive   46 Liberty Drive

17.	51 Mott Place	51 Mott Place
18.	65 Mulberry Lane	65 Mulberry Ave.
19.	2156 Stanley Ave.	2561 Stanley Ave.
20.	47D Channing Way	47D Channing Lane
21.	2C Grant Rd.	2K Grant Rd.
22.	622 Gable Court	622 Grable Court
23.	12 Cooper St.	12 Cooper St.
24.	7F McCrae Way	7F MacCrea Way
25.	47R Lugosi St.	47R Lugozi St.
26.	46F Turner Ave.	46F Turner Ave.
27.	902 Randall Drive	209 Randall Drive
28.	10510 Hutton Place	15100 Hutton Place
29.	55 Quinn St.	55 Quinn Ave.
30.	362 Davis Road	362 Davies Road
31.	15 Andress-Russell Lane	13 Andress-Russell Lane
32.	32 Hepburn Ave.	23 Hepburn Ave.
33.	206A Reeves Ave.	206D Reeves Ave.
34.	311-4c Plymouth Lane	311-4c Plymouth Lane
35.	4D Merrill Ave.	4D Meril Ave.
36.	114 Winding Forest Blvd.	141 Winding Forest Blvd.
37.	1156 Huron St.	1165 Huron St.
38.	721 US Hwy. 19	721 US Hwy. 19
39.	58 Lake Way	58 Lake Ave.
40.	75 No. Wilding Ave.	75 No. Winding Ave.
41.	6511 Delores St.	6511 Delores St.
42.	1078 Veronica Ave.	1078 Veronica Place
43.	2125D Paul Blvd.	2125D Paulus Blvd.
44.	3537 US Hwy. 22	3573 US Hwy. 22

45.	38 Rosewood St.	38 Rosendod St.
46.	56B Woodland Rd.	56D Woodland Rd.
47.	1847 No. Carter Ave.	1847 No. Carter St.
48.	439S Byron Place	439S Byron Place
49.	8R West Dunne Court	8R West Dun Court
50.	19 Sixth St.	19 Sixth Ave.
51.	1K Westminster Rd.	1K Westminster Rd.
52.	2030 US Hwy. 11	2011 US Hwy. 30
53.	115 Park Gate St.	115 Park Gate St.
54.	35 Cloister Court	35 Closster Court
55.	2765 Avenelle Ave.	2765 Avenelle Ave.
56.	2131B Winding Hill Lane	2131B Windinall Lane
57.	65 Brando Terrace	56 Brando Terrace
58.	15 Shakespeare Way	15 Shake Pear Way
59.	2500 W. Chaucer St.	2500 N. Chaucer St.
60.	11R West Renoir Terrace	11R West Renoir Terrace
61.	51311 No. Rivette Rd.	51311 No. Rivette Rd.
62.	17 Wenders Way	17 Wenders Place
63.	12121 Lee Place	12121D Lee Place
64.	5W East Hitchcock St.	5E West Hitchcock St.
65.	407 Cook Lane	407 Cook Lane
66.	14 Quail Run Road	14 Quaile Road
67.	197 Blue Court	197 Blue Place
68.	431 Balliol Way	134 Balliol Way
69.	19 East Bedford Road	19 West Bedford Road
70.	1213 Bayberry Way	1213 Baybury Way
71.	2 So. Old Way Road	25 So. Old Way Road
72.	756 Ford Ave.	756 Ford Ave.

73.	1309 So. Riverview Ave.	1390 So. Riverview Ave.
74.	208 Lincoln Place	20B Lincoln Place
75.	84A Swatter Square	84A Squatter Square
76.	151515 US Hwy. 202-206	151551 US Hwy. 202-206
77.	56 Clobert Terrace	56 Collber Terrace
78.	141F Murnau Lane	141F Murnau Drive
79.	53 Sternberg Street	53 Steinberg Street
80.	6 W. MacArthur Ave.	6 N. MacArthur Ave.
81.	67 Angelika Court	67 Angel Court
82.	35 Washington Place	35 Washington Lane
83.	952D Lunar Lane	952D Lunar Lane
84.	49 Apple Orchard Terrace	49 Apple Tree Terrace
85.	2131 Crow's Mill Road	2113 Crow's Mill Road
86.	242 East Easton Rd.	242 West Easton Rd.
87.	92E Keystone Blvd.	92E Keston Blvd.
88.	223 No. Center St.	223 Center St.
89.	10 Capra Court	10 Capra Court
90.	119A South Day Lane	119F South Day Lane
91.	59 First Ave.	51 Ninth Ave.
92.	215 Gertrude St.	215 Gertrude St.
93.	20 Dance Hall Place	20 Dansall Place
94.	4757B North Dundee Ave.	4757B North Dundee Ave.
95.	44F West Welles Way	44F West Welles Place

TEST 1

Memory for Addresses

(Answer sheets appear in the back of this book.)

TIME: Study 5 Minutes, Work 5 Minutes
88 Questions

DIRECTIONS: Below are five boxes labeled A,B,C,D, and E. Each box contains five addresses. You will be given five minutes to memorize the addresses in the boxes and their locations. After five minutes are up, you will have an additional five minutes to answer the following 88 questions and mark on the answer sheet the letter of the box in which the address belongs. You will not be able to refer back to the boxes once you begin answering the questions.

A	B	C	D	E
3200-4499 Poe	5700-6899 Poe	4100-5699 Poe	3500-4799 Poe	4300-5899 Poe
Samuel	Lake	Louise	Pond	Livingston
4100-5699 Clark	4300-5899 Clark	5700-6899 Clark	3200-4499 Clark	3500-4799 Clark
Palley	Knapp	Aspen	Harper	Larkin
3500-4799 Burger	3200-4499 Burger	4300-5899 Burger	4100-5699 Burger	5700-6899 Burger

1. Lake
2. 4300-5899 Burger
3. Louise
4. Knapp
5. 4300-5899 Poe
6. 4100-5699 Burger
7. Palley
8. Pond
9. 4100-5699 Poe
10. Larkin
11. 3500-4799 Poe
12. 3200-4499 Clark
13. Samuel
14. 3500-4799 Clark
15. 5700-6899 Clark
16. Harper
17. 3200-4499 Poe
18. Livingston
19. 5700-6899 Poe
20. Aspen
21. 4100-5699 Clark
22. 4300-5899 Clark
23. 5700-6899 Burger
24. 3500-4799 Burger
25. 3200-4499 Burger
26. 4300-5899 Burger

27. Larkin

28. Lake

29. 3200-4499 Poe

30. Palley

31. 3500-4799 Poe

32. Knapp

33. 5700-6899 Poe

34. Louise

35. 3200-4499 Clark

36. Harper

37. 4300-5899 Poe

38. Samuel

39. Knapp

40. 4100-5699 Poe

41. 5700-6899 Clark

42. Livingston

43. Pond

44. 3200-4499 Burger

45. 4100-5699 Clark

46. Aspen

47. 3500-4799 Clark

48. 4100-5699 Burger

49. 3500-4799 Poe

50. 3500-4799 Burger

51. Lake

52. 4300-5899 Clark

53. Palley

54. Larkin

55. 4300-5899 Burger

56. Samuel

57. 3200-4499 Poe

58. Harper

59. 5700-6899 Burger

60. Louise

61. Knapp

62. Palley

63. 4100-5699 Clark

64. Pond

65. 3200-4499 Clark

66. Livingston

67. 4100-5699 Poe

68. 5700-6899 Poe

69. 3200-4499 Burger

70. 3500-4799 Burger

71. Aspen

72. Lake

73. Larkin

74. 3500-4799 Poe

75. Harper

76. 4300-5899 Poe

77. Samuel

78. 4300-5899 Clark

79. 5700-6899 Clark

80. 4300-5899 Burger

81. Livingston

82. 3500-4799 Clark

83. 5700-6899 Burger

84. Palley

85. Knapp

86. 4100-5699 Burger

87. Pond

88. Louise

TEST 1

Number Series

(Answer sheets appear in the back of this book.)

TIME: 20 Minutes
24 Questions

DIRECTIONS: For each question, there is a series of numbers that follow some definite order. Look at the series of numbers and decide which two numbers will come next in the series. You will be given five answers to choose from.

1. 1   13   25   37   49   61   73   _____   _____
    (A) 91, 99
    (B) 97, 109
    (C) 112, 120
    (D) 89, 97
    (E) 85, 97

2. 2   3   4   3   6   3   8   3   _____   _____
    (A) 8, 4
    (B) 9, 13
    (C) 3, 10
    (D) 9, 3
    (E) 10, 3

3. 1   2   3   5   8   13   21   _____   _____
    (A) 34, 55
    (B) 35, 43

(C) 42, 84

(D) 55, 76

(E) 35, 54

4.   1   3   4   6   7   9   10   12   _____   _____

(A) 13, 14

(B) 11, 13

(C) 15, 17

(D) 13, 15

(E) 14, 16

5.   2   4   8   16   32   64   128   _____   _____

(A) 130, 132

(B) 256, 512

(C) 512, 652

(D) 260, 520

(E) 232, 464

6.   1   1   2   1   3   1   4   1   _____   _____

(A) 1, 5

(B) 6, 1

(C) 5, 1

(D) 3, 2

(E) 1, 7

7.   1   3   7   15   31   63   127   _____   _____

(A) 254, 508

(B) 256, 510

(C) 253, 507

(D) 255, 511

(E) 250, 510

8. 2   10   18   26   34   42   50   58   _____   _____

(A) 66, 74

(B) 62, 70

(C) 74, 80

(D) 60, 68

(E) 66, 72

9. 2   8   10   8   18   8   26   8   34   8   _____   _____

(A) 8, 34

(B) 34, 9

(C) 42, 8

(D) 8, 42

(E) 9, 42

10. 1   7   2   14   3   21   4   28   _____   _____

(A) 35, 42

(B) 42, 7

(C) 5, 28

(D) 5, 7

(E) 5, 35

11. 13   42   129   390   1,173   3,522   _____   _____

(A) 4,111, 7,211

(B) 10,569, 31,710

(C) 5,411, 10,569

(D) 7,211, 31,710

(E) 10,569, 31,717

12. 2   6   22   86   342   1,366   5,462   21,846   _____   _____

    (A)   85,334, 341,334

    (B)   85,336, 341,334

    (C)   31,334, 41,334

    (D)   35,335, 85,336

    (E)   31,335, 41,336

13. 1   5   9   13   17   21   25   29   _____   _____

    (A)   27, 31

    (B)   33, 37

    (C)   31, 35

    (D)   31, 37

    (E)   32, 36

14. 1   3   11   43   171   683   2,731   10,923   _____   _____

    (A)   43,691, 174,763

    (B)   11,846, 23,822

    (C)   30,788, 60,924

    (D)   46,392, 174,764

    (E)   11,923, 129,323

15. 2   4   7   11   16   22   29   37   _____   _____

    (A)   35, 43

    (B)   41, 58

    (C)   46, 56

    (D)   46, 58

    (E)   92, 184

16. 4   8   12   16   20   24   28   32   _____   _____

    (A)   38, 42

    (B)   38, 40

    (C)   40, 44

    (D)   44, 50

    (E)   36, 40

17. 15   30   45   60   75   90   105   120   _____   _____

    (A)   135, 150

    (B)   150, 135

    (C)   130, 140

    (D)   135, 160

    (E)   125, 135

18. 11   21   31   41   51   61   71   81   _____   _____

    (A)   19, 21

    (B)   90, 101

    (C)   11, 121

    (D)   91, 101

    (E)   91, 111

19. 2   6   18   54   162   486   1,458   4,374   _____   _____

    (A)   5,374, 6,374

    (B)   13,122, 39,366

    (C)   31,122, 39,366

    (D)   16,122, 28,486

    (E)   5,121, 6,366

20. 1.1   2.1   3.1   4.1   5.1   6.l   7.1   8.1   _____   _____

    (A)   9.1, 10.1

    (B)   9.1, 10.01

    (C)   9.1, 10.9

    (D)   10.10, 9.9

    (E)   11.1, 12.1

21. 5   11   23   47   95   191   383   767   _____   _____

    (A)   867, 1,067

    (B)   1,535, 3,071

    (C)   1,530, 1,370

    (D)   1,450, 2,900

    (E)   854, 1,600

22. 3   5   7   5   11   5   15   5   _____   _____

    (A)   17, 5

    (B)   5, 19

    (C)   19, 5

    (D)   17, 19

    (E)   5, 25

23. 1   37   2   37   3   37   4   37   _____   _____

    (A)   37, 5

    (B)   5, 37

    (C)   7, 37

    (D)   5, 35

    (E)   6, 38

24. 2   1   4   3   6   5   8   7   _____   _____

    (A) 9, 10

    (B) 9, 8

    (C) 8, 10

    (D) 9, 11

    (E) 10, 9

TEST 1

Following Oral Directions - Worksheet

(Answer sheets appear in the back of this book.)

TIME: Instructions will be read at approximately 80 words per minute.

DIRECTIONS: Follow the instructions that are read to you. They will not be repeated during the examination. You are to mark your worksheets according to the instructions that are read to you. After each set of instructions, you will be given time to record your answer on your answer sheet. You should have only one space darkened for each number. If you go to darken a space for a number and you have already darkened another space, either erase the first mark and darken the space for your new choice **or** let the original mark remain.

---

1. 245   321   250   340   352

2. A _____   50 _____

3. June   December   September   May

4. E   D   C   B   A
    10:15   11:02   9:43   10:07   9:53

5. E   D   C   B   A
    2   4   5   6   8

6. A _____   B _____   3 _____   D _____

7. New York   Washington   Tulsa   Alabama

8. (19) △46 (58) [82]

9. 08904   07901   08702   08775

10. 16   6   29   9   38   8

TEST 1

ANSWER KEY

Address Checking

1. (A)	15. (D)	29. (D)	43. (D)	57. (D)	71. (D)	85. (D)
2. (A)	16. (A)	30. (D)	44. (D)	58. (D)	72. (A)	86. (D)
3. (D)	17. (A)	31. (D)	45. (D)	59. (D)	73. (D)	87. (D)
4. (D)	18. (D)	32. (D)	46. (D)	60. (A)	74. (D)	88. (D)
5. (A)	19. (D)	33. (D)	47. (D)	61. (A)	75. (D)	89. (A)
6. (D)	20. (D)	34. (A)	48. (A)	62. (D)	76. (D)	90. (D)
7. (D)	21. (D)	35. (D)	49. (D)	63. (D)	77. (D)	91. (D)
8. (A)	22. (D)	36. (D)	50. (D)	64. (D)	78. (D)	92. (A)
9. (D)	23. (A)	37. (D)	51. (A)	65. (A)	79. (D)	93. (D)
10. (A)	24. (D)	38. (A)	52. (D)	66. (D)	80. (D)	94. (A)
11. (D)	25. (D)	39. (D)	53. (A)	67. (D)	81. (D)	95. (D)
12. (A)	26. (A)	40. (D)	54. (D)	68. (D)	82. (D)	
13. (D)	27. (D)	41. (A)	55. (A)	69. (D)	83. (A)	
14. (D)	28. (D)	42. (D)	56. (D)	70. (D)	84. (D)	

Memory for Addresses

1. (B)	14. (E)	27. (E)	40. (C)	53. (A)	66. (E)	79. (C)
2. (C)	15. (C)	28. (B)	41. (C)	54. (E)	67. (C)	80. (C)
3. (C)	16. (D)	29. (A)	42. (E)	55. (C)	68. (B)	81. (E)
4. (B)	17. (A)	30. (A)	43. (D)	56. (A)	69. (B)	82. (E)
5. (E)	18. (E)	31. (D)	44. (B)	57. (A)	70. (A)	83. (E)
6. (D)	19. (B)	32. (B)	45. (A)	58. (D)	71. (C)	84. (A)
7. (A)	20. (C)	33. (B)	46. (C)	59. (E)	72. (B)	85. (B)
8. (D)	21. (A)	34. (C)	47. (E)	60. (C)	73. (E)	86. (D)
9. (C)	22. (B)	35. (D)	48. (D)	61. (B)	74. (D)	87. (D)
10. (E)	23. (E)	36. (D)	49. (D)	62. (A)	75. (D)	88. (C)
11. (D)	24. (A)	37. (E)	50. (A)	63. (A)	76. (E)	
12. (D)	25. (B)	38. (A)	51. (B)	64. (D)	77. (A)	
13. (A)	26. (C)	39. (B)	52. (B)	65. (D)	78. (B)	

Note: There is only an answer key for the "Memory for Addresses" section.

Number Series

1.	(E)	13.	(B)
2.	(E)	14.	(A)
3.	(A)	15.	(C)
4.	(D)	16.	(E)
5.	(B)	17.	(A)
6.	(C)	18.	(D)
7.	(D)	19.	(B)
8.	(A)	20.	(A)
9.	(C)	21.	(B)
10.	(E)	22.	(C)
11.	(B)	23.	(B)
12.	(A)	24.	(E)

Following Oral Directions

(Please see "Detailed Explanations of Answers.")

DETAILED EXPLANATIONS
OF ANSWERS

Test 1

Address Checking

1. alike
2. alike
3. 22a Varrick St.   22a Varick St.
4. 2501 W. Huston **Lane**   2501 W. Huston **Ave.**
5. alike
6. **460** Highway 66   **461** Highway 66
7. 35 **No.** 5th Ave.   35 **So.** 5th Ave.
8. alike
9. 2121 **Broadway**   2121 **Broad Way**
10. alike
11. 247 Church **Blvd.**   247 Church **Rd.**
12. alike
13. 4113**E** No. Campus Rd.   4113**N** No. Campus Rd.
14. **14** Florence Court   **41** Florence Court
15. 46**D** Grandview Place   46**B** Grandview Place
16. alike
17. alike
18. 65 Mulberry **Lane**   65 Mulberry **Ave.**
19. 2**156** Stanley Ave.   2**561** Stanley Ave.
20. 47D Channing **Way**   47D Channing **Lane**
21. 2**C** Grant Rd.   2**K** Grant Rd.
22. 622 Gable Court   622 Grable Court
23. alike
24. 7F McCrae Way   7F MacCrea Way
25. 47R Lugosi St.   47R Lugozi St.
26. alike

27. **902** Randall Drive   **209** Randall Drive
28. **10510** Hutton Place   **15100** Hutton Place
29. 55 Quinn **St.**   55 Quinn **Ave.**
30. 362 Davis Road   362 Davies Road
31. 15 Andress-Russell Lane   13 Andress-Russell Lane
32. **32** Hepburn Ave.   **23** Hepburn Ave.
33. 206**A** Reeves Ave.   206**D** Reeves Ave.
34. alike
35. 4D Mer**rill** Ave.   4D Meril Ave.
36. **114** Winding Forest Blvd.   **141** Winding Forest Blvd.
37. 11**56** Huron St.   11**65** Huron St.
38. alike
39. 58 Lake **Way**   58 Lake **Ave.**
40. 75 No. W**ild**ing Ave.   75 No. W**ind**ing Ave.
41. alike
42. 1078 Veronica **Ave.**   1078 Veronica **Place**
43. 2125D Paul Blvd.   2125D Paul**us** Blvd.
44. 35**37** US Hwy. 22   35**73** US Hwy. 22
45. 38 Rose**wood** St.   38 Rose**ndod** St.
46. 56**B** Woodland Rd.   56**D** Woodland Rd.
47. 1847 No. Carter **Ave.**   1847 No. Carter **St.**
48. alike
49. 8R West Dun**ne** Court   8R West Dun Court
50. 19 Sixth **St.**   19 Sixth **Ave.**
51. alike
52. 20**30** US Hwy. **11**   2011 US Hwy. **30**
53. alike
54. 35 Cloister Court   35 Closster Court
55. alike
56. 2131B Windin**g Hill** Lane   2131B Windin**all** Lane
57. **65** Brando Terrace   **56** Brando Terrace
58. 15 **Shakespeare** Way   15 **Shake Pear** Way
59. 2500 **W.** Chaucer St.   2500 **N.** Chaucer St.
60. alike
61. alike
62. 17 Wenders **Way**   17 Wenders **Place**
63. 12121 Lee Place   12121**D** Lee Place

64.	5**W** **East** Hitchcock St.	5**E** **West** Hitchcock St.
65.	alike	
66.	14 Quail **Run** Road	14 Quail**e** Road
67.	197 Blue **Court**	197 Blue **Place**
68.	431 Balliol Way	134 Balliol Way
69.	19 **East** Bedford Road	19 **West** Bedford Road
70.	1213 Bay**b**erry Way	1213 Bay**bury** Way
71.	2 So. Old Way Road	25 So. Old Way Road
72.	alike	
73.	1309 So. Riverview Ave.	1390 So. Riverview Ave.
74.	208 Lincoln Place	20B Lincoln Place
75.	84A Swatter Square	84A S**qu**atter Square
76.	151515 US Hwy. 202-206	151551 US Hwy. 202-206
77.	56 **Clobert** Terrace	56 **Collber** Terrace
78.	141F Murnau **Lane**	141F Murnau **Drive**
79.	53 Sternberg Street	53 Steinberg Street
80.	6 **W.** MacArthur Ave.	6 **N.** MacArthur Ave.
81.	67 Angel**ika** Court	67 Angel Court
82.	35 Washington **Place**	35 Washington **Lane**
83.	alike	
84.	49 Apple **Orchard** Terrace	49 Apple **Tree** Terrace
85.	2131 Crow's Mill Road	2113 Crow's Mill Road
86.	242 **East** Easton Rd.	242 **West** Easton Rd.
87.	92E Keysto**ne** Blvd.	92E Keston Blvd.
88.	223 **No.** Center St.	223 Center St.
89.	alike	
90.	119**A** South Day Lane	119**F** South Day Lane
91.	5**9** **First** Ave.	5**1** **Ninth** Ave.
92.	alike	
93.	20 **Dance Hall** Place	20 **Dansall** Place
94.	alike	
95.	44F West Welles **Way**	44F West Welles **Place**

Number Series

1. **(E)** This is a single series increasing in steps of 12. So the correct answer is (E) 85, 97.

2. **(E)** This is a single series increasing in steps of 2, with a constant (3) between terms. So the correct answer is (E) 10, 3.

3. **(A)** This is a Fibonacci sequence: each term, after the first, is obtained by adding together the preceding two terms. [For example, 3 = 1 + 2 and 5 = 2 + 3.] Therefore the correct answer is (A) 34, 55.

4. **(D)** There are two alternating series here (1, 4, 7, etc. and 3, 6, 9, etc.), each increasing in steps of 3. The correct answer is (D) 13, 15.

5. **(B)** This series consists of consecutive powers of 2; each number is obtained by multiplying the preceding one by 2. So the correct answer is (B) 256, 512.

6. **(C)** This is essentially a single series consisting of consecutive integers (1,2,3, etc.), with a constant (1) between terms. So the correct answer is (C) 5, 1.

7. **(D)** One easy way to continue this series is to multiply each term (after 1) by 2 and subtract 1 from the result. The correct answer is (D) 255, 511.

8. **(A)** This is a single series, with terms increasing in steps of 8. So the correct answer is (A) 66, 74.

9. **(C)** This is essentially a single series, increasing in steps of 8, with a constant (8) intervening between terms. So the correct answer is (C) 42, 8.

10. **(E)** There are two alternating series here. The first (1,2,3, etc.) increases in steps of 1, while each term in the second series (7, 14, 21, etc.) is obtained by adding 7 to the preceding number. So the correct answer is (E) 5, 35.

11. **(B)** In this series, each term, starting from the second, is obtained by multiplying the preceding number by 3, and then adding 3 to that result. For example, $[(13 \times 3) + 3 = 42]$. The correct response is (B) 10,569, 31,710.

12. **(A)** In this series, multiply each term by 4 and subtract 2 from the result. So the correct answer is (A) 87,382, 349,526.

13. **(B)** In this series, the terms increase in steps of 4. So the correct answer is (B) 33, 37.

14. **(A)** In this series, the difference between consecutive terms is growing by a factor of 4. To obtain a new term, beginning from the third, multiply the difference between the preceding two terms by 4 and add the result to the immediately preceding term. [For example, 43 = {(11 – 3) × 4} + 11.] So the correct answer is (A) 43,691, 174,763.

15. **(C)** The difference between consecutive terms in this series increases by 1. [For example, 4 – 2 = 2; 7 – 4 = 3; 11 – 7 = 4, etc.] So the correct response is (C) 46, 56.

16. **(E)** This series consists of consecutive multiples of 4. (The terms increase in steps of 4.) So the correct answer is (E) 36, 40.

17. **(A)** This series consists of consecutive multiples of 15. (The terms increase in steps of 15.) So the correct answer is (A) 135, 150.

18. **(D)** The terms in this series increase in steps of 10. The correct response is (D) 91, 101.

19. **(B)** There are two alternating series here (2, 18, 162, etc., and 6, 54, 486, etc.), each increasing by a factor of 9. To obtain a new term in one series, multiply the preceding term in that series by 9. [For example, 18 = 2 × 9 and 54 = 6 × 9.] So the correct answer is (B) 13,122, 39,366.

20. **(A)** The numbers in this series increase in steps of 1.0. So the correct response is (A) 9.1, 10.1.

21. **(B)** The difference between consecutive terms in this series increases by a factor of 2. To obtain a new term, beginning from the third, multiply the difference between the preceding two terms by 2 and add the result to the immediately preceding term. [For example, 23 = {(11 – 5) × 2} + 11.] So the correct answer is (B) 1,535, 3,071.

22. **(C)** Beginning with 3, add 4, and separate all numbers by the number 5. The correct response is (C) 19, 5.

23. **(B)** There is essentially only one series, consisting of consecutive integers (1,2,3, etc.), with a constant (37) intervening between consecutive terms. The correct response is (B) 5, 37.

24. **(E)**   There are two alternating series here: the first consists of consecutive even numbers (2, 4, 6, etc.) and the second consists of consecutive odd numbers (1, 3, 5, etc.). The correct answer is (E) 10, 9.

Following Oral Directions

This is how your worksheet should look:

1. **A** 245   **B** 321   **C** 250   **D** 3④0   **E** 352

2. A __25__   50 __B__

3. June   December   September   May

4. E   D   C   B   A
    10:15   11:02   9:43   10:07   9:53

5. E   D   C   B   A
    2   4   5   6   8

6. A __24__   B __56__   3 __C__   D __76__

7. New York   Washington   Tulsa   Alabama

8. (19)   △D 46   58   ☐B 82

9. 0890④   0⑦901   08702   08775

10. △16E   6   (29)   9   ☐38   8

In this section, please note that the solution to each problem is preceded by the actual instructions read by the examiner.

Examine sample one. (Pause 2-3 seconds) Write the letter A as in "apple" through E as in "elephant" in alphabetical order above each of these numbers. (Pause 5 seconds) If the number under the letter E as in "elephant" is more than the sum of the number under C as in "cat" plus 100, go to number 12 on the answer sheet and fill in the letter C as in "cat." (Pause 5 seconds) If it is equal to or less than the number under C as in "cat" plus 100, go to number 21 and darken the oval for B as in "boy." (Pause 5 seconds)

ANSWER: Since the number under E (352) is more than the sum of the number under C plus 100 (250 +100 = 350), go to number 12 on your answer sheet and fill in the oval for C.

Examine sample one again. (Pause 2-3 seconds) Find the second highest even number. (Pause 2 seconds) If this is under A as in "apple," C as in "cat," or E as in "elephant," circle the first two digits of this number. (Pause 2 seconds) If it is under B as in "boy" or D as in "dog," circle the last two digits. (Pause 2 seconds) Darken the corresponding letter/number combination on your answer sheet. (Pause 5 seconds)

ANSWER: The second highest even number is 340. Since it is under D, circle the last two digits (40). Darken the corresponding number/letter combination on your answer sheet—40 D.

Examine sample two. (Pause 2-3 seconds) If Monday comes before Friday and Tuesday, write the letter B as in "boy" next to the number 50. (Pause 2 seconds) Otherwise, write the letter C as in "cat" in the same space. (Pause 2 seconds) Now go to the number 14 on your answer sheet and darken the space for E as in "elephant." (Pause 5 seconds)

ANSWER: Since Monday comes before Friday and Tuesday, write the letter B next to the number 50. Now go to the number 14 on your answer sheet and darken the oval for E.

Examine sample two again. (Pause 2-3 seconds) Write the number equivalent to one-half of 50 on the space next to the letter shown. (Pause 2 seconds) Darken the corresponding number/letter combination on your answer sheet. (Pause 5 seconds)

ANSWER: Write the number equivalent to one-half of 50 (25) on the space next to the letter shown (A). Darken the corresponding number/letter combination—25 A.

Examine sample three. (Pause 2-3 seconds) If any of these months are adjacent to each other during the year, go to number 47 on your answer sheet and darken the oval for D as in "dog." (Pause 5 seconds) Otherwise, go to the same number and darken the oval for A as in "apple." (Pause 5 seconds)

ANSWER: Since May and June are adjacent to each other during the year, go to number 47 on your answer sheet and darken the oval for D.

Examine sample three again. (Pause 2-3 seconds) If two or more of these months encompass two different seasons, go to numbers 51 and 32 on your answer sheet and darken the spaces for A as in "apple" in both of them. (Pause 7 seconds) Otherwise, go to 42 and darken the same letter. (Pause 5 seconds)

ANSWER: Since the four months listed encompass all four seasons, go to numbers 51 and 32 on your answer sheet and darken the ovals for A

Examine sample four. (Pause 2-3 seconds) Each letter represents a house on the same route, and the number shows what time the mailman reached each house on a particular day. If the mailman arrived at house B as in "boy" more than one-half hour before he arrived at house D as in "dog," go to number 59 on your answer sheet and darken the oval for C as in "cat." (Pause 7 seconds) Otherwise, go to 95 and darken the same letter. (Pause 5 seconds)

ANSWER: Since the mailman arrived at house B (10:07) more than one-half hour before he arrived at house D (11:02), go to 59 on your answer sheet and darken the circle for C.

Examine sample four again. (Pause 2-3 seconds) If the earliest time shown ends with an odd number, go to that number on your answer sheet and darken the oval for B as in "boy." (Pause 2 seconds) If it ends with an even number, go to that number plus one on your answer sheet and darken the circle for E as in "elephant." (Pause 5 seconds)

ANSWER: Since the earliest time shown (9:43) ends with an odd number (43), go to that number on your answer sheet and darken the oval for B.

Examine sample five. (Pause 2-3 seconds) If the number under C as in "cat" is one more than the number under B as in "boy" but one less than the number under D as in "dog," go to number 23 on your answer sheet and darken the letter A as in "apple." (Pause 7 seconds) Otherwise, go to number 31 and darken the same letter. (Pause 5 seconds)

ANSWER: Since the number under C (5) is not one more than the number under B (6) nor one less than the number under D (4), go to number 31 and darken the oval for A.

Examine sample five again. (Pause 2-3 seconds) Find the number under C as in "cat" on your answer sheet. Now darken the oval for the letter over the number four in the sample. (Pause 5 seconds) Find the number under D as in "dog," and darken the oval for the letter over number five in the sample. (Pause 5 seconds)

ANSWER: Find the number under C (5) and darken the oval for the letter over the number 4 (D). You should have darkened 4 D. Find the number under D (4) and darken the oval for the letter over 5 (C). You should have darkened 5 C.

Examine sample six. (Pause 2-3 seconds) Write the third letter of the alphabet on the space next to the only number in the sample. (Pause 2 seconds) Darken this number/letter combination on your answer sheet. (Pause 5 seconds)

ANSWER: Go to number 3 (the only number in the sample) and darken the oval for C (the third letter of the alphabet).

Examine sample six again. (Pause 2-3 seconds) Write the numbers 24, 56, and 76, in that order, on the spaces next to the letters. (Pause 5 seconds) Darken these combinations on your answer sheet. (Pause 5 seconds)

ANSWER: Go to 24 on your answer sheet and darken the oval for A. Go to 56 on your answer sheet and darken the oval for B. Go to 76 on your answer sheet and darken the oval for D.

Examine sample seven. (Pause 2-3 seconds) If any of the names in the sample could be the name of a state or a city, go to number 15 on your answer sheet and darken the space for B as in "boy." (Pause 5 seconds) If they are all only cities, go to number 49 on your answer sheet and darken the space for E as in "elephant." (Pause 2 seconds) If they are all only states, go to number 60 and darken the oval for D as in "dog." (Pause 5 seconds)

ANSWER: Since New York and Washington can be the names of both a state and a city, go to number 15 on your answer sheet and darken the oval for B.

Examine sample seven again. (Pause 2-3 seconds) If the second word of the first name has the same number of letters as the third name listed, go to number 17 on your answer sheet and darken the letter for B as in "boy." (Pause 7 seconds) Otherwise, go to number 26 and darken the space for the same letter. (Pause 5 seconds)

ANSWER: Since the second word of the first name (York) does not have the same number of letters in the third name listed (Tulsa), go to number 26 and darken the oval for B.

Examine sample seven again. (Pause 2-3 seconds) If the last place mentioned is north of the first place mentioned, go to number 44 on your answer sheet and darken the space for A as in "apple." (Pause 5 seconds) If it is south, go to number 41 and darken the space for D as in "dog." (Pause 5 seconds)

ANSWER: Since the last place mentioned (Alabama) is south of the first place mentioned (New York), go to number 41 on your answer sheet and darken the oval for D.

Examine sample eight. (Pause 2-3 seconds) If all the numbers in the triangle are odd numbers, put the letter B as in "boy" in the second circle. (Pause 2 seconds) If all the odd numbers are in circles, put the letter B as in "boy" in the square. (Pause 2 seconds) Darken the corresponding number/letter combination on your answer sheet. (Pause 5 seconds)

ANSWER: There is only one odd number (19) and it is in the circle. Therefore, put the letter B in the square and darken the corresponding number/letter combination—82 B.

Examine sample three again. (Pause 2-3 seconds) If the third month shown has more letters than the second but less than the fourth, go to number 68 on your answer sheet and darken the oval for C as in "cat." (Pause 7 seconds) If it has more than any other month shown, go to the same number and darken the space for D as in "dog." (Pause 5 seconds)

ANSWER: Since the third month shown (September) has more letters (9) than any of the other months shown, go to number 68 and darken the oval for D.

Examine sample eight again. (Pause 2-3 seconds) If the second number is more than the sum of the numbers in circles, put the letter C as in "cat" in the triangle. (Pause 7 seconds) If not, put the letter D as in "dog" in the triangle. (Pause 2 seconds) Darken the corresponding number/letter combination. (Pause 5 seconds)

ANSWER: Since the second number (46) is not more than the sum of the numbers in the circles (19 + 58 = 77), put the letter D in the triangle. Darken the corresponding number/letter combination—46 D.

Examine sample nine. (Pause 2-3 seconds) These numbers represent zip codes from different towns in the same state. The lower the number, the farther south the town. Find the town that is farthest south. (Pause 2 seconds) Circle the second and third digits. (Pause 2 seconds) Go to the number in the circle on your answer sheet and darken A as in "apple." (Pause 5 seconds)

ANSWER: The second zip code listed (07901) is the lowest number and therefore the farthest south. Circle the second and third digits (79). Go to the number 79 on your answer sheet and darken A.

Examine sample four again. (Pause 2-3 seconds) If the time under B as in "boy" is earlier than the time under E as in "elephant" but later than the time under A as in "apple," go to the number equivalent to the minute after the hour on your answer sheet and darken the letter B as in "ball." (Pause 5 seconds) Otherwise, go to the number corresponding to the minutes after the hour under E as in "elephant" and darken the circle for B as in "boy." (Pause 5 seconds)

ANSWER: The time under B (10:07) is earlier than the time under E (10:15) but later than the time under A (9:53). Therefore, go to the number equivalent to the minute after the hour (7) on your answer sheet and darken the oval for B.

Examine sample nine again. (Pause 2-3 seconds) Find the town that is farthest north. Circle the fourth and fifth digits. (Pause 2 seconds) Now find the number in the circle on your answer sheet and darken E as in "elephant." (Pause 5 seconds)

ANSWER: The first zip code listed (08904) is the highest number and therefore the farthest north. Circle the fourth and fifth digits (04). Go to number 4 on your answer sheet and darken E. However, you should have already darkened the oval for D. You have two choices — erase your mark for D and darken E or let E stand and do not darken the oval for D.

Examine sample ten. (Pause 2-3 seconds) If the second number in the sample is the second largest and the second to last number is the second smallest, write the letter C as in "cat" beside the first number. (Pause 5 seconds) If not, write the letter E as in "elephant" beside that number. (Pause 2 seconds) Darken the selected number/letter combination on your answer sheet. (Pause 5 seconds)

ANSWER: Since the second number in the sample (6) is not the second largest (29 is) and the second to the last number (38) is not the second smallest (8 is), write the letter E beside the first number 16. Darken the selected number/ letter combination on your answer sheet—16 E.

Examine sample five again. (Pause 2-3 seconds) On your answer sheet, find the number that is equivalent to the sum of the number under C as in "cat," and the number under B as in "boy." (Pause 2 seconds) Darken the oval for D as in "dog." (Pause 5 seconds)

ANSWER: On your answer sheet, find the number that is equivalent to the sum of the number under C and the number under B (5 + 6 = 11). Darken the oval for D.

Examine sample ten again. (Pause 2-3 seconds) If the two smallest numbers add up to less than the third number from the left, go to number 71 on your answer sheet and darken the circle for D as in "dog." (Pause 7 seconds) Otherwise, go to the same number on your answer sheet and darken the oval for A as in "apple." (Pause 5 seconds)

ANSWER: Since the two smallest numbers add up to (6 + 8 = 14) less than the third number from the left (29), go to number 71 on your answer sheet and darken the oval for D.

Examine sample ten again. (Pause 2-3 seconds) Draw a square, circle, and triangle around the fifth number shown, the third number shown, and the first number shown, respectively. (Pause 5 seconds) Go to the same number that is in the circle on your answer sheet and darken the letter D as in "dog." (Pause 2 seconds) Go to the same number that is in the circle on your answer sheet and darken the letter C as in "cat." (Pause 5 seconds)

ANSWER: Go to the same number you should have written in the circle on your answer sheet (29) and darken the oval for D.

POSTAL EXAM
Test 1 - Following Oral Directions
ANSWER KEY

#	Answer		#	Answer		#	Answer
1.	A B C D E		34.	A B C D E		67.	A B C D E
2.	A B C D E		35.	A B C D E		68.	A B C **D** E
3.	A B **C** D E		36.	A B C D E		69.	A B C D E
4.	A B C **D** **E**		37.	A B C D E		70.	A B C D E
5.	A B **C** **D** E		38.	A B C D E		71.	A B C **D** E
6.	A B C D **E**		39.	A B C D E		72.	A B C D E
7.	A **B** C D E		40.	A B C **D** E		73.	A B C D E
8.	A B C D E		41.	A B C **D** E		74.	A B C D E
9.	A B C D E		42.	A B C D E		75.	A B C D E
10.	A B C D E		43.	A **B** C D E		76.	A B C **D** E
11.	A B C **D** E		44.	A B C D E		77.	A B C D E
12.	A B **C** D E		45.	A B C D E		78.	A B C D E
13.	A B C D E		46.	A B C **D** E		79.	**A** B C D E
14.	A B C D **E**		47.	A B C **D** E		80.	A B C D E
15.	A **B** C D E		48.	A B C D E		81.	A B C D E
16.	A B C D **E**		49.	A B C D E		82.	A **B** C D E
17.	A B C D E		50.	A B C D E		83.	A B C D E
18.	A B C D E		51.	**A** B C D E		84.	A B C D E
19.	A B C D E		52.	A B C D E		85.	A B C D E
20.	A B C D E		53.	A B C D E		86.	A B C D E
21.	A B C D E		54.	A B C D E		87.	A B C D E
22.	A B C D E		55.	A B C D E		88.	A B C D E
23.	A B C D E		56.	A **B** C D E		89.	A B C D E
24.	**A** B C D E		57.	A B C D E		90.	A B C D E
25.	**A** B **C** D E		58.	A B C D E		91.	A B C D E
26.	A **B** C D E		59.	A B **C** D E		92.	A B C D E
27.	A B C D E		60.	A B C D E		93.	A B C D E
28.	A B C D E		61.	A B C D E		94.	A B C D E
29.	A B C **D** E		62.	A B C D E		95.	A B C D E
30.	A B C D E		63.	A B C D E		96.	A B C D E
31.	**A** B C D E		64.	A B C D E		97.	A B C D E
32.	**A** B C D E		65.	A B C D E		98.	A B C D E
33.	A B C D E		66.	A B C D E			

Test 2

TEST 2

Address Checking

(Answer sheets appear in the back of this book.)

TIME: 6 Minutes
        95 Questions

DIRECTIONS: In this section you will be asked to compare two lists of addresses, deciding if they are alike or different. If the addresses are alike, you will mark oval "A" on your answer sheet; if they are different, you will mark oval "D" on your answer sheet.

1. 213 University Court   213 University Court

2. 48 Earl Terrace   48 Earlie Terrace

3. 100a Kellogg Square   100d Kellogg Square

4. 22b Euston Street   22b Euston Street

5. 1345 Avenue A   1234 Avenue A

6. 64 Perdue Place   64 Perdue Place

7. 250001 Route 22   25001 Route 22

8. 402a North Fourth Ave.   402a North Fourth Ave.

9. 22 Tendril Place   22 Tendril Place

10. 6115 Central Ave.   1556 Central Ave.

11. 5837 Shoeshine St.   5837 Shoeshine St.

12. 2 Larkspur Blvd.   2 Larkspur Blvd.

13. 12f West Mrytal   12f West Mirtle

14. 77 Massie Place   777 Massie Place

15. 2019 Seattle Rd.   2019 Seattle Blvd.

16. 500 East Hanover Lane   500 East Hanover Lane

17.	12 North Sunnyvale St.	12 North Sunnyvale St.
18.	82r Juniper Place	82r Juniper Place
19.	2020 W. North Ave.	2020 N. West Ave.
20.	932 Tunison Court	932 Tunison Court
21.	12b Heddon Terrace	12b Heddon Terrace
22.	2 Highway 11	22 Highway 1
23.	14 Sandy Way	14 Sandune Way
24.	97 Swainton St.	97 Swainsson St.
25.	202g Cantalope Place	202g Cantalope Ave.
26.	67483 Shew Road	67483 Shew Road
27.	208G Wysteria Way	208G Wysteria Way
28.	46 West Janine St.	46 West Janie St.
29.	3 So. Telegraph Rd.	3 So. Telegraph Line Rd.
30.	42 Orwell Ave.	24 Orwell Ave.
31.	11112 Sudder Place	11112 Sutter Place
32.	202S So. Stelton Rd.	202S So. Stelton Rd.
33.	29 Tennis Way	29 Tennie's Way
34.	88 So. Lawn Blvd.	88 No. Lawn Blvd.
35.	17c Mastiff Terrace	17c Mastiff Terrace
36.	84 Cloud Street	84 Cloud Street
37.	466 Route 514	466 Route 514
38.	2S N. Boating Place	25 N. Boating Place
39.	2b Westfield Way	2b Westfield Way
40.	2145 Woznick Rd.	2145 Woznick Rd.
41.	379 Teacup Lane	379 Teapot Lane
42.	37640f Packard Ave.	36470 Packard Ave.
43.	67B W. Northern St.	67B W. Northern St.

44.	78376 Highway 14	78376 Highway 14
45.	Newberry Vt. 12921	Newberry Vt. 12921
46.	88 So. Swan St.	88 So. Swan St.
47.	Oleanta, NY 29025	Oneonta, NY 29025
48.	25 Woodbridge Ave.	25 Woodbridge Ave.
49.	314b Banbury Rd.	314b Bambiry Rd.
50.	29 W. Cycle Ave.	29 W. Cycle Ave.
51.	2002 Cedar Terrace	202 Cedar Terrace
52.	457 Host Street	458 Host Street
53.	191 Washington Drive	191 Washington Drive
54.	1300 (E) Beach Ave.	1300 (E) Beach Drive
55.	220 Revere Blvd.	220 Revere Blvd.
56.	705 Brigantine Blvd.	1705 Brigantine Blvd.
57.	31a Mine St.	31b Mine St.
58.	225 Hagen Rd.	225 Hagen Rd.
59.	516 Cavery Drive	516 Cavery Ave.
60.	529 N. Checkpoint Place	529M Checkpoint Place
61.	New Brunswick, NJ 08903	New Brunswick, NJ 08901
62.	22 Shipmaster Drive	22 Shipmaster Drive
63.	47 Yale Ave.	47 Yale Ave.
64.	134b Louis Place	134 (E) Louis Place
65.	205 Harrison Ave.	205 Harrison Ave.
66.	23 Maple Ave.	23 Maple Ave.
67.	47 W. May St.	74 W. May St.
68.	500 Mountain Ave.	500 Mountain Ave.
69.	20 (E) Stone St.	20 W. Stone St.
70.	22b Prosper St.	2b Prosper St.

71.	65 Hope Rd.	65 Hope Way
72.	15 Edgebrook Ct.	14 Edgebrook Ct.
73.	133 Hamilton Ave. Apt 99	133 Hamilton Ave. Apt 9
74.	149b George St.	149b George St.
75.	Highland Park, NJ 08904	Highland Park, NJ 08904
76.	Salina, KS 72430	Salina, KS 72430
77.	481k (E) 68th St.	481k W. 68th St.
78.	18 Tennent Ave.	18 Tennent Ave.
79.	181 Pineyrun Road	181 Pineyrun Road
80.	486 Rt. 1 North	486 Rt. 1 North
81.	Detroit, MI 29254	Detroit, MI 29452
82.	4855 Guilden Terrace	4855 Guilden Place
83.	Bronx, NY 17115	Bronx, NY 11577
84.	26 Global Lane	26 Global Lane
85.	41b South Elk Rd.	41s South Elk Rd.
86.	24651 Diane Court	24651 Diane Court
87.	76e East Bishop St.	76e East Bishop St.
88.	20240 North Holly Road	2240 North Holly Road
89.	8 How Lane	8 How Place
90.	214 Cape Circle	214 Cape Court
91.	29 Diamond St.	29 Daisy St.
92.	837492 Highway 21	837492 Highway 21
93.	32 Texas Ave.	32 Texas Ave.
94.	88 Bright St.	88 Bright St.
95.	7654 Welton Lane	7654 Wulton Lane

TEST 2

Memory for Addresses

(Answer sheets appear in the back of this book.)

TIME: Study 5 Minutes, Work 5 Minutes
88 Questions

> **DIRECTIONS:** Below are five boxes labeled A,B,C,D, and E. Each box contains five addresses. You will be given five minutes to memorize the addresses in the boxes and their locations. After five minutes are up, you will have an additional five minutes to answer the following 88 questions and mark on the answer sheet the letter of the box in which the address belongs. You will not be able to refer back to the boxes once you begin answering the questions.

A	B	C	D	E
2100-3599 Hyde	4100-5699 Hyde	5600-6799 Hyde	1200-2899 Hyde	6200-7899 Hyde
James	Drake	Cogswell	New Market	Reading
5600-6799 Riva	1200-2899 Riva	2100-3599 Riva	6200-7899 Riva	4100-5699 Riva
Stout	Dawson	Donaldson	Dover	Oakbrook
1200-2899 Shirley	5600-6799 Shirley	6200-7899 Shirley	4100-5699 Shirley	2100-3599 Shirley

1. Dawson
2. 5600-6799 Hyde
3. Oakbrook
4. 6200-7899 Riva
5. 1200-2899 Shirley
6. James
7. Reading
8. 2100-3599 Hyde
9. Cogswell
10. 1200-2899 Hyde
11. 5600-6799 Shirley
12. Drake
13. New Market
14. 4100-5699 Riva
15. Stout
16. 6200-7899 Shirley
17. 5600-6799 Riva
18. Dover
19. 1200-2899 Riva
20. 4100-5699 Hyde
21. 6200-7899 Hyde
22. Donaldson
23. 2100-3599 Riva
24. 2100-3599 Shirley
25. 4100-5699 Shirley
26. 1200-2899 Shirley
27. Oakbrook

28. Dawson

29. 5600-6799 Shirley

30. 2100-3599 Hyde

31. 6200-7899 Riva

32. Cogswell

33. Reading

34. 1200-2899 Hyde

35. James

36. 5600-6799 Hyde

37. 6200-7899 Shirley

38. New Market

39. 4100-5699 Riva

40. 6200-7899 Hyde

41. Drake

42. Donaldson

43. 5600-6799 Riva

44. Dover

45. 2100-3599 Riva

46. 2100-3599 Shirley

47. Stout

48. 1200-2899 Shirley

49. 4100-5699 Shirley

50. 5600-6799 Hyde

51. Dawson

52. 2100-3599 Hyde

53. 6200-7899 Riva

54. 4100-5699 Hyde

55. Cogswell
56. Donaldson
57. Oakbrook
58. 1200-2899 Riva
59. James
60. 1200-2899 Hyde
61. New Market
62. 6200-7899 Shirley
63. 2100-3599 Riva
64. 5600-6799 Riva
65. Dover
66. Reading
67. 4100-5699 Riva
68. Stout
69. Cogswell
70. 5600-6799 Shirley
71. Drake
72. 4100-5699 Hyde
73. 1200-2899 Shirley
74. 5600-6799 Hyde
75. New Market
76. 6200-7899 Hyde
77. 6200-7899 Riva
78. 4100-5699 Riva
79. James
80. Donaldson
81. 6200-7899 Shirley

82. Drake

83. 2100-3599 Hyde

84. 4100-5699 Shirley

85. 2100-3599 Shirley

86. Cogswell

87. Dawson

88. Stout

TEST 2

Number Series

(Answer sheets appear in the back of this book.)

TIME: 20 Minutes
24 Questions

DIRECTIONS: For each question, there is a series of numbers that follow some definite order. Look at the series of numbers and decide which two numbers will come next in the series. You will be given five answers to choose from.

1.   2   1   4   3   6   5   8   7   _____   _____

   (A)   10, 9

   (B)   9, 10

   (C)   10, 12

   (D)   9, 11

   (E)   10, 11

2.   1   2   5   6   9   10   13   _____   _____

   (A)   16, 17

   (B)   11, 14

   (C)   15, 18

   (D)   15, 17

   (E)   14, 17

3.   1   3   1   4   2   6   2   8   _____   _____

   (A)   3, 10

   (B)   3, 12

(C) 29, 32

(D) 3, 9

(E) 4, 10

4.   1   2   2   3   3   4   4   5   _____   _____

(A) 6, 2

(B) 1, 5

(C) 5, 6

(D) 6, 7

(E) 6, 8

5.   7   5   12   10   22   20   _____   _____

(A) 44, 42

(B) 40, 42

(C) 42, 40

(D) 40, 60

(E) 40, 64

6.   1   11   2   22   3   33   4   44   _____   _____

(A) 6, 65

(B) 5, 55

(C) 5, 6

(D) 66, 55

(E) 55, 5

7.   1   7   2   14   3   21   4   28   _____   _____

(A) 5, 35

(B) 16, 56

(C) 6, 42

(D) 5, 25

(E) 6, 38

8. 1   2   2   5   3   10   4   17   _____   _____

(A) 5, 18

(B) 6, 36

(C) 25, 100

(D) 5, 29

(E) 5, 26

9. 1   3   4   5   7   12   9   11   20   _____   _____

(A) 13, 26

(B) 22, 24

(C) 22, 25

(D) 13, 15

(E) 12, 13

10. 1   4   13   40   121   364   1,093   3,280   _____   _____

(A) 9,841, 29,524

(B) 4,280, 5,280

(C) 6,260, 12,421

(D) 1,216, 2,432

(E) 16, 32

11. 1   2   4   2   7   2   10   2   _____   _____

(A) 2, 13

(B) 13, 2

(C) 14, 2

(D) 13, 3

(E) 13, 16

12. 1   12   2   21   3   12   4   21   _____   _____

(A) 13, 5

(B) 5, 13

(C) 5, 12

(D) 12, 5

(E) 5, 21

13. $1/_2$ 1 $1^1/_2$ 2 $2^1/_2$ 3 $3^1/_2$ 4 $4^1/_2$ _____   _____

(A) 5, $5^1/_2$

(B) $5^1/_2$, 6

(C) 5, $6^1/_2$

(D) $5^1/_2$, $6^1/_2$

(E) 6, 7

14. 2   10   50   250   1,250   6,250   _____   _____

(A) 31,250, 156,250

(B) 7,750, 9,257

(C) 30,750, 15,000

(D) 12,250, 24,750

(E) 12,500, 62,500

15. 5   2   10   2   15   2   20   2   _____   _____

(A) 30, 2

(B) 40, 4

(C) 25, 2

(D) 2, 25

(E) 40, 2

16. 10   20   30   40   50   60   70   80   _____   _____

    (A)   87, 97

    (B)   100, 90

    (C)   100, 120

    (D)   900, 110

    (E)   90, 100

17. 4   6   10   18   34   66   130   258   _____   _____

    (A)   402, 700

    (B)   388, 646

    (C)   514, 1,026

    (D)   1,026, 5,014

    (E)   316, 628

18. 1   12   23   34   45   56   67   78   _____   _____

    (A)   91, 101

    (B)   98, 111

    (C)   87, 98

    (D)   89, 100

    (E)   76, 87

19. 1   .05   2   .05   3   .05   4   .05   _____   _____

    (A)   6, .07

    (B)   5, .05

    (C)   .05, 4

    (D)   8, 10

    (E)   40, 500

20. 2   3   5   6   8   9   11   12   _____   _____

    (A)   13, 14
    (B)   14, 15
    (C)   16, 18
    (D)   14, 16
    (E)   13, 15

21. 2   6   18   54   162   486   1,458   _____   _____

    (A)   4,374, 13,122
    (B)   2,916, 5,238
    (C)   437, 1,312
    (D)   1,944, 3,402
    (E)   2,016, 4,212

22. 1   2   3   5   6   7   9   10   _____   _____

    (A)   12, 14
    (B)   11, 12
    (C)   11, 14
    (D)   11, 13
    (E)   14, 15

23. 1   2   4   5   7   8   10   11   _____   _____

    (A)   12, 14
    (B)   13, 15
    (C)   13, 14
    (D)   12, 15
    (E)   12, 13

24. 2   1   2   3   2   5   2   7   _____   _____
    (A) 10, 12
    (B) 2, 10
    (C) 9, 2
    (D) 2, 14
    (E) 2, 9

TEST 2

Following Oral Directions - Worksheet

(Answer sheets appear in the back of this book.)

TIME: Instructions will be read at approximately 80 words per minute.

> **DIRECTIONS:** Follow the instructions that are read to you. They will not be repeated during the examination. You are to mark your worksheets according to the instructions that are read to you. After each set of instructions, you will be given time to record your answer on your answer sheet. You should have only one space darkened for each number. If you go to darken a space for a number and you have already darkened another space, either erase the first mark and darken the space for your new choice **or** let the original mark remain.

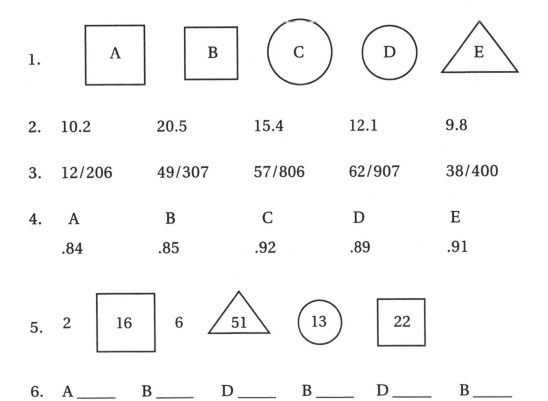

1.   A   B   C   D   E

2.   10.2   20.5   15.4   12.1   9.8

3.   12/206   49/307   57/806   62/907   38/400

4.   A   B   C   D   E
     .84   .85   .92   .89   .91

5.   2   16   6   51   13   22

6.   A____   B____   D____   B____   D____   B____

7. A 08833-0125   D 08923-0130

    B 08933-0125   E 08833-0120

    C 08833-0130

8. 87B   44C   36C   11D   77B   21D   19A

9. R ____   S ____   T ____   U ____   V ____

TEST 2

ANSWER KEY

Address Checking

1. (A)	15. (D)	29. (D)	43. (A)	57. (D)	71. (D)	85. (D)
2. (D)	16. (A)	30. (D)	44. (A)	58. (A)	72. (D)	86. (A)
3. (D)	17. (A)	31. (D)	45. (A)	59. (D)	73. (D)	87. (A)
4. (A)	18. (A)	32. (A)	46. (A)	60. (D)	74. (A)	88. (D)
5. (D)	19. (D)	33. (D)	47. (D)	61. (D)	75. (A)	89. (D)
6. (A)	20. (A)	34. (D)	48. (A)	62. (A)	76. (A)	90. (D)
7. (D)	21. (A)	35. (A)	49. (D)	63. (A)	77. (D)	91. (D)
8. (A)	22. (D)	36. (A)	50. (A)	64. (D)	78. (A)	92. (A)
9. (A)	23. (D)	37. (A)	51. (D)	65. (A)	79. (A)	93. (A)
10. (D)	24. (D)	38. (D)	52. (D)	66. (A)	80. (A)	94. (A)
11. (A)	25. (D)	39. (A)	53. (A)	67. (D)	81. (D)	95. (D)
12. (A)	26. (A)	40. (A)	54. (D)	68. (A)	82. (D)	
13. (D)	27. (A)	41. (D)	55. (A)	69. (D)	83. (D)	
14. (D)	28. (D)	42. (D)	56. (D)	70. (D)	84. (A)	

Memory for Addresses

1. (B)	14. (E)	27. (E)	40. (E)	53. (D)	66. (E)	79. (A)
2. (C)	15. (A)	28. (B)	41. (B)	54. (B)	67. (E)	80. (C)
3. (E)	16. (C)	29. (B)	42. (C)	55. (C)	68. (A)	81. (C)
4. (D)	17. (A)	30. (A)	43. (A)	56. (C)	69. (C)	82. (B)
5. (A)	18. (D)	31. (D)	44. (D)	57. (E)	70. (B)	83. (A)
6. (A)	19. (B)	32. (C)	45. (C)	58. (B)	71. (B)	84. (D)
7. (E)	20. (B)	33. (E)	46. (E)	59. (A)	72. (B)	85. (E)
8. (A)	21. (E)	34. (D)	47. (A)	60. (D)	73. (A)	86. (C)
9. (C)	22. (C)	35. (A)	48. (A)	61. (D)	74. (C)	87. (B)
10. (D)	23. (C)	36. (C)	49. (D)	62. (C)	75. (D)	88. (A)
11. (B)	24. (E)	37. (C)	50. (C)	63. (C)	76. (E)	
12. (B)	25. (D)	38. (D)	51. (B)	64. (A)	77. (D)	
13. (D)	26. (A)	39. (E)	52. (A)	65. (D)	78. (E)	

Note: There is only an answer key for the "Memory for Addresses" section.

Number Series

1.	(A)	13.	(A)
2.	(E)	14.	(A)
3.	(D)	15.	(C)
4.	(C)	16.	(E)
5.	(C)	17.	(C)
6.	(B)	18.	(D)
7.	(A)	19.	(B)
8.	(E)	20.	(B)
9.	(D)	21.	(A)
10.	(A)	22.	(D)
11.	(B)	23.	(C)
12.	(C)	24.	(E)

Following Oral Directions

(Please see "Detailed Explanation of Answers.")

DETAILED EXPLANATIONS OF ANSWERS

Test 2

Address Checking

1. alike
2. 48 Earl Terrace   48 Earl**ie** Terrace
3. 100**a** Kellogg Square   100**d** Kellogg Square
4. alike
5. **1345** Avenue A   **1234** Avenue A
6. alike
7. 2500**0**1 Route 22   25001 Route 22
8. alike
9. alike
10. **6115** Central Ave.   **1556** Central Ave.
11. alike
12. alike
13. 12f West **Mrytal**   12f West **Mirtle**
14. 77 Massie Place   777 Massie Place
15. 2019 Seattle **Rd.**   2019 Seattle **Blvd.**
16. alike
17. alike
18. alike
19. 2020 **W. North** Ave.   2020 **N. West** Ave.
20. alike
21. alike
22. 2 Highway 1**1**   2**2** Highway 1
23. 14 Sandy Way   14 Sand**une** Way
24. 97 Swainton St.   97 Swains**s**on St.
25. 202g Cantalope **Place**   202g Cantalope **Ave.**
26. alike
27. alike

28. 46 West Janine St.   46 West Janie St.
29. 3 So. Telegraph Rd.   3 So. Telegraph **Line** Rd.
30. **42** Orwell Ave.   **24** Orwell Ave.
31. 11112 Su**dd**er Place   11112 Su**tt**er Place
32. alike
33. 29 Tennis Way   29 Tenni**e's** Way
34. 88 **So.** Lawn Blvd.   88 **No.** Lawn Blvd.
35. alike
36. alike
37. alike
38. 2**S** N. Boating Place   2**5** N. Boating Place
39. alike
40. alike
41. 379 Tea**cup** Lane   379 Tea**pot** Lane
42. 37**640f** Packard Ave.   36**470** Packard Ave.
43. alike
44. alike
45. alike
46. alike
47. O**lea**nta, NY 29025   O**neo**nta, NY 29025
48. alike
49. 314b Ban**bury** Rd.   314b Bam**biry** Rd.
50. alike
51. 2002 Cedar Terrace   202 Cedar Terrace
52. 457 Host Street   45**8** Host Street
53. alike
54. 1300 (E) Beach **Ave.**   1300 (E) Beach **Drive**
55. alike
56. 705 Brigantine Blvd.   **1**705 Brigantine Blvd.
57. 31**a** Mine St.   31**b** Mine St.
58. alike
59. 516 Cavery **Drive**   516 Cavery **Ave.**
60. 529 **N.** Checkpoint Place   529**M** Checkpoint Place
61. New Brunswick, NJ 0890**3**   New Brunswick, NJ 0890**1**
62. alike
63. alike
64. 134**b** Louis Place   134 **(E)** Louis Place

65. alike
66. alike
67. **47** W. May St.   **74** W. May St.
68. alike
69. 20 **(E)** Stone St.   20 **W.** Stone St.
70. 22b Prosper St.   2b Prosper St.
71. 65 Hope **Rd.**   65 Hope **Way**
72. 15 Edgebrook Ct.   14 Edgebrook Ct.
73. 133 Hamilton Ave. Apt **99**   133 Hamilton Ave. Apt. 9
74. alike
75. alike
76. alike
77. 481k **(E)** 68th St.   481k **W.** 68th St.
78. alike
79. alike
80. alike
81. Detroit, MI **29254**   Detroit, MI **29452**
82. 4855 Guilden **Terrace**   4855 Guilden **Place**
83. Bronx, NY 1**7115**   Bronx, NY 1**1577**
84. alike
85. 41**b** South Elk Rd.   41**s** South Elk Rd.
86. alike
87. alike
88. **2**0240 North Holly Road   2240 North Holly Road
89. 8 How **Lane**   8 How **Place**
90. 214 Cape **Circle**   214 Cape **Court**
91. 29 **Diamond** St.   29 **Daisy** St.
92. alike
93. alike
94. alike
95. 7654 Welton Lane   7654 Wulton Lane

Number Series

1. **(A)** Beginning with 2, subtract 1 and add 3 to make the series; therefore, choice (A) 10, 9 is correct.

2. **(E)** Beginning with 1, alternately add 1 and then 3 to the number. Therefore, choice (E) 14, 17 is correct.

3. **(D)** In this series, beginning with 1, the first number is multiplied first by 3 then the number is repeated and then it is multiplied by 4; therefore, choice (D) 3, 9 is correct.

4. **(C)** Beginning with 1, add 1 and then repeat the number, then add 1 and repeat the number again. Therefore, choice (C) 5, 6 is the correct response.

5. **(C)** Beginning with 7, subtract 2, and then add the first and second digits to make the next number, then subtract 2 again, and then add the third and fourth digits. Following this pattern, (C) 42, 40 is the correct response.

6. **(B)** There are two alternating series. The first begins with 1 and then adds 1 each time. The second multiplies the previous number in the first series by 11, so choice (B) 5, 55 is the correct response.

7. **(A)** Once again there are two alternating series. The first increases in increments of 1, and the second multiplies the preceding number in the first series by 7. The correct response is (A) 5, 35.

8. **(E)** In this combination of alternating series, the first begins with 1 and proceeds by increments of 1, and the second multiplies the preceding number in the first series by itself and then adds 1. Therefore, the correct response is (E) 5, 26.

9. **(D)** This has two series alternating, with two of the first pattern followed by one number from the second. The first pattern is comprised of consecutive odd numbers. The second pattern begins with 4 and adds 8 to each number. Therefore, (D) 13, 15 is the correct response.

10. (A) Beginning with 1 this series involves multiplying the numeral by 3 and adding 1. Therefore, the correct response is (A) 9,841, 29,524.

11. (B) This series begins with 1, followed each time by the number 2, and then proceeds in increments of 3. Therefore, the correct response is (B) 13, 2.

12. (C) Beginning with the number 1, the series then increases by 1. The second series repeats 12 and then 21 in between the numerals of the first series. The correct response is (C) 5, 12.

13. (A) This series begins with one-half, and adds one-half of each number, so the correct response is (A) 5, $5\frac{1}{2}$.

14. (A) This number series begins with 2 and is multiplied each time by 5. The correct response is (A) 31,250, 156,250.

15. (C) A series starting with 5 and increasing by increments of 5 is separated by the number 2, so the correct response is (C) 25, 2.

16. (E) Beginning with 10, 10 is added to each number. The correct response is (E) 90, 100.

17. (C) Starting with 4, subtract 2, and then add this number to the previous number. The correct response is (C) 514, 1,026.

18. (D) Starting with 1, add 11 to each number. The next numbers in the series are (D) 89, 100.

19. (B) A series beginning with 1 and increasing in increments of 1 is separated by the number .05. Therefore, the correct response is (B) 5, .05.

20. (B) First add 1 to the numeral, and then add 2, and repeat the pattern. The next numbers in the series are (B) 14, 15.

21. **(A)** Beginning with 2, multiply each number by 3. The correct response is (A) 4,374, 13,122.

22. **(D)** Beginning with 1, add 1, then 1 again, and then 2. The correct response is (D) 11, 13.

23. **(C)** Beginning with 1, add first 1 and then 2 to the number, so that the correct response is (C) 13, 14.

24. **(E)** A series of increasing odd numbers beginning with 1 is alternated with the number 2. The correct response is (E) 2, 9.

Following Oral Directions

This is how your worksheet should look:

1.

2.   10.2   20.5   15.4   12.1   9.8

3.   12/206   <u>49</u>/307   57/806   62/907   38/400

4.   A   B   C   D   E

     .84   .85   .92   .89   (.91)

5.   2 16   6   13

6.   A____   B <u>76</u>   D <u>35</u>   B____   D <u>37</u>   B <u>51</u>

7.   A 08833-0125   D 08933-0130

     B 08933-0125   E 08833-0120

     C 08833-0130

8.   87B   44C   36C   11D   77B   21D   19A

9.   R <u>12</u>   S <u>14</u>   T <u>16</u>   U <u>18</u>   V <u>20</u>

In this section, please note that the solution to each problem is preceded by the actual instructions read by the examiner.

Examine sample one. (Pause 2-3 seconds) Write the number 44 in the triangle if the letter C as in "cat" is in the smaller of the two circles shown. (Pause 2 seconds) Otherwise write the number 47 in the small box and the number 74 in the larger box. (Pause 2 seconds) Darken the corresponding number/letter combination. (Pause 5 seconds)

ANSWER: Since the letter C is in the bigger circle, write the number 47 in the small box and the number 74 in the larger box. Darken the corresponding number/letter combinations (47 B and 74 A).

Examine sample one again. (Pause 2-3 seconds) If there are two triangles, write the number 21 in the smallest circle shown. If not, write the same number in the largest circle shown and the number 41 in the smallest circle shown. (Pause 5 seconds)

ANSWER: Since there is only one triangle shown, write the number 21 in the largest circle shown and the number 41 in the smallest circle shown.

Examine sample two. (Pause 2-3 seconds) These numbers represent the average speeds it takes to sort one foot of mail into letters or flats. Write the letter A as in "apple" under the number second from the left if it is the second fastest speed. (Pause 2 seconds) If it is the second slowest speed write the letter D as in "dog." (Pause 2 seconds) If neither of these is true, go to number 20 and darken the oval for C as in "cat." (Pause 5 seconds)

ANSWER: The second number from the left (20.5) is not the second fastest speed (15.4) nor the second lowest speed (10.2). Therefore, go to number 20 and the darken oval for C.

Examine sample two again. (Pause 2-3 seconds) Go to the slowest speed. Add the digits of the number together. (Pause 2 seconds) Go to the number formed by their sum on the answer sheet and darken the oval for A as in "apple." (Pause 5 seconds)

ANSWER: Go to the slowest speed (9.8). Add the digits of the number together (9 + 8 = 17). Go to the number formed by their sum (17) on the answer sheet and darken the oval for A.

Examine sample three. (Pause 2-3 seconds) The first two numbers are route numbers, and the last three represent the number of houses on the route. If the first two numbers are 50 and above, the route is urban; if 49 or below, it is a rural route. Find the route with the most houses. (Pause 2 seconds) If it is a rural route, go to the route number on your answer sheet and darken the oval for D as in "dog." (Pause 2 seconds) If it is a city route, go to number 49 and darken the oval for B as in "boy." (Pause 5 seconds)

ANSWER: The route with the most houses is 62/907. Since the route number, 62, is above 50, it is considered an urban, or city, route. Therefore, go to number 49 and darken the oval for B. However, if you answered the previous problem correctly, you should have already darkened oval B for number 49.

Examine sample three again. (Pause 2-3 seconds) If there are more rural than city routes, go to the second from the left, and underline the route number. (Pause 2 seconds) Go to that number on your answer sheet and darken B as in "boy." (Pause 2 seconds) If there are more urban routes, go to the same number and darken D as in "dog." (Pause 5 seconds)

ANSWER: There are more urban routes. Go to the second from the left and underline the route number (49). Go to that number on your answer sheet and darken the oval for B.

Examine sample four. (Pause 2-3 seconds) These numbers represent the customer satisfaction index for postal service for several different regions. Find the route which has the highest index for percentage of customer satisfaction. (Pause 2 seconds) Darken the combination immediately to the left of it on your answer sheet. (Pause 5 seconds)

ANSWER: The route that has the highest index for percentage of customers (.92) is C. Darken the combination immediately to the left of it (85 B) on your answer sheet.

Examine sample four again. (Pause 2-3 seconds) Circle the second lowest percentage of customer satisfaction if it is greater than 90. (Pause 2 seconds) If not, circle the second highest percentage of satisfaction. (Pause 2 seconds) Go to this combination on your answer sheet, and darken the appropriate number/letter combination. (Pause 5 seconds)

ANSWER: The second lowest percentage of customer satisfaction (.85) is not greater than 90. Circle the second highest percentage of satisfaction (.91). Go to this combination on your answer sheet (91 E) and darken the appropriate number/letter combination.

Examine sample five. (Pause 2-3 seconds) Find the sum of any numbers that are not enclosed in geometrical shapes. (Pause 2 seconds) Go to this number on the answer sheet and darken the oval for D as in "dog." (Pause 5 seconds)

ANSWER: Numbers 2 and 6 are not enclosed in geometrical shapes. The sum of these numbers is 8. Go to the number 8 on your answer sheet and darken the oval for D.

Examine sample five again. (Pause 2-3 seconds) If the number in the large box is greater than the number in the triangle and the circle, write the letter A as in "apple" in the large box. (Pause 5 seconds) If not, write the letter E as in "elephant" in the small box. (Pause 2 seconds) Darken the corresponding number/letter combination on your answer sheet. (Pause 5 seconds)

ANSWER: Since the number in the large box (16) is not greater than the number in the triangle and the circle, write the letter E in the small box. Darken the corresponding number/letter combination (22 E) on your answer sheet.

Examine sample five again. (Pause 2-3 seconds) If the largest even number is enclosed in the same geometric shape as the smallest odd number, go to number 88 and darken the letter B as in "boy." (Pause 5 seconds) If this is not true, write the letter C as in "cat" in the triangle. (Pause 2 seconds) Darken the corresponding number/letter combination on your answer sheet. (Pause 5 seconds)

ANSWER: Since the largest even number (22) is enclosed in a box not a circle like the smallest odd number (13), write the letter C in the triangle. Darken the corresponding number/letter combination (51 C).

Examine sample six. (Pause 2-3 seconds) Write the even numbers between 75 and 79 next to any B as in "boy" and the odd numbers between 34 and 38 next to any D as in "dog." (Pause 7 seconds) Darken the corresponding number/letter combination on your answer sheet. (Pause 5 seconds)

ANSWER: Go to numbers 76 and 78 (the even numbers between 75 and 79) on your answer sheet and darken the ovals for B (76 B and 78 B). Go to numbers 35 and 37 (the odd numbers between 34 and 38) on your answer sheet and darken the ovals for D (35 D and 37 D).

Examine sample six again. (Pause 2-3 seconds) Find the letter that only appears one time. Write the number 8 on the line next to it. (Pause 2 seconds) Darken the corresponding number/letter combination on your answer sheet. (Pause 5 seconds)

ANSWER: The letter "A" only appears one time. Write 8 next to A on the worksheet and darken the number/letter combination.

Examine sample six again. (Pause 2-3 seconds) If the fourth letter from the left is the fourth letter of the alphabet, write the number 51 next to the first D as in "dog." (Pause 5 seconds) If not, write the same number next to the last B as in "boy." (Pause 5 seconds)

ANSWER: Since the fourth letter (B) is not the fourth letter of the alphabet, write the number 51 next to the last B on your worksheet.

Examine sample seven. (Pause 2-3 seconds) These numbers represent different zip codes and post office boxes, the last four numbers being the post office boxes. Find the highest post office box number for the 08823 zip code. (Pause 2 seconds) Go to number 55 on your answer sheet and darken this number. (Pause 5 seconds)

ANSWER: This is a tricky question. There is no 08823 zip code listed. Therefore, you cannot answer the question.

Examine sample seven again. (Pause 2-3 seconds) Draw boxes around the third and fourth digits of each zip to form new numbers. (Pause 2 seconds) If these numbers are either the same or exactly 10 apart, go to the higher of the numbers and darken the letter E as in "elephant." (Pause 2 seconds) Otherwise, go to the smaller number and darken the oval for B as in "boy." (Pause 5 seconds)

ANSWER: Since the numbers are either the same or exactly 10 apart, go to the higher of the new numbers (93) on your answer sheet and darken the oval for E.

Examine sample one again. (Pause 2-3 seconds) If N comes after M but before O in the alphabet, go to the first number on the answer sheet and darken the letter in the triangle. (Pause 5 seconds) If any part of this statement is untrue, go to the last number on your answer sheet and darken the same letter. (Pause 5 seconds)

ANSWER: Since N comes after M but before O in the alphabet, go to number 1 on the answer sheet and darken the oval for E, the letter in the triangle.

Examine sample eight. (Pause 2-3 seconds) If the highest number shown is more than the sum of the lowest number shown plus 30, go to the lowest number associated with a D as in "dog" and circle it. (Pause 5 seconds) Otherwise, go to the highest number associated with a C as in "cat" and circle that number. (Pause 2 seconds) Darken the corresponding number/letter combination on your answer sheet. (Pause 5 seconds)

ANSWER: The highest number shown (87) is more than the sum of the lowest number shown plus 30 (11+30=44), go to the lowest number associated with a D (which is 11) and circle it. Darken the corresponding number/letter combination (11 D).

Examine sample eight again. (Pause 2-3 seconds) If the third letter of the alphabet is also with the third number shown, go to the lowest odd number and circle it. (Pause 2 seconds) Darken the corresponding number/letter combination on your answer sheet. (Pause 2 seconds) If the third letter of the alphabet is with the fourth number shown, find the highest odd number and circle that. (Pause 2 seconds) Darken the corresponding number/letter combination on your answer sheet. (Pause 5 seconds)

ANSWER: Since the third letter of the alphabet is also the third letter shown (C), go to the lowest odd number and circle it (it has already been circled). This has already been done. Darken the corresponding number/letter combination (11 D). However, this has already been done. The third letter of the alphabet is not with the fourth number shown.

Examine sample two again. (Pause 2-3 seconds) If the third speed shown is more than the first but less than the fifth, go to number five on your answer sheet and darken the oval for B as in "boy." (Pause 5 seconds) If it is more than the first and fifth, go to number 15 and darken the oval for C as in "cat." (Pause 5 seconds)

ANSWER: The third speed shown (15.4) is more than the first (10.2) and fifth speed (9.8). Therefore., go to number 15 and darken the oval for C.

Examine sample eight again. (Pause 2-3 seconds) Circle the second-highest even number if it is also the second-highest number shown. (Pause 5 seconds) Darken the corresponding number/letter combination. (Pause 2 seconds) Otherwise, go to number 4 and darken the oval for E as in "elephant." (Pause 5 seconds)

ANSWER: Since the second highest even number (36) is not the second highest number shown (77 is), go to number 4 and darken the oval for E.

Here is what the examiner said:

Examine sample nine. (Pause 2-3 seconds) Write the even numbers between 11 and 21 in ascending order in the spaces provided beside the letters. (Pause 5 seconds) Go to the space on your answer sheet corresponding to the number you have written beside the letter T. (Pause 2 seconds) Darken the oval for E as in "elephant." (Pause 5 seconds)

ANSWER: You should have written the number 16 next to the letter T. Go to the space on your answer sheet corresponding to the number and darken the oval for E.

Examine sample nine again. (Pause 2-3 seconds) If the number you have written beside V is 5 or more than the number you have written beside R, go to the space corresponding to the number you have written by S and darken the oval for A as in "apple." (Pause 5 seconds) Otherwise, find the number next to U and darken the oval for D as in "dog." (Pause 5 seconds)

ANSWER: The number you should have written beside V (20) is 5 or more than the number you have written beside R. You should have written 12 beside R (12 + 5 = 17). Go to the space on your answer sheet corresponding to the number you should have written by S (14) and darken the oval for A.

Examine sample two again. (Pause 2-3 seconds) If the fifth speed is less than half of the first speed, go to number 98 on your answer sheet and darken the oval for E as in "elephant." (Pause 5 seconds) If this is not true, but if it is less than half of the second speed shown, go the number 98 on your answer sheet and darken the oval for A as in "apple." (Pause 2 seconds) If it is less than half of the first speed *and* of the second speed, go to number 89 and darken the oval for E as in "elephant." (Pause 5 seconds)

ANSWER: Since the fifth speed (9.8) is more than half of the first speed but it is less than half of the second speed, go to the number 98 on your answer sheet and darken the oval for A.

Examine sample seven again. (Pause 2-3 seconds) If the post office box with the highest number in the 08933 zip code has the same number as the post office box with the highest number in the 08833 zip code, go to the number 1 on your answer sheet and darken the oval with the letter next to the highest post office box in the 08933 zip code. (Pause 7 seconds) If the numbers are not equal, go to number 1 on your answer sheet and darken the oval with the letter next to the lowest post office box in the 08833 zip code. (Pause 5 seconds)

ANSWER: The post office box with the highest number in the 08933 zip code has the same number as the post office box with the highest number in the 08833 zip code (both 130). Go to number 1 on your answer sheet and darken the oval for D (the letter next to the highest post office box in the 08933 zip code).

POSTAL EXAM
Test 2 - Following Oral Directions
ANSWER KEY

1. Ⓐ Ⓑ Ⓒ ● Ⓔ	34. Ⓐ Ⓑ Ⓒ Ⓓ Ⓔ	67. Ⓐ Ⓑ Ⓒ Ⓓ Ⓔ
2. Ⓐ Ⓑ Ⓒ Ⓓ Ⓔ	35. Ⓐ Ⓑ Ⓒ ● Ⓔ	68. Ⓐ Ⓑ Ⓒ Ⓓ Ⓔ
3. Ⓐ Ⓑ Ⓒ Ⓓ Ⓔ	36. Ⓐ Ⓑ Ⓒ Ⓓ Ⓔ	69. Ⓐ Ⓑ Ⓒ Ⓓ Ⓔ
4. Ⓐ Ⓑ Ⓒ Ⓓ ●	37. Ⓐ Ⓑ Ⓒ ● Ⓔ	70. Ⓐ Ⓑ Ⓒ Ⓓ Ⓔ
5. Ⓐ Ⓑ Ⓒ Ⓓ Ⓔ	38. Ⓐ Ⓑ Ⓒ Ⓓ Ⓔ	71. Ⓐ Ⓑ Ⓒ Ⓓ Ⓔ
6. Ⓐ Ⓑ Ⓒ Ⓓ Ⓔ	39. Ⓐ Ⓑ Ⓒ Ⓓ Ⓔ	72. Ⓐ Ⓑ Ⓒ Ⓓ Ⓔ
7. ● Ⓑ Ⓒ Ⓓ Ⓔ	40. Ⓐ Ⓑ Ⓒ Ⓓ Ⓔ	73. Ⓐ Ⓑ Ⓒ Ⓓ Ⓔ
8. ● Ⓑ Ⓒ Ⓓ Ⓔ	41. Ⓐ Ⓑ Ⓒ Ⓓ Ⓔ	74. ● Ⓑ Ⓒ Ⓓ Ⓔ
9. Ⓐ Ⓑ Ⓒ Ⓓ Ⓔ	42. Ⓐ Ⓑ Ⓒ Ⓓ Ⓔ	75. Ⓐ Ⓑ Ⓒ Ⓓ Ⓔ
10. Ⓐ Ⓑ Ⓒ Ⓓ Ⓔ	43. Ⓐ Ⓑ Ⓒ Ⓓ Ⓔ	76. Ⓐ ● Ⓒ Ⓓ Ⓔ
11. Ⓐ Ⓑ Ⓒ ● Ⓔ	44. Ⓐ Ⓑ Ⓒ Ⓓ Ⓔ	77. Ⓐ Ⓑ Ⓒ Ⓓ Ⓔ
12. Ⓐ Ⓑ Ⓒ Ⓓ Ⓔ	45. Ⓐ Ⓑ Ⓒ Ⓓ Ⓔ	78. Ⓐ ● Ⓒ Ⓓ Ⓔ
13. Ⓐ Ⓑ Ⓒ Ⓓ Ⓔ	46. Ⓐ Ⓑ Ⓒ Ⓓ Ⓔ	79. Ⓐ Ⓑ Ⓒ Ⓓ Ⓔ
14. ● Ⓑ Ⓒ Ⓓ Ⓔ	47. Ⓐ ● Ⓒ Ⓓ Ⓔ	80. Ⓐ Ⓑ Ⓒ Ⓓ Ⓔ
15. Ⓐ Ⓑ ● Ⓓ Ⓔ	48. Ⓐ Ⓑ Ⓒ Ⓓ Ⓔ	81. Ⓐ Ⓑ Ⓒ Ⓓ Ⓔ
16. Ⓐ Ⓑ Ⓒ Ⓓ ●	49. Ⓐ ● Ⓒ Ⓓ Ⓔ	82. Ⓐ Ⓑ Ⓒ Ⓓ Ⓔ
17. ● Ⓑ Ⓒ Ⓓ Ⓔ	50. Ⓐ Ⓑ Ⓒ Ⓓ Ⓔ	83. Ⓐ Ⓑ Ⓒ Ⓓ Ⓔ
18. Ⓐ Ⓑ Ⓒ Ⓓ Ⓔ	51. Ⓐ Ⓑ ● Ⓓ Ⓔ	84. Ⓐ Ⓑ Ⓒ Ⓓ Ⓔ
19. Ⓐ Ⓑ Ⓒ Ⓓ Ⓔ	52. Ⓐ Ⓑ Ⓒ Ⓓ Ⓔ	85. Ⓐ ● Ⓒ Ⓓ Ⓔ
20. Ⓐ Ⓑ ● Ⓓ Ⓔ	53. Ⓐ Ⓑ Ⓒ Ⓓ Ⓔ	86. Ⓐ Ⓑ Ⓒ Ⓓ Ⓔ
21. Ⓐ Ⓑ Ⓒ Ⓓ Ⓔ	54. Ⓐ Ⓑ Ⓒ Ⓓ Ⓔ	87. Ⓐ Ⓑ Ⓒ Ⓓ Ⓔ
22. Ⓐ Ⓑ Ⓒ Ⓓ ●	55. Ⓐ Ⓑ Ⓒ Ⓓ Ⓔ	88. Ⓐ Ⓑ Ⓒ Ⓓ Ⓔ
23. Ⓐ Ⓑ Ⓒ Ⓓ Ⓔ	56. Ⓐ Ⓑ Ⓒ Ⓓ Ⓔ	89. Ⓐ Ⓑ Ⓒ Ⓓ Ⓔ
24. Ⓐ Ⓑ Ⓒ Ⓓ Ⓔ	57. Ⓐ Ⓑ Ⓒ Ⓓ Ⓔ	90. Ⓐ Ⓑ Ⓒ Ⓓ Ⓔ
25. Ⓐ Ⓑ Ⓒ Ⓓ Ⓔ	58. Ⓐ Ⓑ Ⓒ Ⓓ Ⓔ	91. Ⓐ Ⓑ Ⓒ Ⓓ ●
26. Ⓐ Ⓑ Ⓒ Ⓓ Ⓔ	59. Ⓐ Ⓑ Ⓒ Ⓓ Ⓔ	92. Ⓐ Ⓑ Ⓒ Ⓓ Ⓔ
27. Ⓐ Ⓑ Ⓒ Ⓓ Ⓔ	60. Ⓐ Ⓑ Ⓒ Ⓓ Ⓔ	93. Ⓐ Ⓑ Ⓒ Ⓓ ●
28. Ⓐ Ⓑ Ⓒ Ⓓ Ⓔ	61. Ⓐ Ⓑ Ⓒ Ⓓ Ⓔ	94. Ⓐ Ⓑ Ⓒ Ⓓ Ⓔ
29. Ⓐ Ⓑ Ⓒ Ⓓ Ⓔ	62. Ⓐ Ⓑ Ⓒ Ⓓ Ⓔ	95. Ⓐ Ⓑ Ⓒ Ⓓ Ⓔ
30. Ⓐ Ⓑ Ⓒ Ⓓ Ⓔ	63. Ⓐ Ⓑ Ⓒ Ⓓ Ⓔ	96. Ⓐ Ⓑ Ⓒ Ⓓ Ⓔ
31. Ⓐ Ⓑ Ⓒ Ⓓ Ⓔ	64. Ⓐ Ⓑ Ⓒ Ⓓ Ⓔ	97. Ⓐ Ⓑ Ⓒ Ⓓ Ⓔ
32. Ⓐ Ⓑ Ⓒ Ⓓ Ⓔ	65. Ⓐ Ⓑ Ⓒ Ⓓ Ⓔ	98. Ⓐ Ⓑ Ⓒ Ⓓ Ⓔ
33. Ⓐ Ⓑ Ⓒ Ⓓ Ⓔ	66. Ⓐ Ⓑ Ⓒ Ⓓ Ⓔ	

Test 3

TEST 3

Address Checking

(Answer sheets appear in the back of this book.)

TIME: 6 Minutes
           95 Questions

DIRECTIONS: In this section you will be asked to compare two lists of addresses, deciding if they are alike or different. If the addresses are alike, you will mark oval "A" on your answer sheet; if they are different, you will mark oval "D" on your answer sheet.

1. 29 Phoebe Terrace   29 Phoebe Terrace

2. 324B W. Tulane St.   224B W. Tulane St.

3. 4151 Oxford Drive   4151 Oxford Drive

4. 2020 Hill Street   2202 Hill Street

5. 2 Route 11 West   2 Route 11 East

6. 121 Tices Lane Apt. 3   121 Tices Lane Apt. 2

7. Metuchen, NJ 08840   Metuchen, NJ 08840

8. 1 Cardinal Blvd.   1 Cardenell Blvd.

9. 1451B W. Lodge St.   1451B W. Lodge St.

10. 932 Hodges Lane   932 Hodges Lane

11. 25 Kentnor St. Apt. 5   5 Kentnor St. Apt. 5

12. 98 Jay Place   98 Jay Road

13. 125 East Chaise Rd.   125 East Chaise Rd.

14. 7 Leigh Lane   7 Lee Lane

15. 616 Washington St.   616 Washington St.

16. 57 (E) Green Place   57 W. Green Place

17.	252 Broad St.	252 Broad St.
18.	191 State Hwy. No. 18	191 State Hwy. No. 18
19.	115 State Hwy. No. 27	115 State Hwy. No. 27
20.	49 W. Henry Rd.	49W Henry Rd.
21.	62 Safran Ave.	62 Safran Ave.
22.	347 Wyckoff Way W.	347W Wyckoff Way
23.	961B Village Dr. East	961B Village Dr. East
24.	406 Royal Oak Ct.	406 Royal Ct.
25.	8T Quincy Cir.	80 Quincy Cir.
26.	12 Cartier Dr.	12 Cartier Dr.
27.	181 Auld Way	181 Auld Way
28.	126 Jeremy Ct.	126 Jeremy St.
29.	153 Throckmaster Lane	153 Throckmaster Lane
30.	409 S. 10th Ave.	4092 10th Ave.
31.	15 Goodwill Place	15 Goodwill Place
32.	62A Commercial Ave.	62A Commercial Ave.
33.	852 US Hwy. No. 1	852 US Hwy. No. 1
34.	3510 Northfield Lane	3510 Northfield Lane
35.	2072 Merrywood Dr.	2072 Merrywood Dr.
36.	1 Iris Ct.	1 Rise Ct.
37.	6A Nelson Rd. South	6A Nelson Rd. South
38.	350 Schoolhouse Rd.	350 Schoolhouse Blvd.
39.	1144D George Ct.	1144G George Ct.
40.	15 Westbury Rd.	15 Westbury Rd.
41.	2380 Cottrell Ave.	2380 Cottrell Ave.
42.	902 So. Look Dr.	902 So. Look Dr.
43.	Jamesburg, NJ 08706	Jamesburg, NJ 08807

44.	2507 Forest Haven Blvd.	2507 Forest Haven Blvd.
45.	8 Kirshner Lane	8 Kirsh Lane
46.	1901 US Hwy. 130	19 US Hwy. 130
47.	5 Newkirk Rd.	5 Newkirk Rd.
48.	1250 S. Deans Lane	1250 S. Dinas Lane
49.	128B Keystone Ct.	1288 Keystone Ct.
50.	211F Amboy Ave.	211F Amboy St.
51.	1155 St. Georges Rd.	1155 St. Georges Rd.
52.	421 Old Bridge Tpk.	421 Old Bridge Tpk.
53.	1090 King Georges Post Rd.	1090 King Georges Rd
54.	65 W. Prospect St.	65 (E) Prospect St.
55.	247 S. Main St.	274 S. Main St.
56.	214B Spring Hill Rd.	214B Spring Hill Rd.
57.	61 Winding Wood Dr.	61 Winding Wood Ave.
58.	1136 Aaeon Rd. North	1136 Aaron Rd. North
59.	46A Englishtown Rd.	46A Englishtown Rd.
60.	17 Maryknoll Rd.	17 Marybone Rd.
61.	17 So. Grover Ave.	17 So. Grover Ave.
62.	14H Woodbridge Terrace	14H Woodbridge Terrace
63.	393 MacDowell Dr.	393 MacDowell Dr.
64.	2206 Timber Oaks Rd.	2260 Timber Oaks Rd.
65.	705C Jesse Way	705C Jesse Way
66.	15 Marlin Rd.	15 Maitlin Rd.
67.	N. Brunswick, NJ 08905	N. Brunswick, NJ 08905
68.	15 S. Main St.	15 S. Main St.
69.	US Hwy. No. 9	US Hwy. No. 90
70.	New Durham & Stelton Rd.	N. Durham & Stelton Rd.

71.	7 Chris St.	7 Chris St.
72.	185 National Rd.	1851 National Rd.
73.	722 US Hwy. 202-206 N.	722 US Hwy. 202-206 S.
74.	15E Maggee Terrace	15E Marge Terrace
75.	250 No. Crescent Ave.	250 No. Crescent Ave.
76.	1 New York Blvd.	1 New York Blvd.
77.	5 West Ave.	5 W. East Ave.
78.	6 Becker Farm Rd.	6 Becker Farm Rd.
79.	21F State Hwy. No. 516	21D State Hwy. No. 516
80.	519 County Hwy. No. 523	519 County Hwy. No. 523
81.	556 Spotswood-Dover Rd.	565 Spotswood-Dover Rd.
82.	Ferry & State Hwy. 17	Ferry & State Hwy. 17
83.	1 Astor Place	1A Star Place
84.	123 Adelaide Ave.	123 Adelaide Ct.
85.	391 No. Oaks Blvd.	391 No. Oaks Blvd.
86.	17N Burney Rd.	17 No. Burney Rd.
87.	1E Twain Ave.	1E Twain Ave.
88.	35 Cabot Way	53 Cabot Way
89.	572 New Durham Rd. West	572 New Durham Rd. West
90.	7A Auer Court	7A Aven Court
91.	281D So. 11th St.	281D So. 11th St.
92.	4 Tulip Dr.	4 Tulip Rd.
93.	1617 N. Birchwood Ct.	1167 N. Birchwood Ct.
94.	9B Brick Plant Rd.	9B Brick Plant Rd.
95.	Broadway and Madison	Broadway and Radison

TEST 3

Memory for Addresses

(Answer sheets appear in the back of this book.)

TIME: Study 5 Minutes, Work 5 Minutes
88 Questions

DIRECTIONS: Below are five boxes labeled A,B,C,D, and E. Each box contains five addresses. You will be given five minutes to memorize the addresses in the boxes and their locations. After five minutes are up, you will have an additional five minutes to answer the following 88 questions and mark on the answer sheet the letter of the box in which the address belongs. You will not be able to refer back to the boxes once you begin answering the questions.

A	B	C	D	E
4700-5599 Tappen	8800-9499 Tappen	1100-1799 Tappen	6100-6599 Tappen	9100-9899 Tappen
Birch	Peartree	Oakcrest	Dunster	Avery
9100-9899 Hamstead	6100-6599 Hamstead	4700-5599 Hamstead	8800-9499 Hamstead	1100-1799 Hamstead
Tottenham	Leicester	Highgate	Ethel	River
1100-1799 Jacksons	9100-9899 Jacksons	8800-9499 Jacksons	4700-5599 Jacksons	6100-6599 Jacksons

1. Dunster
2. 6100-6599 Jacksons
3. Ethel
4. 4700-5599 Jacksons
5. 1100-1799 Jacksons
6. Tottenham
7. 8800-9499 Hamstead
8. Peartree
9. 6100-6599 Hamstead
10. Oakcrest
11. 1100-1799 Hamstead
12. Leicester
13. 9100-9899 Tappen
14. 1100-1799 Tappen
15. Birch
16. 8800-9499 Jacksons
17. 8800-9499 Tappen
18. 4700-5599 Jacksons
19. River
20. 6100-6599 Tappen
21. 9100-9899 Hamstead
22. 4700-5599 Tappen
23. Avery
24. Highgate
25. 9100-9899 Jacksons
26. 4700-5599 Hamstead
27. Dunster

28. 6100-6599 Jacksons

29. 1100-1799 Hamstead

30. 1100-1799 Jacksons

31. Peartree

32. 4700-5599 Jacksons

33. 1100-1799 Tappen

34. Tottenham

35. 9100-9899 Hamstead

36. Ethel

37. Oakcrest

38. 8800-9499 Tappen

39. Avery

40. 6100-6599 Hamstead

41. River

42. 4700-5599 Tappen

43. 8800-9499 Hamstead

44. Highgate

45. Leicester

46. 9100-9899 Tappen

47. 6100-6599 Jacksons

48. Tottenham

49. 8800-9499 Jacksons

50. 6100-6599 Tappen

51. Dunster

52. Peartree

53. Birch

54. 1100-1799 Tappen

55. 4700-5599 Jacksons

56. River

57. Ethel

58. Oakcrest

59. 8800-9499 Tappen

60. 9100-9899 Hamstead

61. 8800-9499 Hamstead

62. Avery

63. Highgate

64. Dunster

65. 6100-6599 Tappen

66. 4700-5599 Tappen

67. Leicester

68. 4700-5599 Jacksons

69. Tottenham

70. Birch

71. 6100-6599 Hamstead

72. 8800-9499 Jacksons

73. 1100-1799 Tappen

74. 6100-6599 Jacksons

75. 9100-9899 Jacksons

76. 1100-1799 Jacksons

77. Peartree

78. 4700-5599 Hamstead

79. 8800-9499 Hamstead

80. 1100-1799 Hamstead

81. 9100-9899 Hamstead

82. 8800-9499 Tappen

83. Oakcrest

84. Birch

85. 9100-9899 Tappen

86. Ethel

87. 9100-9899 Jacksons

88. 1100-1799 Jacksons

TEST 3

Number Series

(Answer sheets appear in the back of this book.)

TIME: 20 Minutes
24 Questions

DIRECTIONS: For each question, there is a series of numbers that follow some definite order. Look at the series of numbers and decide which two numbers will come next in the series. You will be given five answers to choose from.

1. 2   3   3   4   5   5   6   7   _____   _____

   (A) 7, 8

   (B) 8, 9

   (C) 9, 7

   (D) 6, 8

   (E) 7, 9

2. 1   3   2   4   3   5   4   6   _____   _____

   (A) 5, 6

   (B) 7, 8

   (C) 5, 7

   (D) 7, 9

   (E) 5, 8

3. 1   8   2   9   3   10   4   11   _____   _____

   (A) 5, 11

   (B) 5, 12

(C) 6, 12

(D) 11, 5

(E) 5, 10

4.   1   22   3   24   5   26   7   28   _____ _____

(A) 8, 30

(B) 8, 64

(C) 9, 35

(D) 9, 30

(E) 35, 9

5.   88   11   66   33   44   55   22   7 _____ _____

(A) 66, 33

(B) 0, 99

(C) 33, 88

(D) 88, 11

(E) 99, 0

6.   1   100   2   99   3   98   4   97   _____ _____

(A) 5, 98

(B) 6, 95

(C) 97, 4

(D) 96, 5

(E) 5, 96

7.   1   100   3   99   5   98   7   97   _____ _____

(A) 8, 98

(B) 96, 9

(C) 8, 96

(D) 14, 194

(E) 9, 96

8. 2   6   4   12   6   18   8   24   _____ _____

(A) 10, 30

(B) 10, 26

(C) 20, 60

(D) 30, 16

(E) 8, 30

9. 1   15   2   18   3   21   4   24   _____ _____

(A) 5, 25

(B) 5, 27

(C) 6, 36

(D) 25, 5

(E) 12, 48

10. 1   1   11   2   2   11   3   3   _____ _____

(A) 12, 48

(B) 4, 48

(C) 11, 4

(D) 5, 25

(E) 4, 11

11. 100   98   1   3   96   94   5   7   _____ _____

(A) 6, 92

(B) 8, 10

(C) 92, 90

(D) 7, 9

(E) 90, 9

12. 1   10   2   20   3   30   4   40   _____ _____

    (A) 5, 25

    (B) 6, 60

    (C) 50, 5

    (D) 5, 50

    (E) 25, 5

13. 202   177   152   127   102   77   52 _____ _____

    (A) 41, 30

    (B) 66, 55

    (C) 26, 13

    (D) 75, 52

    (E) 27, 2

14. 10,000   9,000   1   2   3   8,000   7,000   4

    _____   _____

    (A) 5, 6

    (B) 6,000, 5,000

    (C) 6,000, 5

    (D) 7, 7,000

    (E) 5, 5,000

15. 1   111   3   111   4   111   6   111   _____

    _____

    (A) 7, 222

    (B) 7, 111

    (C) 8, 111

    (D) 8, 10

    (E) 5, 7

16. 1   2   3   2   5   2   7   2   _____ _____

    (A) 9, 2

    (B) 14, 2

    (C) 9, 11

    (D) 14, 28

    (E) 2, 2

17. 2   3   4   3   6   3   8   3   _____ _____

    (A) 10, 12

    (B) 3, 3

    (C) 3, 10

    (D) 10, 3

    (E) 12, 10

18. 1   3   6   8   11   13   16   18   _____ _____

    (A) 20, 22

    (B) 36, 72

    (C) 24, 26

    (D) 23, 21

    (E) 21, 23

19. 1   100   6   95   11   90   16   8   5   _____ _____

    (A) 90, 12

    (B) 80, 32

    (C) 21, 80

    (D) 45, 48

    (E) 20, 24

20. 25,000   2   5,000   4   1,000   6   200   8

     _____   _____

    (A)   10, 12

    (B)   400, 800

    (C)   2,000, 10

    (D)   40, 10

    (E)   10, 100

21. 5   10   99   98   15   20   97   9   _____

     _____

    (A)   25, 30

    (B)   95, 93

    (C)   95, 94

    (D)   25, 50

    (E)   25, 100

22. 1   6   2   7   3   8   4   9   _____   _____

    (A)   10, 11

    (B)   5, 10

    (C)   10, 5

    (D)   5, 11

    (E)   8, 18

23. 100   12   99   12   98   12   97   12   _____

     _____

    (A)   24, 194

    (B)   96, 12

    (C)   14, 16

    (D)   12, 12

    (E)   96, 95

24. 200   189   178   167   156   145   134   123
     _____   _____

(A) 111, 100

(B) 246, 552

(C) 134, 145

(D) 112, 101

(E) 150, 250

TEST 3

Following Oral Directions - Worksheet

(Answer sheets appear in the back of this book.)

TIME: Instructions will be read at approximately 80 words per minute.

DIRECTIONS: Follow the instructions that are read to you. They will not be repeated during the examination. You are to mark your worksheets according to the instructions that are read to you. After each set of instructions, you will be given time to record your answer on your answer sheet. You should have only one space darkened for each number. If you go to darken a space for a number and you have already darkened another space, either erase the first mark and darken the space for your new choice **or** let the original mark remain.

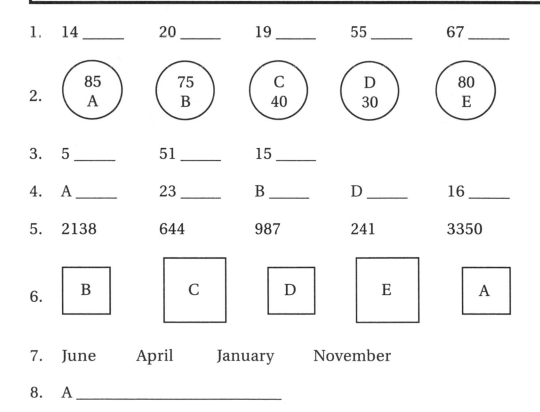

1. 14 _____   20 _____   19 _____   55 _____   67 _____

2. (85 A)   (75 B)   (C 40)   (D 30)   (80 E)

3. 5 _____   51 _____   15 _____

4. A _____   23 _____   B _____   D _____   16 _____

5. 2138   644   987   241   3350

6. [B]   [C]   [D]   [E]   [A]

7. June   April   January   November

8. A _____

B _____

C _____

D _____

E _____

9. 25/48   28/56

10. 304 B Elmwood   220 Foster   314 Peyton   253 Stanwick

11. [A] △C ◯D △E [D] △A

TEST 3

ANSWER KEY

Address Checking

1. (A)	15. (A)	29. (A)	43. (D)	57. (D)	71. (A)	85. (A)
2. (D)	16. (D)	30. (D)	44. (A)	58. (D)	72. (D)	86. (D)
3. (A)	17. (A)	31. (A)	45. (D)	59. (A)	73. (D)	87. (A)
4. (D)	18. (A)	32. (A)	46. (D)	60. (D)	74. (D)	88. (D)
5. (D)	19. (A)	33. (A)	47. (A)	61. (A)	75. (A)	89. (A)
6. (D)	20. (D)	34. (A)	48. (D)	62. (A)	76. (A)	90. (D)
7. (A)	21. (A)	35. (A)	49. (D)	63. (A)	77. (D)	91. (A)
8. (D)	22. (D)	36. (D)	50. (A)	64. (D)	78. (A)	92. (D)
9. (A)	23. (A)	37. (A)	51. (A)	65. (A)	79. (D)	93. (D)
10. (A)	24. (D)	38. (D)	52. (A)	66. (D)	80. (A)	94. (A)
11. (D)	25. (D)	39. (D)	53. (D)	67. (A)	81. (D)	95. (D)
12. (D)	26. (A)	40. (A)	54. (D)	68. (A)	82. (A)	
13. (A)	27. (A)	41. (A)	55. (D)	69. (D)	83. (D)	
14. (D)	28. (D)	42. (A)	56. (A)	70. (D)	84. (D)	

Memory for Addresses

1. (D)	14. (C)	27. (D)	40. (B)	53. (A)	66. (A)	79. (D)
2. (E)	15. (A)	28. (E)	41. (E)	54. (C)	67. (B)	80. (E)
3. (D)	16. (C)	29. (E)	42. (A)	55. (D)	68. (D)	81. (A)
4. (D)	17. (B)	30. (A)	43. (D)	56. (E)	69. (A)	82. (B)
5. (A)	18. (D)	31. (B)	44. (C)	57. (D)	70. (A)	83. (C)
6. (A)	19. (E)	32. (D)	45. (B)	58. (C)	71. (B)	84. (A)
7. (D)	20. (D)	33. (C)	46. (E)	59. (B)	72. (C)	85. (E)
8. (B)	21. (A)	34. (A)	47. (E)	60. (A)	73. (C)	86. (D)
9. (B)	22. (A)	35. (A)	48. (A)	61. (D)	74. (E)	87. (B)
10. (C)	23. (E)	36. (D)	49. (C)	62. (E)	75. (B)	88. (A)
11. (E)	24. (C)	37. (C)	50. (D)	63. (C)	76. (A)	
12. (B)	25. (B)	38. (B)	51. (D)	64. (D)	77. (B)	
13. (E)	26. (C)	39. (E)	52. (B)	65. (D)	78. (C)	

Note: There is only an answer key for the "Memory for Addresses" section.

Number Series

1.	(A)	13.	(E)
2.	(C)	14.	(A)
3.	(B)	15.	(B)
4.	(D)	16.	(A)
5.	(B)	17.	(D)
6.	(E)	18.	(E)
7.	(E)	19.	(C)
8.	(A)	20.	(D)
9.	(B)	21.	(A)
10.	(C)	22.	(B)
11.	(C)	23.	(B)
12.	(D)	24.	(D)

Following Oral Directions

(Please see "Detailed Explanations of Answers.")

DETAILED EXPLANATIONS OF ANSWERS

Test 3

Address Checking

1. alike
2. **324B** W. Tulane St.   **224B** W. Tulane St.
3. alike
4. **2020** Hill Street   **2202** Hill Street
5. 2 Route 11 **West**   2 Route 11 **East**
6. 121 Tices Lane Apt. **3**   121 Tices Lane Apt. **2**
7. alike
8. 1 Card**inal** Blvd.   1 Card**enell** Blvd.
9. alike
10. alike
11. **25** Kentor St. Apt. 5   **5** Kentor St. Apt. 5
12. 98 Jay **Place**   98 Jay **Road**
13. alike
14. 7 L**eigh** Lane   7 L**ee** Lane
15. alike
16. 57 **(E)** Green Place   57 **W.** Green Place
17. alike
18. alike
19. alike
20. 49 **W.** Henry Rd.   49**W** Henry Rd.
21. alike
22. 347 Wyckoff Way **W.**   347 **W** Wyckoff Way
23. alike
24. 406 Royal **Oak** Ct.   406 Royal Ct.
25. **8T** Quincy Cir.   **80** Quincy Cir.
26. alike

27.	alike	
28.	126 Jeremy **Ct.**	126 Jeremy **St.**
29.	alike	
30.	409 **S.** 10th Ave.	409**2** 10th Ave.
31.	alike	
32.	alike	
33.	alike	
34.	alike	
35.	alike	
36.	1 **Iris** Ct.	1 **Rise** Ct.
37.	alike	
38.	350 Schoolhouse **Rd.**	350 Schoolhouse **Blvd.**
39.	1144**D** George Ct.	1144**G** George Ct.
40.	alike	
41.	alike	
42.	alike	
43.	Jamesburg, NJ 08**706**	Jamesburg, NJ 08**807**
44.	alike	
45.	8 Kirsh**ner** Lane	8 Kirsh Lane
46.	19**01** US Hwy. 130	19 US Hwy. 130
47.	alike	
48.	1250 S. **Deans** Lane	1250 S. **Dinas** Lane
49.	128**B** Keystone Ct.	128**8** Keystone Ct.
50.	alike	
51.	alike	
52.	alike	
53.	1090 King Georges **Post** Rd.	1090 King Georges Rd.
54.	65 **W.** Prospect St.	65 **(E)** Prospect St.
55.	**247** S. Main St.	**274** S. Main St.
56.	alike	
57.	61 Winding Wood **Dr.**	61 Winding Wood **Ave.**
58.	1136 Aaeon Rd. North	1136 Aaron Rd. North
59.	alike	
60.	17 Mary**knoll** Rd.	17 Mary**bone** Rd.
61.	alike	
62.	alike	
63.	alike	

64. 2206 Timber Oaks Rd.   2260 Timber Oaks Rd.
65. alike
66. 15 Ma**r**lin Rd.   15 Ma**it**lin Rd.
67. alike
68. alike
69. US Hwy. No. 9   US Hwy. No. **90**
70. **New** Durham & Stelton Rd.   **N.** Durham & Stelton Rd.
71. alike
72. 185 National Rd.   1851 National Rd.
73. 722 US Hwy. 202-206 **N.**   722 US Hwy. 202-206 **S.**
74. 15E **Maggee** Terrace   15E **Margie** Terrace
75. alike
76. alike
77. 5 **West** Ave.   5 **W. East** Ave.
78. alike
79. 21**F** State Hwy. No. 516   21**D** State Hwy. No. 516
80. alike
81. 5**56** Spotswood-Dover Rd.   5**65** Spotswood-Dover Rd.
82. alike
83. 1 **Astor** Place   1**A Star** Place
84. 123 Adelaide **Ave.**   123 Adelaide **Ct.**
85. alike
86. 17**N** Burney Rd.   17 **No.** Burney Rd.
87. alike
88. **35** Cabot Way   **53** Cabot Way
89. alike
90. 7A **Auer** Court   7A **Aven** Court
91. alike
92. 4 **Tulip Dr.**   4 **Tolip Rd.**
93. 1**61**7 N. Birchwood Ct.   1**16**7 N. Birchwood Ct.
94. alike
95. Broadway and **Madison**   Broadway and **Radison**

Number Series

1. **(A)** Beginning with 2, add 1 to each number, repeating every other number one extra time. The correct response is (A) 7, 8.

2. **(C)** Beginning with 1, add 2, and then subtract 1, and repeat this pattern. The correct response is (C) 5, 7.

3. **(B)** Beginning with 1, add 7, and then subtract 6. Repeat this pattern. Therefore, the correct response is (B) 5, 12.

4. **(D)** This is a series of odd numbers, with the sum of each number and 21 alternating with the numbers. The correct response is (D) 9, 30.

5. **(B)** There are two alternating series here: the first begins with 88 and decreases by 22, the second begins with 11 and increases by 22. The correct response is (B) 0, 99.

6. **(E)** A series beginning with 1 and increasing by 1 is alternated with a series beginning with 100 and decreasing by 1, so the correct answer is (E) 5, 96.

7. **(E)** The first series begins with 1 and is increased by 2, and the second begins with 100 and is decreased by 1. Therefore, the correct response is (E) 9, 96.

8. **(A)** Beginning with 2, alternate between increasing consecutive even numbers and multiplying the last consecutive even number by 3. The pattern would go like this: **2,** $2 \times 3 =$ **6, 4,** $4 \times 3 =$ **12,** etc. The correct response is (A) 10, 30.

9. **(B)** Beginning with 1, increase by increments of 1. Alternate this sequence with another sequence that takes each of these numbers, adds 4, and multiplies that sum by 3. The pattern would go like this: **1,** $(1 + 4) \times 3 =$ **15, 2,** $(2 + 4) \times 3 =$ **18,** etc. The correct response is (B) 5, 27.

10. **(C)**   The first series begins with 1 and is increased by increments of 1, but each number is repeated twice. The pattern is separated by the number 11. The correct response is (C) 11, 4.

11. **(C)**   These two series alternate two numbers at a time. The first begins with 100 and subtracts 2 and the second begins with 1 and adds 2. The correct response is (C) 92, 90.

12. **(D)**   Each number in a series beginning with 1 and increasing by 1 is alternated with that number multiplied by 10. Therefore the correct response is (D) 5, 50.

13. **(E)**   Beginning with 202, 25 is subtracted from each number; therefore, the correct response is (E) 27, 2.

14. **(A)**   Two numbers of one series are alternated with three numbers of the next. The first begins with 10,000 and is decreased by 1,000 each time. The second series begins with 1 and is increased by 1. The correct response is (A) 5, 6.

15. **(B)**   A series which increases alternately by adding 1 or 2 is separated by the number 111. The correct response is (B) 7, 111.

16. **(A)**   This is a series of increasing odd numbers separated by the number 2. Therefore, the correct response is (A) 9, 2.

17. **(D)**   This is a series of increasing even numbers separated by the number 3, so the correct response is (D) 10, 3.

18. **(E)**   Beginning with 1, add 2 and then 3 to the numbers, so that the next numbers in the series are (E) 21, 23.

19. **(C)**   This pattern has two alternating series, one beginning with 1 and increasing by 5, and the other beginning with 100 and decreasing by 5. Therefore, the correct response is (C) 21, 80.

20. **(D)**   This pattern has two alternating series, the first beginning with 25,000 divided by 5, and the second beginning with 2 and increased by adding 2. The correct response is (D) 40, 10.

21. **(A)**   This pattern has two series alternating two numbers at a time: the first begins with 5 and adds 5, and the second begins with 99 and subtracts 1. The correct response is (A) 25, 30.

22. **(B)**   Beginning with 1, add 5 and then subtract 4. The correct response is (B) 5, 10.

23. **(B)**   Beginning with 100, this series is decreased by 1 and separated by the number 12. The correct response is (B) 96, 12.

24. **(D)**   Beginning with 200, this series is decreased by 11. Therefore, the correct response is (D) 112, 101.

Following Oral Directions

This is how your worksheet should look:

1. 14 **A**   20 **D**   19 ____   55 **C**   67 ____

2. ⊘ 85 A   ⊘ 75 B   ⊘ C 40   ⊘ D 30   ⊘ 80 E

3. 5 **D**   51 **A**   15 **B**

4. A **2**   23 **D**   B **26**   D **2**   16 **A**

5. 2138   644   987   241   3350
    A   **B**   **C**   **D**   **E**

6. ☐ B   ☐ **13** C   ☐ **80** D   ☐ **17** E   ☐ **24** A

7. June   April   January   November

8. A ___**10**___
    B ___**43**___
    C _____
    D **18**___
    E _____

9. 25/48   28/56
    ᴅ

10. 304 B Elmwood   220 Foster   314 Peyton   253 Stanwick

11. **46** A   C   **47** D   E D   **37** A

In this section, please note that the solution to each problem is preceded by the actual instructions read by the examiner.

Examine sample one. (Pause 2-3 seconds) These figures represent the number of parcels delivered by different carriers on the same day. If the difference between the most and the least is more than 20, write the letter D as in "dog" next to number 20. (Pause 2 seconds) If the difference is 20 or less, write the letter D as in "dog" next to number 19. (Pause 2 seconds) Darken the corresponding number/letter combination on your answer sheet. (Pause 5 seconds)

ANSWER: Taking the highest and lowest numbers, we find that their difference (67-14=53) is greater than 20. Therefore, the letter D should be written next to the number 20 on the answer sheet—20 D.

Examine sample one again. (Pause 2-3 seconds) If the second smallest number of parcels delivered was less than 10, write the letter B as in "boy" next to the greatest number of parcels delivered. (Pause 2 seconds) If the second smallest number of parcels delivered was more than 10 but less than 20, write the letter C as in "cat" next to the second highest number. (Pause 2 seconds) If neither of these statements is true, write the letter A as in "apple" next to the second smallest number. Darken the corresponding oval on your answer sheet. (Pause 5 seconds)

ANSWER: Since the second smallest number (19) is less than 20, the letter C should be written next to the second highest number (55). The letter C should also be filled-in at number 55 on the answer sheet—55 C.

Examine sample two. (Pause 2-3 seconds) The numbers in the circles represent mail volume index figures. Those shown above the letters represent above-average mail volumes, and those shown below the letters represent below-average mail volume. If circle A as in "apple" has the highest mail volume, find the number on your answer sheet that corresponds to the number in the circle and darken the letter A as in "apple." (Pause 5 seconds) If not, go to the number which is the same as the highest volume, and darken the letter which appears in that oval. (Pause 5 seconds)

ANSWER: Since the circle A has a mail volume greater than any other circle (85>75, 40, 30, 80), the letter A should be darkened at number 85 on the answer sheet—85A.

Examine sample two again. (Pause 2-3 seconds) If circles C as in "cat" and E as in "elephant" have above-average volumes, go to number 21 on your answer sheet and darken the oval for D as in "dog." (Pause 2 seconds) If circles C as in "cat" and D as in "dog" have below-average volumes, go to number 8 on your answer sheet and darken the oval for B as in "boy." (Pause 5 seconds)

ANSWER: Since the mail volume for C and D are written below each letter, they are below-average volumes. The letter B should be darkened at number 8—8B.

Examine sample three. (Pause 2-3 seconds) Write the letter B as in "boy" next to the second smallest number shown, the letter A as in "apple" next to the largest number shown, and the letter D as in "dog" next to the smallest number shown. (Pause 5 seconds) Darken all of these number/letter combinations on your answer sheet. (Pause 5 seconds)

ANSWER: Since 51 is greater than 15, which is greater than 5, the letter A should be filled-in at number 51, the letter B should be filled-in at number 15, and the letter D should be filled-in at number 5 on the answer sheet—51A, 15B, and 5D.

Examine sample three again. (Pause 2-3 seconds) If the product of the first and third numbers is less than the second number, go to number 12 on your answer sheet and darken the letter A as in "apple." (Pause 5 seconds) If the product of the first and third numbers is more than the second number, go to number 22 on your answer sheet and darken the letter E as in "elephant." (Pause 5 seconds)

ANSWER: Since the product of the first and third numbers (5 x 15 = 75) is greater than the second number (51), the letter E should be filled-in at number 22 on the answer sheet—22E.

Examine sample three again. (Pause 2-3 seconds) If the sum of all three numbers is less than or equal to 100, go to number 92 on your answer sheet and darken the letter A as in "apple." (Pause 5 seconds) If the sum of all three numbers is more than 200, go to number 91 on your answer sheet and darken the letter B as in "boy." (Pause 5 seconds) If neither of these statements is true, go to number 29 and darken A as in "apple." (Pause 5 seconds)

ANSWER: Since the sum of the three numbers (5 + 51 + 15 = 71) is less than 100, the letter A should be filled-in at number 92 on the answer sheet—92A.

Examine sample four. (Pause 2-3 seconds) Write the number 26 next to the second letter of the alphabet. (Pause 2 seconds) Darken the corresponding number/letter combination on your answer sheet. (Pause 5 seconds)

ANSWER: Since B is the second letter of the alphabet, the number 26 should be written next to it. The letter B should also be filled-in at number 26 on the answer sheet—26B.

Examine sample four again. (Pause 2-3 seconds) Write the first letter shown next to the last number shown and the last letter shown next to the first number shown. (Pause 5 seconds) Darken the corresponding number/letter combination on your answer sheet. (Pause 5 seconds)

ANSWER: Since A is the first letter shown, it should be written next to the number 16. Similarly, the last letter shown, D, should be written next to the number 23. Lastly, the letter A should be filled-in at number 16 and the letter D should be filled-in at number 23 on the answer sheet—16A and 23D.

Examine sample four again. (Pause 2-3 seconds) If, after you answer the last two questions, every number or letter shown has something written next to it, go to number 1 on your answer sheet and darken the oval for E as in "elephant." (Pause 2 seconds) If there is a number left with nothing written next to it, write the letter C as in "cat" next to it. If there is a letter left, write the number 2 next to it. (Pause 2 seconds) Darken the corresponding number/letter combination on your answer sheet. (Pause 5 seconds)

ANSWER: Since the space after the letter A and the letter D are still blank (the number 23 should have the letter D next to it, the letter B should have the number 26 next to it, and the number 16 should have the letter A next to it) write the number 2 on the remaining empty lines. Lastly, either the letter A or D should be darkened at number 2 (remember that you may have only one letter filled-in per question)—2A or 2D.

Examine sample five. (Pause 2-3 seconds) These figures represent the number of letters delivered by different carriers on a certain day. Write the letters A as in "apple" through E as in "elephant" in alphabetical order, one under each number. (Pause 5 seconds) Go to the number on your answer sheet represented by the first two digits of the highest number and darken the oval for the letter you have written under it. (Pause 5 seconds)

ANSWER: When the directions told you to write the letters A through E alphabetically, you should have paired the numbers and letters in this way: (2138/A, 644/B, 987/C, 241/D, & 3350/E). You then had to choose the highest number (3350) and use its first two digits (33) to find the number to go to on the answer sheet where you would fill-in the letter E—33E.

Examine sample five again. (Pause 2-3 seconds) The higher numbers represent city routes; the lower represent rural routes. Circle the last two digits of the number representing the most rural route. (Pause 2 seconds) Find this number on your answer sheet and darken the oval for the letter you have written under it. (Pause 5 seconds)

ANSWER: It is important in this problem to take into consideration the entire range of numbers. Look at the first sentence as a kind of general range, the higher numbers represent cities, the lower numbers, rural routes. It is not important to concern yourself with medians in this question. Since 241 is the lowest number, it would have to be the lowest rural route, you would single-out 41 and fill-in the letter D—41D.

Examine sample six. (Pause 2-3 seconds) Write the number 80 in the box with the fourth letter of the alphabet in it. (Pause 2 seconds) Darken the corresponding number/letter combination on your answer sheet. (Pause 5 seconds)

ANSWER: You should have written the number 80 in the box with the letter D in it. The letter D also should have been darkened at number 80 on your answer sheet—80D.

Examine sample six again. (Pause 2-3 seconds) Write the numbers 13 and 17, in that order, in the two largest boxes. (Pause 2 seconds) Darken the corresponding number/letter combination on your answer sheet. (Pause 5 seconds) Now if the first letter shown in a small box is the first letter of the alphabet, write the number 42 in that box. (Pause 2 seconds) If the last letter shown in a small box is the first letter of the alphabet, write the number 24 in that box.

(Pause 2 seconds) Darken the number/letter combination on your answer sheet. (Pause 5 seconds)

ANSWER: You should have written the number 13 in the box labeled C and the number 17 in the box labeled E. You should have then darkened in the letter C at number 13 and E at number 17 on your answer sheet. Since the letter shown in the last box is the letter A, you should have written the number 24 with it. The letter A should have been filled-in at number 24 on your answer sheet—24A.

Examine sample seven. (Pause 2-3 seconds) If either of the first two months shown could be classified as fall months, go to number five on your answer sheet and darken the oval for D as in "dog." (Pause 2 seconds) If either of them could be classified as spring months, go to the same number but darken the oval for E as in "elephant." (Pause 5 seconds)

ANSWER: Since the month of April occurs during spring, you should have gone to 5 on your answer sheet and darkened the letter E—5E. However, 5D should have already been darkened. You can erase 5D and darken 5E or do not erase 5D and do not darken 5E.

Examine sample seven again. (Pause 2-3 seconds) If more than two of the months have a vowel as their second letter, go to the number 35 on your answer sheet and darken the oval for B as in "boy." (Pause 2-3 seconds) Otherwise, go to the same number and darken the oval for E as in "elephant." (Pause 5 seconds)

ANSWER: Since three of the months listed have vowels for their second letters, you should have gone to number 35 on your answer sheet and darkened the letter B—35B.

Examine sample eight. (Pause 2-3 seconds) Write the number 10 on the longest line, 18 on the shortest line, and 43 on the second line from the top. (Pause 5 seconds) Darken these number/letter combinations on your answer sheet. (Pause 5 seconds)

ANSWER: You should have written the number 10 on line A, number 18 on line D, and number 43 on line B. After that, you should have gone and darkened the letters for the corresponding numbers—10A, 18D, and 43B.

Examine sample eight again. (Pause 2-3 seconds) If the second longest line shown is the second letter of the alphabet, write the number 50 on that line. (Pause 2 seconds) If not, go to number 50 and darken the oval for E as in "elephant." (Pause 5 seconds)

ANSWER: Since the second longest line is letter E (and not B), you should have gone to number 50 on your answer sheet and darkened the letter E—50E.

Examine sample one again. (Pause 2-3 seconds) If the third number shown is more than the second but less than the fifth, write the letter B as in "boy" next to the smallest number shown. (Pause 2 seconds) If the third number is less than the second, write the letter A as in "apple" next to the smallest number. (Pause 2 seconds) Darken the corresponding number/letter combination on your answer sheet. (Pause 5 seconds)

ANSWER: Since the third number (19) is less than the second (20), the letter A should be written next to the smallest number (14). The letter A should also be darkened at number 14 on the answer sheet—14A.

Examine sample nine. (Pause 2-3 seconds) The first set of numbers represents the price of a small post office box for half a year or a year, and the second set represents the price of a large post office box for half a year or a year. If either of the second numbers in the set is more than two times as big as the first number in the set, go to the largest number in that set and write the letter D as in "dog." (Pause 5 seconds) If this statement is not true, go to the smallest number in either set and write the same letter under it. (Pause 2 seconds) Darken the number/letter combination you have chosen on your answer sheet. (Pause 5 seconds)

ANSWER: Since neither of the sets of first numbers doubled is less than their second numbers (25 x 2 = 50>48 and 28 x 2= 56=56), you should have found the smallest number (25) and written the letter D underneath it. You should have continued by darkening the letter D at number 25 on your answer sheet—25D.

Examine sample ten. (Pause 2-3 seconds) These are four addresses in the same town. Even numbers are on the south side of the street, and odd numbers are on the north. If the third and fourth addresses given are on the north side, go to number 65 on your answer sheet and darken the oval for A as in "apple." (Pause 2 seconds) If either of these addresses is on the south side, go to the same number, but darken the oval for B as in "boy." (Pause 5 seconds)

ANSWER: Since the third address number is 253 it can only be on the south side of town, so you should have gone to number 65 on your answer sheet and filled-in the letter B—65B.

Examine sample ten again. (Pause 2-3 seconds) If two or more of the names of streets have the same number of letters, go to the number on your answer sheet equivalent to the first two digits of the first number and darken the oval for D as in "dog." (Pause 5 seconds) If none of the names has the same number of letters, go to the number on your answer sheet equivalent to the last two digits of the last number and darken the oval for the same letter. (Pause 5 seconds)

ANSWER: Since two of the street names have the same number of letters (Foster — 6 and Peyton — 6), you should have gone to the first two digits of the first number listed (30 from 304) and darkened the letter D—30D.

Examine sample ten again. (Pause 2-3 seconds) If the names appear in alphabetical order, go to the last space on your answer sheet and darken the oval of the fifth letter of the alphabet. (Pause 2 seconds) If they are not alphabetical, go to number 31 and darken the letter C as in "cat." (Pause 5 seconds)

ANSWER: Since the names of the streets are listed in alphabetical order (Elmwood, Foster, Peyton, Stanwick), you should have gone to the last space on your answer sheet (number 98) and filled-in the letter E—98E.

Examine sample eleven. (Pause 2-3 seconds) If any letters appear in both a box and a triangle, write the numbers 46 and 37, in that order, in those two shapes. (Pause 5 seconds) Darken the corresponding number/letter combination on your answer sheet. (Pause 5 seconds)

ANSWER: Since the letter A is within a box and a triangle, write the number 46 in the box and 37 in the triangle. You should have continued to darken the letter A at both numbers 37 and 46—37A and 46A.

Examine sample eleven again. (Pause 2-3 seconds) If there are always seven days in a week, four weeks in a month and twelve months in a year, write the number 47 in the only shape that appears once. (Pause 2 seconds) If any part of this statement is not true, write the numbers 60, 61, and 62 in the shape that appears three times. (Pause 5 seconds) Darken the corresponding number/letter combination on your answer sheet. (Pause 5 seconds)

ANSWER: Since there are always seven days in a week, four weeks in a month, and twelve months in a year, you should have written the number 47 in the circle (as it is the only shape that appears once). You should have then gone to number 47 on your answer sheet and darkened the letter D (as it was contained within the circle)—47D.

POSTAL EXAM
Test 3 - Following Oral Directions
ANSWER KEY

#	Answer	#	Answer	#	Answer
1.	—	34.	—	67.	—
2.	A, D	35.	B	68.	—
3.	—	36.	—	69.	—
4.	—	37.	A	70.	—
5.	D, E	38.	—	71.	—
6.	—	39.	—	72.	—
7.	—	40.	—	73.	—
8.	B	41.	D	74.	—
9.	—	42.	—	75.	—
10.	A	43.	B	76.	—
11.	—	44.	—	77.	—
12.	—	45.	—	78.	—
13.	C	46.	A	79.	—
14.	A	47.	D	80.	D
15.	B	48.	—	81.	—
16.	A	49.	—	82.	—
17.	E	50.	E	83.	—
18.	D	51.	A	84.	—
19.	—	52.	—	85.	A
20.	D	53.	—	86.	—
21.	—	54.	—	87.	—
22.	E	55.	C	88.	—
23.	D	56.	—	89.	—
24.	A	57.	—	90.	—
25.	D	58.	—	91.	—
26.	B	59.	—	92.	A
27.	—	60.	—	93.	—
28.	—	61.	—	94.	—
29.	—	62.	—	95.	E
30.	D	63.	—	96.	—
31.	—	64.	—	97.	—
32.	—	65.	B	98.	E
33.	E	66.	—		

Test 4

TEST 4

Address Checking

(Answer sheets appear in the back of this book.)

TIME: 6 Minutes
95 Questions

DIRECTIONS: In this section you will be asked to compare two lists of addresses, deciding if they are alike or different. If the addresses are alike, you will mark oval "A" on your answer sheet; if they are different, you will mark oval "D" on your answer sheet.

1. 5001 US Hwy. No. 46   5001 US Hwy. No. 46
2. 1 So. Martin Ave.   1 So. Martin Ave.
3. 4401 Clinton Ave.   4041 Clinton Ave.
4. 11 Progress Court   11 Progress St.
5. US Hwy. 1 & Old Post Rd.   US Hwy. 1 & Old Post Rd.
6. 64 Plum St.   64 Plume St.
7. 861 South Ave.   861 South Ave.
8. 30J Montgomery Ct.   305 Montgomery Ct.
9. 62 Vernon Way   62 Vernon Way
10. 19 Princes Drive   19 Princes Drive
11. 14 Walker Ave.   14 Walker Ave.
12. 66L Claridge Place   661 Claridge Place
13. 14 Wysteria Dr.   14 Wisteria Dr.
14. 16 Dancaster Ct.   6 Dancaster Ct.
15. 926 Ellis Pkwy.   926 Ellis Pkwy.
16. 21B Oliver Ave.   213 Oliver Ave.

17.	224 Raymond Rd.	224 Raymond Rd.
18.	294 Bromley Place	294 Browley Place
19.	100 McCaw Dr.	100 McCaw Dr.
20.	11 Phillips Dr.	11 Phillips Dr.
21.	47 Providence Blvd.	47 Providence Rd.
22.	166 Stafford Rd.	16B Stafford Rd.
23.	1 Gates Ave. West	1 Gates Ave. West
24.	28 June St.	28 July St.
25.	76 Kingsland Circle	76 Kingsland Circle
26.	46 Lewis Place	46 Louis Place
27.	140D Harding Ave.	140D Harding Ave.
28.	1 Chalet Drive	1 Chalet Drive
29.	8A Glynn Court	8A Glynn Court
30.	47 John F. Kennedy Dr.	74 John F. Kennedy Dr.
31.	37 Susan Lane	37 Susan Place
32.	213 S. Fulton St.	213B Fulton St.
33.	201 West Locust Ave.	201 West Locust Ave.
34.	128 Kane Ave.	128 Cane Ave.
35.	24 Ernston Rd. Apt. 4	24 Earnest Rd. Apt. 4
36.	2104 N. Oaks Blvd.	2104 N. Oaks Blvd.
37.	16 Brown Ct.	161 Brown Ct.
38.	11B Bayshore Dr.	11B Bayshore Dr.
39.	6 Cornwall Ct.	6 Cornwall St.
40.	37 Flagger Terrace	37 Flagger Terrace
41.	22 County Hwy. N. 516	22 County Hwy. N. 561
42.	3 Dennett Rd.	3 Dennett Rd.
43.	20A Westminster Blvd.	204 Westminster Blvd.

44.	228 Dunhams Corner Rd.	228 Dunhams Corner Rd.
45.	10 W. Reed St.	10 W. Reed St.
46.	2 Angelika Ct.	2 Angelica Rd.
47.	24A Rossmoor Dr.	24A Rossmoor Dr.
48.	16 TigerLily Ct.	16 TigerLily Ct.
49.	2 Dogwood Dr.	2 Dogwood Dr.
50.	1463 Paunee Rd.	1463 Pownee Rd.
51.	151 Mary Ave.	151 Mary Ave.
52.	1388 Hollywood Ave.	138B Hollywood Ave.
53.	75 So. Rolph Place	75 So. Rolph Place
54.	40 Meadow Ct.	40 Meadow Ct.
55.	990C Aurora Rd.	990C Aurena Rd.
56.	563 Park Dr.	563 Park Place
57.	2 N. Baldwin St.	2 N. Baldwin St.
58.	303 S. 2nd Ave.	303 S. 2nd Ave.
59.	10E (E) Garden Way	10D (E) Garden Way
60.	12 N. 5th Ave. Apt. 2D	12 N. 5th Ave. Apt 2G
61.	5 Topaz Lane	5 Topaz Lane
62.	262 Scott Ct.	262 Scott Ct.
63.	675 US Hwy. No. 1	756 US Hwy. No. 1
64.	17 Seminary Place	17 Seminary Place
65.	15 Railroad Ave.	15 Ralroad Ave.
66.	850 Port Reading Ave.	850 Reading Ave.
67.	10 Whittier Dr. Apt. 2C	10 Whittin Dr. Apt. 2C
68.	2411 Greenhollow Dr.	2411 Greenhollow Dr.
69.	21 Heritage Terrace	12 Heritage Terrace
70.	18 Traci Lane	18 Traci Lane

71.	82 Creemer Ave.	82 Creamer Ave.
72.	52 Larch Ct. Apt. 5M	52 Larch Ct. Apt. 5M
73.	14D 4th Ave.	14D 4th Ave.
74.	10 Collasuido Ct.	10 Collasundo Ct.
75.	220 Forsgate Dr.	202 Forsgate Dr.
76.	Rt. 1 & Rt. 18	Rt. 1 & Rt. 18
77.	49K Reading Rd.	49K Reading Blvd.
78.	109 Belluscio Circle	109 Belluscio Circle
79.	120 Homes Park Ave	120 Homes Park Ave
80.	7 Kate Terrace	7 Katie Terrace
81.	171 Picadilly Place	171 Picadilly Place
82.	7 Long St.	7L Long St.
83.	26 Jaime Ct.	26 Jamee Ct.
84.	34 Bartman Rd.	34 Bartman Rd.
85.	14 Hana Rd.	14 Hana Rd.
86.	178 Chestnut Ave.	178D Chestnut Ave.
87.	511 Newbrunswick Ave.	511 Brunswick Ave.
88.	6 Jeffery Circle	6 Jeffery Circle
89.	Wood Ave. & Oak Tree Rd.	Wood Ave. & Old Oak Rd.
90.	55B Halfacre Rd.	55B Halfacre Rd.
91.	15 Tamrac Dr.	15 Tamrac Rd.
92.	23 Southpine Blvd.	23 Southpine Blvd.
93.	7 Bond Place	7 Bond Street
94.	75 Coventry Circle	75 Coventry Circle
95.	7 Greening Way	7 Greening Way

TEST 4

Memory for Addresses

(Answer sheets appear in the back of this book.)

TIME: Study 5 Minutes, Work 5 Minutes
88 Questions

DIRECTIONS: Below are five boxes labeled A,B,C,D, and E. Each box contains five addresses. You will be given five minutes to memorize the addresses in the boxes and their locations. After five minutes are up, you will have an additional five minutes to answer the following 88 questions and mark on the answer sheet the letter of the box in which the address belongs. You will not be able to refer back to the boxes once you begin answering the questions.

A	B	C	D	E
1200-2299 Major	3500-3899 Major	7800-8599 Major	8700-9299 Major	2000-2899 Major
Willett	Heinrich	Cottonwood	Marcone	Fitch
7800-8599 Center	2000-2899 Center	8700-9299 Center	3500-3899 Center	1200-2299 Center
Peach	Ernston	Ethel	Janine	Bennetts
3500-3899 Thorpe	7800-8599 Thorpe	1200-2299 Thorpe	2000-2899 Thorpe	8700-9299 Thorpe

1. 1200-2299 Major
2. 7800-8599 Center
3. Ethel
4. Fitch
5. 1200-2299 Major
6. 8700-9299 Thorpe
7. Heinrich
8. 8700-9299 Center
9. 3500-3899 Major
10. Peach
11. 8700-9299 Major
12. 2000-2899 Thorpe
13. Ernston
14. 2000-2899 Center
15. Marcone
16. 3500-3899 Thorpe
17. 3500-3899 Center
18. Cottonwood
19. 7800-8599 Major
20. Willett
21. 7800-8599 Thorpe
22. Janine
23. 1200-2299 Center
24. Bennetts
25. 2000-2899 Major
26. 7800-8599 Center
27. Heinrich

28. Ernston

29. Peach

30. 1200-2299 Thorpe

31. 2000-2899 Thorpe

32. 8700-9299 Thorpe

33. 3500-3899 Major

34. Fitch

35. 8700-9299 Major

36. 1200-2299 Major

37. Marcone

38. 7800-8599 Major

39. 1200-2299 Center

40. Ethel

41. Willett

42. Cottonwood

43. 2000-2899 Center

44. Bennetts

45. Janine

46. 7800-8599 Thorpe

47. 8700-9299 Center

48. 3500-3899 Center

49. 3500-3899 Thorpe

50. 1200-2299 Thorpe

51. 2000-2899 Thorpe

52. 7800-8599 Center

53. 2000-2899 Major

54. 8700-9299 Thorpe

55. Peach

56. Fitch

57. 3500-3899 Major

58. Heinrich

59. 8700-9299 Major

60. 1200-2299 Major

61. 1200-2299 Center

62. Ernston

63. Marcone

64. 7800-8599 Major

65. 2000-2899 Center

66. Bennetts

67. Ethel

68. Willett

69. 7800-8599 Thorpe

70. Janine

71. 7800-8599 Center

72. 3500-3899 Center

73. Heinrich

74. 3500-3899 Major

75. 8700-9299 Center

76. 3500-3899 Thorpe

77. 2000-2899 Major

78. Peach

79. 1200-2299 Center

80. Ernston

81. Cottonwood

82. 8700-9299 Major

83. 7800-8599 Center

84. 8700-9299 Thorpe

85. 3500-3899 Center

86. 7800-8599 Major

87. 7800-8599 Thorpe

88. 2000-2899 Thorpe

TEST 4

Number Series

(Answer sheets appear in the back of this book.)

TIME: 20 Minutes
24 Questions

DIRECTIONS: For each question, there is a series of numbers that follow some definite order. Look at the series of numbers and decide which two numbers will come next in the series. You will be given five answers to choose from.

1. 1   7   5   11   9   15   13   19   _____   _____
    (A) 17, 21
    (B) 21, 23
    (C) 17, 23
    (D) 25, 23
    (E) 29, 39

2. 2   4   5   6   8   9   10   12   _____   _____
    (A) 14, 16
    (B) 12, 13
    (C) 11, 13
    (D) 14, 13
    (E) 13, 14

3. 1   2   3   2   4   2   6   2   _____   _____
    (A) 3, 4

(B) 7, 2

(C) 3, 5

(D) 8, 10

(E) 8, 2

4. 1   15   29   43   57   71   85   99   _____

_____

(A) 113, 127

(B) 181, 362

(C) 115, 130

(D) 101, 121

(E) 112, 124

5. 0   0   10   0   20   0   30   0   _____   _____

(A) 0, 40

(B) 60, 0

(C) 0, 60

(D) 40, 0

(E) 40, 50

6. 109   98   87   76   65   54   43   32   _____

_____

(A) 21, 10

(B) 20, 10

(C) 31, 21

(D) 22, 12

(E) 22, 11

7. 200   2   196   6   192   10   188   14   _____
    _____

    (A) 177, 166

    (B) 18, 22

    (C) 20, 182

    (D) 184, 18

    (E) 12, 10

8. 2   4   6   11   13   15   20   _____   _____

    (A) 22, 27

    (B) 25, 30

    (C) 21, 23

    (D) 28, 33

    (E) 22, 24

9. 100   98   97   95   94   92   91   89   _____
    _____

    (A) 87, 85

    (B) 86, 83

    (C) 88, 86

    (D) 85, 80

    (E) 76, 69

10. 100   1   95   3   90   5   85   7   _____
    _____

    (A) 90, 5

    (B) 80, 9

    (C) 80, 5

    (D) 9, 11

    (E) 80, 75

11. 1   8   2   16   3   24   4   32   _____   _____

    (A) 6, 12

    (B) 6, 48

    (C) 5, 45

    (D) 5, 40

    (E) 8, 16

12. 1   2   5   4   9   8   13   16   _____   _____

    (A) 15, 18

    (B) 26, 18

    (C) 17, 32

    (D) 17, 34

    (E) 32, 64

13. 1   3   2   8   3   9   4   16   _____   _____

    (A) 5, 15

    (B) 6, 36

    (C) 5, 25

    (D) 15, 5

    (E) 32, 64

14. 1   2   4   7   11   16   22   29   _____   _____

    (A) 31, 33

    (B) 37, 46

    (C) 35, 37

    (D) 31, 42

    (E) 31, 46

15. 12   5   12   10   12   15   12   20   _____ _____

    (A) 12, 25

    (B) 12, 30

    (C) 25, 30

    (D) 12, 12

    (E) 22, 24

16. 200   185   170   155   140   125   110   95   _____ _____

    (A) 90, 85

    (B) 85, 75

    (C) 93, 91

    (D) 80, 65

    (E) 90, 80

17. 1   2   3   2   4   6   3   6   _____ _____

    (A) 8, 10

    (B) 9, 4

    (C) 9, 12

    (D) 5, 10

    (E) 8, 16

18. 1   8   2   9   3   10   4   11   _____ _____

    (A) 6, 8

    (B) 13, 15

    (C) 5, 12

    (D) 22, 24

    (E) 8, 22

19. 1   2   3   6   4   5   6   15   _____   _____

    (A) 8, 9

    (B) 10, 12

    (C) 20, 25

    (D) 7, 8

    (E) 12, 30

20. 1   2   2   3   4   12   5   6   _____   _____

    (A) 12, 24

    (B) 10, 12

    (C) 7, 8

    (D) 7, 9

    (E) 30, 7

21. 1   100   2   200   3   300   4   400   _____ _____

    (A) 500, 5

    (B) 5, 6

    (C) 500, 600

    (D) 500, 1,000

    (E) 5, 500

22. 6   7   9   13   21   37   69   133   _____ _____

    (A) 261, 517

    (B) 266, 522

    (C) 233, 333

    (D) 220, 310

    (E) 135, 137

23. 1   1   3   4   9   7   18   10   _____   _____

    (A) 20, 36

    (B) 54, 30

    (C) 21, 54

    (D) 54, 13

    (E) 12, 14

24. 2   50   100   4   150   200   6   250   _____ _____

    (A) 300, 8

    (B) 300, 350

    (C) 8, 300

    (D) 12, 350

    (E) 24, 1,000

TEST 4

Following Oral Directions - Worksheet

(Answer sheets appear in the back of this book.)

TIME: Instructions will be read at approximately 80 words per minute.

DIRECTIONS: Follow the instructions that are read to you. They will not be repeated during the examination. You are to mark your worksheets according to the instructions that are read to you. After each set of instructions, you will be given time to record your answer on your answer sheet. You should have only one space darkened for each number. If you go to darken a space for a number and you have already darkened another space, either erase the first mark and darken the space for your new choice **or** let the original mark remain.

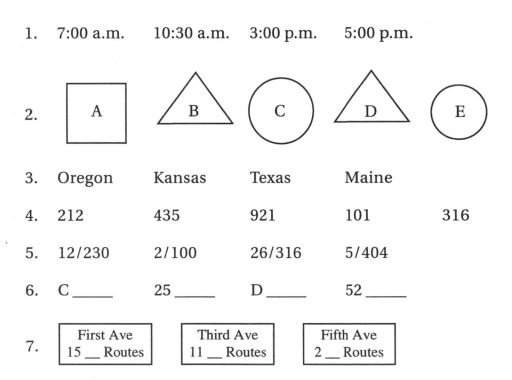

1. 7:00 a.m.   10:30 a.m.   3:00 p.m.   5:00 p.m.

2. A   B   C   D   E

3. Oregon   Kansas   Texas   Maine

4. 212   435   921   101   316

5. 12/230   2/100   26/316   5/404

6. C _____   25 _____   D _____   52 _____

7. First Ave 15 __ Routes   Third Ave 11 __ Routes   Fifth Ave 2 __ Routes

8. 2435679   2432121   2445658   2432159

9. | Monday | Tuesday | Wednesday | Thursday | Friday |
    |--------|---------|-----------|----------|--------|
    | 12 | 21 | 33 | 46 | 52 |

10. 2 _____   5 _____   16 _____   8 _____   4 _____

TEST 4

ANSWER KEY

Address Checking

1. (A)	15. (A)	29. (A)	43. (D)	57. (A)	71. (D)	85. (A)
2. (A)	16. (D)	30. (D)	44. (A)	58. (A)	72. (A)	86. (D)
3. (D)	17. (A)	31. (D)	45. (A)	59. (D)	73. (A)	87. (D)
4. (D)	18. (D)	32. (D)	46. (D)	60. (D)	74. (D)	88. (A)
5. (A)	19. (A)	33. (A)	47. (A)	61. (A)	75. (D)	89. (D)
6. (D)	20. (A)	34. (D)	48. (A)	62. (A)	76. (A)	90. (A)
7. (A)	21. (D)	35. (D)	49. (A)	63. (D)	77. (D)	91. (D)
8. (D)	22. (D)	36. (A)	50. (D)	64. (A)	78. (A)	92. (A)
9. (A)	23. (A)	37. (D)	51. (A)	65. (D)	79. (A)	93. (D)
10. (A)	24. (D)	38. (A)	52. (D)	66. (D)	80. (D)	94. (A)
11. (A)	25. (A)	39. (D)	53. (A)	67. (D)	81. (A)	95. (A)
12. (D)	26. (D)	40. (A)	54. (A)	68. (A)	82. (D)	
13. (D)	27. (A)	41. (D)	55. (D)	69. (D)	83. (D)	
14. (D)	28. (A)	42. (A)	56. (D)	70. (A)	84. (A)	

Memory for Addresses

1. (C)	14. (B)	27. (B)	40. (C)	53. (E)	66. (E)	79. (E)
2. (A)	15. (D)	28. (B)	41. (A)	54. (E)	67. (C)	80. (B)
3. (C)	16. (A)	29. (A)	42. (C)	55. (A)	68. (A)	81. (C)
4. (E)	17. (D)	30. (C)	43. (B)	56. (E)	69. (B)	82. (D)
5. (A)	18. (C)	31. (D)	44. (E)	57. (B)	70. (D)	83. (A)
6. (E)	19. (C)	32. (E)	45. (D)	58. (B)	71. (A)	84. (E)
7. (B)	20. (A)	33. (B)	46. (B)	59. (D)	72. (D)	85. (D)
8. (C)	21. (B)	34. (E)	47. (C)	60. (A)	73. (B)	86. (C)
9. (B)	22. (D)	35. (D)	48. (D)	61. (E)	74. (B)	87. (B)
10. (A)	23. (E)	36. (A)	49. (A)	62. (B)	75. (C)	88. (D)
11. (D)	24. (E)	37. (D)	50. (C)	63. (D)	76. (A)	
12. (D)	25. (E)	38. (C)	51. (D)	64. (C)	77. (E)	
13. (B)	26. (A)	39. (E)	52. (A)	65. (B)	78. (A)	

Note: There is only an answer key for the "Memory for Addresses" section.

Number Series

1.	(C)	13.	(A)
2.	(E)	14.	(B)
3.	(B)	15.	(A)
4.	(A)	16.	(D)
5.	(D)	17.	(B)
6.	(A)	18.	(C)
7.	(D)	19.	(D)
8.	(E)	20.	(E)
9.	(C)	21.	(E)
10.	(B)	22.	(A)
11.	(D)	23.	(D)
12.	(C)	24.	(A)

Following Oral Directions

(Please see "Detailed Explanations of Answers.")

DETAILED EXPLANATIONS
OF ANSWERS

Test 4

Address Checking

1. alike
2. alike
3. 44**01** Clinton Ave.   40**41** Clinton Ave.
4. 11 Progress **Court**   11 Progress **St.**
5. alike
6. 64 Plum St.   64 Plum**e** St.
7. alike
8. 30**J** Montgomery Ct.   30**5** Montgomery Ct.
9. alike
10. alike
11. alike
12. 66**L** Claridge Place   66**1** Claridge Place
13. 14 W**y**steria Dr.   14 Wisteria Dr.
14. **16** Dancaster Ct.   **6** Dancaster Ct.
15. alike
16. 21**B** Oliver Ave.   21**3** Oliver Ave.
17. alike
18. 294 Brom**l**ey Place   294 Brow**l**ey Place
19. alike
20. alike
21. 47 Providence **Blvd.**   47 Providence **Rd.**
22. 16**6** Stafford Rd.   16**B** Stafford Rd.
23. alike
24. 28 J**une** St.   28 J**uly** St.
25. alike
26. 46 Le**wis** Place   46 Lo**uis** Place
27. alike

28. alike
29. alike
30. **47** John F. Kennedy Dr.   **74** John F. Kennedy Dr.
31. 37 Susan **Lane**   37 Susan **Place**
32. 213 **S.** Fulton St.   213**B** Fulton St.
33. alike
34. 128 **Kane** Ave.   128 **Cane** Ave.
35. 24 **Ernston** Rd. Apt. 4   24 **Earnest** Rd. Apt. 4
36. alike
37. 16 Brown Ct.   161 Brown Ct.
38. alike
39. 6 Cornwall **Ct.**   6 Cornwall **St.**
40. alike
41. 22 County Hwy. N. **516**   22 County Hwy. N. **561**
42. alike
43. 20**A** Westminster Blvd.   20**4** Westminster Blvd.
44. alike
45. alike
46. 2 Angel**ika** **Ct.**   2 Angel**ica** **Rd.**
47. alike
48. alike
49. alike
50. 1463 **Paunee** Rd.   1463 **Pownee** Rd.
51. alike
52. 138**8** Hollywood Ave.   138**B** Hollywood Ave.
53. alike
54. alike
55. 990C Aur**or**a Rd.   990C Aur**en**a Rd.
56. 563 Park **Dr.**   563 Park **Place**
57. alike
58. alike
59. 10**E** (E) Garden Way   10**D** (E) Garden Way
60. 12 N. 5th Ave. Apt. 2**D**   12 N. 5th Ave. Apt. 2**G**
61. alike
62. alike
63. **675** US Hwy. No. 1   **756** US Hwy. No. 1
64. alike

65.	15 Railroad Ave.	15 Ralrod Ave.
66.	850 **Port** Reading Ave.	850 Reading Ave.
67.	10 Whitt**ier** Dr. Apt. 2C	10 Whitt**in** Dr. Apt. 2C
68.	alike	
69.	**21** Heritage Terrace	**12** Heritage Terrace
70.	alike	
71.	82 Creemer Ave.	82 Creamer Ave.
72.	alike	
73.	alike	
74.	10 Collasuido Ct.	10 Collasundo Ct.
75.	**220** Forsgate Dr.	**202** Forsgate Dr.
76.	alike	
77.	49 K Reading **Rd.**	49 K Reading **Blvd.**
78.	alike	
79.	alike	
80.	7 Kate Terrace	7 Katie Terrace
81.	alike	
82.	7 Long St.	7L Long St.
83.	26 Ja**ime** Ct.	26 Ja**mee** Ct.
84.	alike	
85.	alike	
86.	178 Chestnut Ave.	178**D** Chestnut Ave.
87.	511 **Newb**runswick Ave.	511 **Brunswick** Ave.
88.	alike	
89.	Wood Ave. & **Oak Tree** Rd.	Wood Ave. & **Old Oak** Rd.
90.	alike	
91.	15 Tamrac **Dr.**	15 Tamrac **Rd.**
92.	alike	
93.	7 Bond **Place**	7 Bond **Street**
94.	alike	
95.	alike	

Number Series

1. **(C)** This series is formed by adding 6 to the first number, then subtracting 2 from the sum of the number and 6, and then repeating the pattern. Therefore, the next numbers in the pattern are (C) 17, 23.

2. **(E)** The pattern in this problem is formed by adding 2 and then 1 and then 1, and then repeating this procedure. Therefore, the correct answer is (E) 13, 14.

3. **(B)** This series is made by adding alternately 2 or 1, and by separating these numbers each time with the number 2. Therefore, the next numbers in the series are (B) 7, 2.

4. **(A)** Beginning with 1, the pattern is formed by adding 14 to each previous number. Therefore, the correct answer is (A) 113, 127.

5. **(D)** Starting with 0, add 10 each time to form this pattern, but separate the numbers by repeating 0. The correct answer is (D) 40, 0.

6. **(A)** Beginning with 109, form this pattern by subtracting 11 each time. Therefore, the correct answer is (A) 21, 10.

7. **(D)** There are two alternating series here. The first begins with 200 and subtracts 4 each time, and the second begins with 2 and adds 4 each time. Therefore, the correct response is (D) 184, 18.

8. **(E)** Beginning with 2, form this pattern by adding 2, and then 2 again, and then 5, and then repeat this procedure. Therefore, the correct answer is (E) 22, 24.

9. **(C)** Beginning with 100, alternate subtracting 2 with subtracting 1, and then repeat. The correct answer is (C) 88, 86.

10. **(B)**   There are two alternating patterns here. The first begins with 100 and subtracts 5 each time, and the second begins with 1 and adds 2 each time. Therefore, the correct answer is (B) 80, 9.

11. **(D)**   In this alternating series, beginning with 1 and progressing upward by 1, each number is coupled with itself multiplied by 8. Therefore, the correct answer is (D) 5, 40.

12. **(C)**   There are two alternating series. The first begins with 1 and adds 4 each time, and the second begins with 2 and multiplies by 2 each time. Therefore, the correct answer is (C) 17, 32.

13. **(A)**   Beginning with 1 and increasing by 1, each number is coupled with the result of being multiplied alternately by 3 and then 4. The correct answer is (A) 5, 15.

14. **(B)**   Form this series by adding first 1, then 2, then 3, etc., increasing the number to be added by 1 each time. The correct answer is (B) 37, 46.

15. **(A)**   A series repeating the number 12 is separated by a series beginning with 5 and increasing by 5. The correct answer is (A) 12, 25.

16. **(D)**   Beginning with 200, form this series by subtracting 15 from each previous number. The correct answer is (D) 80, 65.

17. **(B)**   This is a series of three numbers starting with an integer followed by its next two multiples. The first integer of each set is the first integer of the previous set plus 1. The correct answer is (B) 9, 4.

18. **(C)**   Alternating a series beginning with 1, and increasing by 1 each time, is the sum of the previous number and 8. Therefore, the correct response is (C) 5, 12.

19. **(D)**   This is a series of numbers beginning with 1 and increasing by 1 interrupted after each set of three numbers with the sum of those numbers. Therefore, the correct answer is (D) 7, 8.

20. **(E)**   You are presented with a series of sets, each containing three numbers. In each set, the third number is the product of the first two. The first number of each set is the first integer of the previous set plus 2. The correct result is (E) 30, 7.

21. **(E)**   A series beginning with 1 and increasing by 1 is alternated with the product of each number and 100. The correct answer is (E) 5, 500.

22. **(A)**   Beginning with 6, each number is multiplied by 2, and then 5 is subtracted from the product of the previous two numbers; therefore, the correct answer is (A) 261, 517.

23. **(D)**   This shows two alternating series, each beginning with 1. The first is increased by adding 3 each time, and the second is increased by multiplying each number by 3. The correct answer is (D) 54, 13.

24. **(A)**   There are two alternating series, the first beginning with 2 and increasing by 2 each time, and the second, which appears two numbers at a time, beginning with 50 and increasing by 50 each time. Therefore, the correct answer is (A) 300, 8.

Following Oral Directions

This is how your worksheet should look:

1. 7:00 a.m.   10:30 a.m.   3:00 p.m.   5:00 p.m.

2.

3. Oregon   Kansas   Texas   Maine

4. 212   435   921   101   316
                                                   B   D

5. 12/230   2/100   26/316   5/404

6. C **52**   25 _____   D _____   52 _____

7.
First Ave	Third Ave	Fifth Ave
15 __ Routes	11 __ Routes	2 __ Routes

8. 243**5**679   243**21**21   244**5**658   243**21**59

9. Monday   Tuesday   Wednesday   Thursday   Friday
    12   21**E**   33   46   52

10. 2 _____   5 _____   16 _____   8 __**C**__   4 _____

In this section, please note that the solution to each problem is preceded by the actual instructions read by the examiner.

Examine sample one. (Pause 2-3 seconds) These numbers represent the times that mail is collected from a certain mailbox. If the earliest time is more than 12 hours earlier than the latest time, write the letter E as in "elephant" on the line below the earliest time. (Pause 5 seconds) If not, write the letter B as in "boy" under the latest time. (Pause 2 seconds) Using the first two digits of the time you have selected, go to that space on the answer sheet and darken the corresponding number/letter combination. (Pause 5 seconds)

ANSWER: The earliest time for mail collection, 7:00 a.m., is not 12 hours earlier than the latest time that mail is collected, 5:00 p.m. (it is only a 10 hour difference). Since 5:00 p.m. is the latest time and the first two digits of the time you selected is 50, go to that space on your answer sheet and darken the corresponding number/letter combination—50 B.

Examine sample one again. (Pause 2-3 seconds) If fewer of the collection times are in the morning, put the letter D as in "dog" under the third time and A as in "apple" under the second time. (Pause 2 seconds) If the number of collection times in the afternoon is greater or equal to the number in the morning, put the same letters in the same order beneath the middle two times. (Pause 2 seconds) Go to the spaces on the answer sheet equivalent to the first digits of the times you have chosen and darken the number/letter combination. (Pause 5 seconds)

ANSWER: The number of collection times in the afternoon is equal to the number of collection times in the morning. Put A under 10:30 a.m. and D under 3:00 p.m. on your worksheet. Go to the spaces on the answer sheet equivalent to the first digits of the times you have chosen (1 and 3) and darken the number/letter combinations—1 A and 3 D.

Examine sample two. (Pause 2-3 seconds) If the last three figures shown are the smallest, write the number 92 inside the first circle shown and darken the corresponding number/letter combination on your answer sheet. (Pause 5 seconds) If not, write the same number in the first box shown and darken that combination on the answer sheet. (Pause 5 seconds)

ANSWER: The last three figures shown are not the smallest. Write number 92 in the first box and darken the number/letter combination on your answer sheet—92 A.

Examine sample two again. (Pause 2-3 seconds) If the triangles are among the smallest shapes shown, put the number 51 in the first triangle and 75 in the second, and darken the corresponding number/letter combination on your answer sheet. (Pause 5 seconds) If not, add five to each of these numbers, write this in the triangles, and mark these combinations on your answer sheet. (Pause 7 seconds)

ANSWER: The triangles are among the smallest shapes shown. Put the number 51 in the first triangle and 75 in the second and darken the corresponding number/letter combinations on your answer sheet—51 B and 75 D.

Examine sample three. (Pause 2-3 seconds) If the third state is farther south than the first state and to the east of the last state, go to number 32 on your answer sheet and darken the letter D as in "dog." (Pause 5 seconds) If both of these things are not true, go to the number 23 on your answer sheet and darken the letter C as in "cat." (Pause 2 seconds) If only one of these things is not true, go to the number 13 and darken the letter B as in "boy." (Pause 5 seconds)

ANSWER: Texas is farther south than Oregon but is not east of Maine. Since one of these conditions is not true, go to the number 13 on your answer sheet and darken the oval for B.

Examine sample three again. (Pause 2-3 seconds) If all of these states have the same number of letters in their names, go to number 41 on your answer sheet and darken the letter B as in "boy." (Pause 5 seconds) If this is not true, go to number 14 and darken the same letter. (Pause 5 seconds)

ANSWER: All of the states do not have the same number of letters in their names- Texas and Maine have five; Oregon and Kansas have six. Therefore, go to number 14 on your answer sheet and darken the oval for B.

Examine sample four. (Pause 2-3 seconds) If the largest even number is placed in the sequence before the smallest odd number, write the letter C as in "cat" under the largest even number. (Pause 2 seconds) If not, write the letter B as in "boy" under the smallest odd number. (Pause 2 seconds) Taking the last two digits of the number you have marked, go to that space on your answer sheet and darken the corresponding number/letter combination. (Pause 5 seconds)

ANSWER: The largest even number, 316, is not placed in the sequence before the smallest odd number, 101. Write the letter B under 101 on your worksheet. Taking the last two digits you have marked (01), go to number 1 on your answer sheet and darken the oval for B. Note that the oval for A should already be darkened. You have two choices—erase answer A and darken the oval for B or do not erase answer A and do not darken the oval for B.

Examine sample five. (Pause 2-3 seconds) Each pair of numbers in the sample represents a route number and the number of houses on that route. Routes numbered 10 or below are on the north side of town; those numbered 11 or above are on the south side. If the route with the most stops is on the north side of town, go to the number on your answer sheet corresponding to that route number and darken the letter B as in "boy." (Pause 5 seconds) If the route with the most stops is on the south side, go to that number on your answer sheet and darken the letter D as in "dog." (Pause 5 seconds)

ANSWER: The route with the most stops (404) is on the north side of town. We know it is on the north side of town because it is numbered 5 and routes numbered 10 or below are on the north side of town. Go to the number on your answer sheet corresponding to that route number and darken the oval for B— 5B.

Examine sample five again. (Pause 2-3 seconds) If more of the routes shown are on the south side of town, go to the number 57 on your answer sheet and darken the letter A as in "apple" (Pause 2 seconds) If more are on the north side of town, go to the same number and darken the letter B as in "boy." (Pause 2 seconds) If neither of these statements is true, darken the letter C as in "cat" at both number 21 and number 42 on your answer sheet. (Pause 5 seconds)

ANSWER: Since two of the routes are on the north side of town and two are on the south side of town, darken the letter C for numbers 21 and 42 on your answer sheet—21 C & 42C.

Examine sample four again. (Pause 2-3 seconds) If the third number in the series is greater than the sum of the first and the fourth numbers, write the letter D as in "dog" under the last number. (Pause 2 seconds) If not, write the same letter under the second number. (Pause 2 seconds) Taking the first two digits of the number you have marked, go to that space on the answer sheet and darken the corresponding number/letter combination. (Pause 5 seconds)

ANSWER: Since the third number in the series (921) is greater than the sum of the first and fourth numbers (212 + 101 = 313), write the letter D on your worksheet under the last number (316). Taking the first two digits (31) of the number you marked (316), go to that space on your answer sheet and darken the corresponding number/letter combination—31 D.

Examine sample four again. (Pause 2-3 seconds) If there are more even numbers in the sequence, go to the last odd number on your answer sheet and darken the circle A as in "apple." (Pause 2 seconds) If there are more odd numbers in the sequence, go to the second even number on your answer sheet and darken the oval for E as in "elephant." (Pause 5 seconds)

ANSWER: Since there are more odd numbers than even numbers in the sequence, go to the second even number on your answer sheet (4) and darken the oval for E.

Examine sample six. (Pause 2-3 seconds) If the second number shown is more than twice but less than three times greater than the first number shown, write the last number next to the letter C as in "cat." (Pause 2 seconds) Darken the corresponding number/letter combination on your answer sheet. (Pause 2 seconds) If this is not true, write the first number shown next to the letter D as in "dog" and darken the corresponding number/letter combination on your answer sheet. (Pause 5 seconds)

ANSWER: Since the second number shown (52) is more than twice (25 x 2 = 50) but less than three times (25 x 3= 75) the first number shown, write the last number (52) next to the first letter (C) on your worksheet. Darken the corresponding number letter combination on your answer sheet—52 C.

Examine sample seven. (Pause 2-3 seconds) These boxes represent the number of routes originating from postal substations in a particular city. If Third Avenue has less than twice as many routes as Fifth Avenue, write the letter E as in "elephant" in the First Avenue box. (Pause 5 seconds) Go to the number on your answer sheet corresponding to the number of routes in this box and darken the number/letter combination. (Pause 2 seconds) If this is not true, go to number 22 on your answer sheet and darken the letter C as in "cat." (Pause 5 seconds)

ANSWER: Third Avenue does not have less than twice as many routes as Fifth Avenue. Third Avenue has 11 routes. Fifth Avenue has two routes, (twice as many would be four). Go to number 22 on your answer sheet and darken the oval for C.

Examine sample seven again. (Pause 2-3 seconds) If the sequence is organized from smallest number of routes to largest number of routes, go to the second box and write the letter D as in "dog." (Pause 2 seconds) Find the number on your answer sheet equal to the number of routes in this box and darken the correct number/letter combination. (Pause 2 seconds) If this statement is not true, darken the same combination anyway. (Pause 5 seconds)

ANSWER: Since the sequence is not organized in from smallest number of routes to largest number of routes, find the number on your answer sheet equal to the number of routes in the second box (11) and darken the oval for D—11 D.

Examine sample eight. (Pause 2-3 seconds) If each of these numbers has the same first three digits, go to number 59 on your answer sheet and darken the letter B as in "boy." (Pause 2 seconds) If not, go to the number corresponding to the last two digits of the fourth number and darken the letter C as in "cat." (Pause 5 seconds)

ANSWER: Since the first three digits of the numbers listed are different, go to the number corresponding to the last two digits (59) of the fourth number (2432159) and darken the oval for C—59 C.

Examine sample eight again. (Pause 2-3 seconds) Underline the fourth and fifth digits of each number. (Pause 2 seconds) Consider the two-digit numbers you have underlined. If the sum of the second and fourth is greater than the first, go to the number of the first on your answer sheet and darken the letter D as in "dog." (Pause 5 seconds) If not, go to the number of the third and darken the same letter. (Pause 5 seconds)

ANSWER: Remember that you are considering the two-digit numbers you have underlined. Since the sum of the second and fourth (21 + 21 = 42) is not greater than the first (56), go to the number of the third (56) on your answer sheet and darken the oval for D—56 D.

Examine sample two again. (Pause 2-3 seconds) If there are more circles than any other shape, put the number 24 in the largest circle and darken the corresponding number/letter combination. (Pause 5 seconds) If not, put the same number in the smallest circle and mark your answer sheet accordingly. (Pause 5 seconds)

ANSWER: There are an equal amount of circles and triangles. Therefore, put 24 in the smallest circle and mark your answer sheet accordingly—24 E.

Examine sample nine. (Pause 2-3 seconds) If Monday comes before Tuesday but after Thursday, write the letter B as in "boy" next to the number 33. (Pause 5 seconds) If not, write the letter E as in "elephant" next to the number 21. (Pause 5 seconds)

ANSWER: Since Monday comes before Tuesday but after Thursday, write the letter E next to number 21 on your worksheet. You are not to mark any combination on your answer sheet.

Examine sample nine again. (Pause 2-3 seconds) If the fourth day listed in the sample has the same number of letters as the third day or the fifth day, go to number 17 on your answer sheet and darken the oval for B as in "boy." (Pause 5 seconds) If not, darken the oval for B as in "boy" in number 20. (Pause 5 seconds)

ANSWER: Since the fourth day (Thursday, 8 letters) listed does not have the same number of letters as the third day (Wednesday, 9 letters) or the fifth day (Friday, 6 letters), go to number 20 on your answer sheet and darken the oval for B.

Examine sample nine again. (Pause 2-3 seconds) If the first letter of the first day precedes alphabetically the first letter of the last day, go to number 76 on your answer sheet and darken the oval for D as in "dog." (Pause 5 seconds) If not, go to number 67 and darken the oval for A as in "apple." (Pause 5 seconds)

ANSWER: Since the first letter (M) of the first day (Monday) does not precede alphabetically the first letter (F) of the last day (Friday) go to number 67 on your answer sheet and darken the oval for A.

Examine sample ten. (Pause 2-3 seconds) If the sum of the first and the last numbers shown is an even number, write the letter C as in "cat" next to the fourth number in the sample. (Pause 5 seconds) Darken that number/letter combination on your answer sheet. (Pause 2 seconds) If it is an odd number, write the letter A as in "apple" next to the first number and darken the corresponding number/letter combination on your answer sheet. (Pause 5 seconds)

ANSWER: Since the sum of the first and last numbers shown (2 + 4 = 6) is an even number, write the letter C next to the fourth number on your worksheet (8). Darken that number/letter combination on your answer sheet—8 C.

Examine sample ten again. (Pause 2-3 seconds) If the fourth number is exactly twice the first number and half the third, write the letter E as in "elephant" beside the last number. (Pause 7 seconds) Add 3 to this number, go to the sum on your answer sheet, and darken the corresponding number/letter combination on your answer sheet. (Pause 5 seconds) If this is not true, go to the number that is half the fourth number plus 2, and darken the oval for C as in "cat." (Pause 7 seconds)

ANSWER: The fourth number (8) is not exactly twice the first number (2) and not half the third number (16), go to the number on your answer sheet that is half the fourth number plus 2 (8/2 + 2 = 6) and darken the oval for C—6 C.

Examine sample six again. (Pause 2-3 seconds) If the first letter shown is the fourth letter of the alphabet, write this letter next to the second number shown. (Pause 2 seconds) Add three to the number. Darken the corresponding number/letter combination on your answer sheet. (Pause 5 seconds) If not, go to number 53 on your answer sheet and darken the letter E as in "elephant." (Pause 5 seconds)

ANSWER: Since the first letter shown (C) is not the fourth letter of the alphabet, go to number 53 on your answer sheet and darken the oval for E.

POSTAL EXAM
Test 4 - Following Oral Directions
ANSWER KEY

1. ● ● Ⓒ Ⓓ Ⓔ	34. Ⓐ Ⓑ Ⓒ Ⓓ Ⓔ	67. ● Ⓑ Ⓒ Ⓓ Ⓔ
2. Ⓐ Ⓑ Ⓒ Ⓓ Ⓔ	35. Ⓐ Ⓑ Ⓒ Ⓓ Ⓔ	68. Ⓐ Ⓑ Ⓒ Ⓓ Ⓔ
3. Ⓐ Ⓑ Ⓒ Ⓓ Ⓔ	36. Ⓐ Ⓑ Ⓒ Ⓓ Ⓔ	69. Ⓐ Ⓑ Ⓒ Ⓓ Ⓔ
4. Ⓐ Ⓑ Ⓒ Ⓓ ●	37. Ⓐ Ⓑ Ⓒ Ⓓ Ⓔ	70. Ⓐ Ⓑ Ⓒ Ⓓ Ⓔ
5. Ⓐ ● Ⓒ Ⓓ Ⓔ	38. Ⓐ Ⓑ Ⓒ Ⓓ Ⓔ	71. Ⓐ Ⓑ Ⓒ Ⓓ Ⓔ
6. Ⓐ Ⓑ ● Ⓓ Ⓔ	39. Ⓐ Ⓑ Ⓒ Ⓓ Ⓔ	72. Ⓐ Ⓑ Ⓒ Ⓓ Ⓔ
7. Ⓐ Ⓑ Ⓒ Ⓓ Ⓔ	40. Ⓐ Ⓑ Ⓒ Ⓓ Ⓔ	73. Ⓐ Ⓑ Ⓒ Ⓓ Ⓔ
8. Ⓐ Ⓑ ● Ⓓ Ⓔ	41. Ⓐ Ⓑ Ⓒ Ⓓ Ⓔ	74. Ⓐ Ⓑ Ⓒ Ⓓ Ⓔ
9. Ⓐ Ⓑ Ⓒ Ⓓ Ⓔ	42. Ⓐ Ⓑ ● Ⓓ Ⓔ	75. Ⓐ Ⓑ Ⓒ ● Ⓔ
10. ● Ⓑ Ⓒ Ⓓ Ⓔ	43. Ⓐ Ⓑ Ⓒ Ⓓ Ⓔ	76. Ⓐ Ⓑ Ⓒ Ⓓ Ⓔ
11. Ⓐ Ⓑ Ⓒ ● Ⓔ	44. Ⓐ Ⓑ Ⓒ Ⓓ Ⓔ	77. Ⓐ Ⓑ Ⓒ Ⓓ Ⓔ
12. Ⓐ Ⓑ Ⓒ Ⓓ Ⓔ	45. Ⓐ Ⓑ Ⓒ Ⓓ Ⓔ	78. Ⓐ Ⓑ Ⓒ Ⓓ Ⓔ
13. Ⓐ ● Ⓒ Ⓓ Ⓔ	46. Ⓐ Ⓑ Ⓒ Ⓓ Ⓔ	79. Ⓐ Ⓑ Ⓒ Ⓓ Ⓔ
14. Ⓐ ● Ⓒ Ⓓ Ⓔ	47. Ⓐ Ⓑ Ⓒ Ⓓ Ⓔ	80. Ⓐ Ⓑ Ⓒ Ⓓ Ⓔ
15. Ⓐ Ⓑ Ⓒ Ⓓ Ⓔ	48. Ⓐ Ⓑ Ⓒ Ⓓ Ⓔ	81. Ⓐ Ⓑ Ⓒ Ⓓ Ⓔ
16. Ⓐ Ⓑ Ⓒ Ⓓ Ⓔ	49. Ⓐ Ⓑ Ⓒ Ⓓ Ⓔ	82. Ⓐ Ⓑ Ⓒ Ⓓ Ⓔ
17. Ⓐ Ⓑ Ⓒ Ⓓ Ⓔ	50. Ⓐ ● Ⓒ ● Ⓔ	83. Ⓐ Ⓑ Ⓒ Ⓓ Ⓔ
18. Ⓐ Ⓑ Ⓒ Ⓓ Ⓔ	51. Ⓐ ● Ⓒ Ⓓ Ⓔ	84. Ⓐ Ⓑ Ⓒ Ⓓ Ⓔ
19. Ⓐ Ⓑ Ⓒ Ⓓ Ⓔ	52. Ⓐ Ⓑ ● Ⓓ Ⓔ	85. Ⓐ Ⓑ Ⓒ Ⓓ Ⓔ
20. Ⓐ ● Ⓒ Ⓓ Ⓔ	53. Ⓐ Ⓑ Ⓒ Ⓓ ●	86. Ⓐ Ⓑ Ⓒ Ⓓ Ⓔ
21. Ⓐ Ⓑ ● Ⓓ Ⓔ	54. Ⓐ Ⓑ Ⓒ Ⓓ Ⓔ	87. Ⓐ Ⓑ Ⓒ Ⓓ Ⓔ
22. Ⓐ Ⓑ ● Ⓓ Ⓔ	55. Ⓐ Ⓑ Ⓒ Ⓓ Ⓔ	88. Ⓐ Ⓑ Ⓒ Ⓓ Ⓔ
23. Ⓐ Ⓑ Ⓒ Ⓓ Ⓔ	56. Ⓐ Ⓑ Ⓒ ● Ⓔ	89. Ⓐ Ⓑ Ⓒ Ⓓ Ⓔ
24. Ⓐ Ⓑ Ⓒ Ⓓ ●	57. Ⓐ Ⓑ Ⓒ Ⓓ Ⓔ	90. Ⓐ Ⓑ Ⓒ Ⓓ Ⓔ
25. Ⓐ Ⓑ Ⓒ Ⓓ Ⓔ	58. Ⓐ Ⓑ Ⓒ Ⓓ Ⓔ	91. Ⓐ Ⓑ Ⓒ Ⓓ Ⓔ
26. Ⓐ Ⓑ Ⓒ Ⓓ Ⓔ	59. Ⓐ Ⓑ ● Ⓓ Ⓔ	92. ● Ⓑ Ⓒ Ⓓ Ⓔ
27. Ⓐ Ⓑ Ⓒ Ⓓ Ⓔ	60. Ⓐ Ⓑ Ⓒ Ⓓ Ⓔ	93. Ⓐ Ⓑ Ⓒ Ⓓ Ⓔ
28. Ⓐ Ⓑ Ⓒ Ⓓ Ⓔ	61. Ⓐ Ⓑ Ⓒ Ⓓ Ⓔ	94. Ⓐ Ⓑ Ⓒ Ⓓ Ⓔ
29. Ⓐ Ⓑ Ⓒ Ⓓ Ⓔ	62. Ⓐ Ⓑ Ⓒ Ⓓ Ⓔ	95. Ⓐ Ⓑ Ⓒ Ⓓ Ⓔ
30. Ⓐ Ⓑ Ⓒ Ⓓ Ⓔ	63. Ⓐ Ⓑ Ⓒ Ⓓ Ⓔ	96. Ⓐ Ⓑ Ⓒ Ⓓ Ⓔ
31. Ⓐ Ⓑ Ⓒ ● Ⓔ	64. Ⓐ Ⓑ Ⓒ Ⓓ Ⓔ	97. Ⓐ Ⓑ Ⓒ Ⓓ Ⓔ
32. Ⓐ Ⓑ Ⓒ Ⓓ Ⓔ	65. Ⓐ Ⓑ Ⓒ Ⓓ Ⓔ	98. Ⓐ Ⓑ Ⓒ Ⓓ Ⓔ
33. Ⓐ Ⓑ Ⓒ Ⓓ Ⓔ	66. Ⓐ Ⓑ Ⓒ Ⓓ Ⓔ	

Postal Examination

Test 5

TEST 5

Address Checking

(Answer sheets appear in the back of this book.)

TIME: 6 Minutes
95 Questions

DIRECTIONS: In this section you will be asked to compare two lists of addresses, deciding if they are alike or different. If the addresses are alike, you will mark oval "A" on your answer sheet; if they are different, you will mark oval "D" on your answer sheet.

---

1. 750 State Hwy. No. 34   750 State Hwy. No. 34
2. 2902 Stonehedge Rd.   2902 Stonehenge Rd.
3. 8 Falmouth Rd. Apt. 23C   8 Falmouth Rd. Apt. 23C
4. 15 Jupiter Court   15 Jupiter Court
5. 37 Water St.   37 Walter St.
6. 4B Thrush Dr.   43 Thrush Dr.
7. 7 Wirt St.   7 Wirt St.
8. 410 Spotswood-Matawan Rd.   4210 Spotswood-Matawan Rd.
9. 6 Yorketowne Dr.   6 Yorketowne Dr.
10. Dover Rd. & Fairview Ave.   Dover Rd. & Fairview Ave.
11. 497 St Hwy. No. 27   497 St Hwy. No. 7
12. 2003 US Hwy. 130   203 US Hwy. 130
13. 1107 Connery Blvd.   1107 Connery Blvd.
14. 23 W. Prospect St.   23 (E) Prospect St.
15. 100 Belchase Dr.   100 Belchase Dr.
16. 3391 Route 516   3391 Route 561

17.	2001-A N. Wood Lane	2001-A N. Wood Lane
18.	1 Brunswick Woods Dr.	1 Brunswick Woods Dr.
19.	A-2 Cornwall Rd.	A-2 Cornwall Dr.
20.	Grove & Livingston Ave.	Groven & Livingston Ave.
21.	186-A Smith St.	186-A Smith St.
22.	Vail St & Union Ave	Vail St & Union Ave
23.	1 Stockton Ave.	1 Stockton Ave.
24.	3 Progress Cir.	3 Progress Ct.
25.	1 Haussling Pl.	1 Housling Pl.
26.	415 Gonzalez Lane	415 Gonzalez Lane
27.	48B Mimi Rd.	48B Mimi Rd.
28.	55D Avenue C	55C Avenue D
29.	503 Chester Ct.	503 Chestnut Ct.
30.	109B Diamond Lane	1093 Diamond Lane
31.	380 West Halsey Rd.	380 West Halsey Rd.
32.	170 Garretson Cir.	170 Garnetson Cir.
33.	5 Barkley Ct.	5 Berkley Ct.
34.	7-0 (E) Garden Way	7-0 (E) Garden Way
35.	34 Reservoir Ave.	34 Reservoir Ave.
36.	32 Kingsbridge Ave.	32 Kingsbridge Ave.
37.	31 E. 233rd St. Apt. 5D	30 E. 233rd St. Apt. 5D
38.	58 Wilk Rd.	58 Wilk Rd.
39.	807 Old Raritan Rd	807 Raritan Rd
40.	55 Smullen St.	5S Smullen St.
41.	21 Quick Way	21 Quink Way
42.	5 Biernacki Ct.	5 Biernacki Ct.
43.	1710 Sunnyview Oval	1710 Sunnyview Oval

44.	15B Red Oak Lane	15B Oak Lane
45.	64 S. Cliff Rd.	64 S. Cliff Rd.
46.	83K Loretta St.	835 Loretta St.
47.	2640 Rellin Dr.	2640 Rellin Dr.
48.	15 W. 65th St.	151 W. 65th St.
49.	39 St. Paul Lane	39 St. Paul Lane
50.	14 Jacobson Rd.	14 Jacobson Rd.
51.	39 Gilford Rd.	39 Gilford Rd.
52.	4603 N. Wells Drive	4603-N Wells Drive
53.	4 Bethany Ct.	4 Bethany Ct.
54.	58 Tanbark Dr.	58 Tarbark Dr.
55.	251-C Alpine Way	251-C Alpine Way
56.	960 US Hwy. No. 9	960 US Hwy. No. 9
57.	135D Selwaren Ave.	135D Selvaren Ave.
58.	10 New Jersey Tpke.	110 New Jersey Tpke.
59.	7 Honeysuckle Ct.	7 Honeysuckle St.
60.	38 Exeter Ave.	38B Exeter Ave.
61.	32 Goodridge Terrace	32 Goodridge Terrace
62.	1014 Lakewood Ave.	1014 Lakewood Ave.
63.	232 S. First Ave.	2332 S. First Ave.
64.	12 Frandson Ave.	12 Frankson Ave.
65.	32B Amberly Ct.	32D Amberly Ct.
66.	155 Chippenham Ct. Apt. 2	155 Chippenham Ct. Apt. 2
67.	3664 St Hwy. No. 18	364 St Hwy. No. 18
68.	10 Peter Dr.	10 Peter Ct.
69.	961-B (E) Disbrow Dr.	961-B (E) Disbrow Dr.
70.	37 Outcalt Rd.	37 Outcalf Rd.

71. 5 Woodbridge Commons Rd.   5 Woodbridge Commons Rd.

72. 157 Luke St. Apt. 1A   157 Luke St. Apt. 1D

73. 286 Hana Rd   286 Hana Rd

74. 9 Clembri Ct.   9 Olembri Ct.

75. 264 So. John St.   264 So. John St.

76. 13 Albert Ave.   133 Albert Ave.

77. 35 Nebel Way   35 Nebel Way

78. 4525 Peru Lane   4525 Pearl Lane

79. 35 Maple Ct.   35 Maple St.

80. 21D Durst Dr.   21D Durst Dr.

81. 51 Dane Rd.   51 Dane Rd.

82. 265 Old Bridge Tpke.   265 Old Bridge Tpke.

83. 2131 Cross Bronx Expwy.   231 Cross Bronx Expwy.

84. 42 Quaid Ave.   42 Quaid Ave.

85. 158 Norris Ave.   158 North Ave.

86. 35-J Sturbridge Rd.   35-J Sturbridge Rd.

87. 2 Mount Ct.   2 Mountain Ct.

88. 1955 US Hwy. No. 1   1955 US Hwy. No. 1

89. 32 W. 10th Ave.   32 W. 10th Ave.

90. 653-A Cranbury Cross Rd.   6537 Cranbury Cross Rd.

91. 4526 Curtis St.   4526 Curtis St.

92. 46 Apple Place   461 Apple Place

93. 1 Gourmet Lane   1 Courvet Lane

94. 37 Seymour Ave.   37 Seymour Ave.

95. 12 Deans Rhode Hall Rd.   12 Deans Rhode Hall Rd.

TEST 5

Memory for Addresses

(Answer sheets appear in the back of this book.)

TIME: Study 5 Minutes, Work 5 Minutes
88 Questions

DIRECTIONS: Below are five boxes labeled A,B,C,D, and E. Each box contains five addresses. You will be given five minutes to memorize the addresses in the boxes and their locations. After five minutes are up, you will have an additional five minutes to answer the following 88 questions and mark on the answer sheet the letter of the box in which the address belongs. You will not be able to refer back to the boxes once you begin answering the questions.

A	B	C	D	E
2200-3599 Rossmoor	7700-8599 Rossmoor	1700-2199 Rossmoor	4300-5199 Rossmoor	3200-4299 Rossmoor
Cleremont	O'Rourke	Tiffany	VanDelft	Judd
4300-5199 Anastasia	3200-4299 Anastasia	7700-8599 Anastasia	1700-2199 Anastasia	2200-3599 Anastasia
Candlelight	Ascot	Palomino	Gardenia	Shepard
7700-8599 Ortley	1700-2199 Ortley	3200-4299 Ortley	2200-3599 Ortley	4300-5199 Ortley

1. Gardenia

2. 7700-8599 Anastasia

3. 1700-2199 Anastasia

4. 2200-3599 Ortley

5. Cleremont

6. 3200-4299 Ortley

7. Judd

8. 1700-2199 Ortley

9. 4300-5199 Rossmoor

10. Candlelight

11. 2200-3599 Anastasia

12. Shepard

13. 4300-5199 Ortley

14. 7700-8599 Rossmoor

15. Ascot

16. 2200-3599 Rossmoor

17. 4300-5199 Anastasia

18. Palomino

19. 3200-4299 Rossmoor

20. 3200-4299 Anastasia

21. O'Rourke

22. 7700-8599 Ortley

23. VanDelft

24. Tiffany

25. 1700-2199 Rossmoor

26. 7700-8599 Anastasia

27. 1700-2199 Anastasia

28. Judd

29. Cleremont

30. Candlelight

31. Gardenia

32. 3200-4299 Ortley

33. 1700-2199 Ortley

34. Shepard

35. 2200-3599 Rossmoor

36. Ascot

37. Palomino

38. 4300-5199 Rossmoor

39. 2200-3599 Anastasia

40. 4300-5199 Ortley

41. 1700-2199 Rossmoor

42. 4300-5199 Anastasia

43. O'Rourke

44. 3200-4299 Rossmoor

45. 3200-4299 Anastasia

46. 7700-8599 Rossmoor

47. 7700-8599 Ortley

48. Judd

49. VanDelft

50. Cleremont

51. 1700-2199 Ortley

52. Candlelight

53. Tiffany

54. 7700-8599 Anastasia

55. 2200-3599 Rossmoor

56. Gardenia

57. Shepard

58. 4300-5199 Anastasia

59. Ascot

60. 3200-4299 Anastasia

61. 2200-3599 Ortley

62. 7700-8599 Ortley

63. Cleremont

64. 2200-3599 Anastasia

65. 3200-4299 Ortley

66. 1700-2199 Anastasia

67. O'Rourke

68. 7700-8599 Rossmoor

69. 4300-5199 Rossmoor

70. Palomino

71. 4300-5199 Ortley

72. 3200-4299 Rossmoor

73. Candlelight

74. 2200-3599 Rossmoor

75. 1700-2199 Ortley

76. 1700-2199 Rossmoor

77. VanDelft

78. Judd

79. Shepard

80. 4300-5199 Anastasia

81. 3200-4299 Anastasia

82. Gardenia

83. Tiffany

84. 2200-3599 Anastasia

85. 7700-8599 Ortley

86. Ascot

87. 1700-2199 Anastasia

88. 2200-3599 Ortley

TEST 5

Number Series

(Answer sheets appear in the back of this book.)

TIME: 20 Minutes
24 Questions

DIRECTIONS: For each question, there is a series of numbers that follow some definite order. Look at the series of numbers and decide which two numbers will come next in the series. You will be given five answers to choose from.

1. 1   64   4   64   7   64   10   64   _____   _____
    (A) 12, 64
    (B) 12, 24
    (C) 64, 13
    (D) 13, 64
    (E) 11, 66

2. 1   3   2   6   3   11   4   18   _____   _____
    (A) 5, 27
    (B) 5, 25
    (C) 5, 26
    (D) 25, 5
    (E) 6, 37

3. 1   5   9   13   17   21   25   29   _____   _____

    (A) 31, 33

    (B) 30, 32

    (C) 33, 37

    (D) 60, 120

    (E) 33, 35

4. 1   5   5   10   9   15   13   20   _____   _____

    (A) 17, 21

    (B) 25, 30

    (C) 25, 27

    (D) 17, 25

    (E) 20, 30

5. 2   4   6   12   14   28   30   60   _____   _____

    (A) 62, 64

    (B) 120, 124

    (C) 135, 70

    (D) 90, 120

    (E) 62, 124

6. 1   50   2   49   3   48   4   47   _____   _____

    (A) 6, 48

    (B) 5, 46

    (C) 85, 170

    (D) 49, 5

    (E) 6, 46

7. 100   4   95   4   90   4   85   4   _____   _____
    (A) 4, 80
    (B) 75, 5
    (C) 75, 4
    (D) 4, 4
    (E) 80, 4

8. 1   1   100   3   3   100   5   5   _____   _____
    (A) 100, 7
    (B) 5, 100
    (C) 7, 9
    (D) 100, 6
    (E) 4, 100

9. 10   6   20   11   30   16   40   21   _____   _____
    (A) 60, 32
    (B) 80, 41
    (C) 42, 80
    (D) 50, 26
    (E) 50, 25

10. 1   7   2   12   3   9   4   24   _____   _____
    (A) 5, 25
    (B) 5, 11
    (C) 6, 48
    (D) 8, 48
    (E) 9, 100

11. 25   5   50   10   75   15   100   20   _____   _____
    (A) 25, 30
    (B) 25, 50
    (C) 125, 25
    (D) 125, 150
    (E) 30, 40

12. 1.1   12.1   23.1   34.1   45.1   56.1   67.1   78.1

    _____   _____
    (A) 77.1, 88.1
    (B) 89.9, 111.1
    (C) 89.1, 100.1
    (D) 87.1, 100.1
    (E) 88.1, 101.1

13. 1   21   2   28   3   35   4   42   _____   _____
    (A) 5, 49
    (B) 5, 25
    (C) 5, 50
    (D) 6, 56
    (E) 8, 64

14. 1   4   3   16   5   36   7   64   _____   _____
    (A) 8, 64
    (B) 9, 100
    (C) 9, 81
    (D) 10, 100
    (E) 11, 144

15. 99   11   88   11   77   11   66   11   _____   _____

    (A) 77, 66

    (B) 55, 44

    (C) 11, 55

    (D) 55, 11

    (E) 22, 110

16. 30   13   60   23   90   33   120   43   _____   _____

    (A) 45, 47

    (B) 240, 86

    (C) 53, 63

    (D) 240, 480

    (E) 150, 53

17. 1   2   2   5   3   8   4   11   _____   _____

    (A) 5, 12

    (B) 5, 15

    (C) 5, 14

    (D) 12, 13

    (E) 12, 24

18. 1   5   4   5   9   5   16   5   _____   _____

    (A) 25, 5

    (B) 5, 25

    (C) 4, 20

    (D) 32, 64

    (E) 32, 5

19. 1   6   16   31   51   76   106   141   _____   _____

    (A) 121, 131

    (B) 181, 226

    (C) 131, 142

    (D) 222, 333

    (E) 141, 151

20. 1   3   7   13   21   31   43   57   _____   _____

    (A) 67, 76

    (B) 124, 248

    (C) 75, 100

    (D) 73, 91

    (E) 61, 75

21. 100   99   97   94   90   85   79   72   _____   _____

    (A) 61, 59

    (B) 62, 52

    (C) 64, 49

    (D) 65, 60

    (E) 64, 55

22. 1   100   5   95   9   90   13   85   _____   _____

    (A) 17, 80

    (B) 15, 90

    (C) 26, 80

    (D) 18, 40

    (E) 80, 17

23. 1   21   22   3   21   22   5   21   _____   _____

    (A) 23, 7

    (B) 7, 22

    (C) 22, 7

    (D) 10, 42

    (E) 6, 22

24. 200   199   195   186   170   145   _____   _____

    (A) 121, 100

    (B) 149, 135

    (C) 90, 45

    (D) 109, 60

    (E) 80, 41

TEST 5

Following Oral Directions - Worksheet

(Answer sheets appear in the back of this book.)

TIME: Instructions will be read at approximately 80 words per minute.

DIRECTIONS: Follow the instructions that are read to you. They will not be repeated during the examination. You are to mark your worksheets according to the instructions that are read to you. After each set of instructions, you will be given time to record your answer on your answer sheet. You should have only one space darkened for each number. If you go to darken a space for a number and you have already darkened another space, either erase the first mark and darken the space for your new choice **or** let the original mark remain.

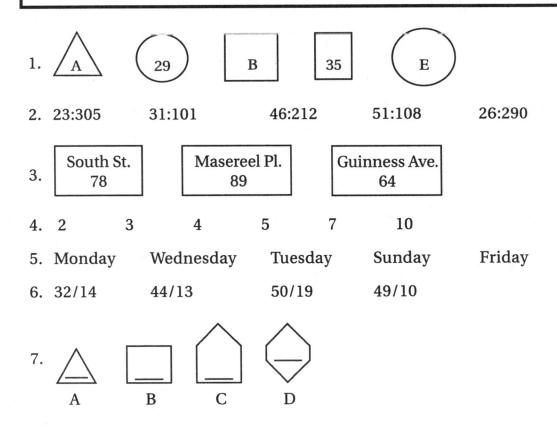

1.

2.   23:305   31:101   46:212   51:108   26:290

3.

4.   2   3   4   5   7   10

5.   Monday   Wednesday   Tuesday   Sunday   Friday

6.   32/14   44/13   50/19   49/10

7.

8. A _____   C _____   15 _____   16 _____

9. Derkins   Duncan   Dandamyr   Dwight

10. 2415   6812   3542   4880

11. 30   40   50   70   80

TEST 5

ANSWER KEY

Address Checking

1. (A)	15. (A)	29. (D)	43. (A)	57. (D)	71. (A)	85. (D)
2. (D)	16. (D)	30. (D)	44. (D)	58. (D)	72. (D)	86. (A)
3. (A)	17. (A)	31. (A)	45. (A)	59. (D)	73. (A)	87. (D)
4. (A)	18. (A)	32. (D)	46. (D)	60. (D)	74. (D)	88. (A)
5. (D)	19. (D)	33. (D)	47. (A)	61. (A)	75. (A)	89. (A)
6. (D)	20. (D)	34. (A)	48. (D)	62. (A)	76. (D)	90. (D)
7. (A)	21. (A)	35. (A)	49. (A)	63. (D)	77. (A)	91. (A)
8. (D)	22. (A)	36. (A)	50. (A)	64. (D)	78. (D)	92. (D)
9. (A)	23. (A)	37. (D)	51. (A)	65. (D)	79. (D)	93. (D)
10. (A)	24. (D)	38. (A)	52. (D)	66. (A)	80. (A)	94. (A)
11. (D)	25. (D)	39. (D)	53. (A)	67. (D)	81. (A)	95. (A)
12. (D)	26. (A)	40. (D)	54. (D)	68. (D)	82. (A)	
13. (A)	27. (A)	41. (D)	55. (A)	69. (A)	83. (D)	
14. (D)	28. (D)	42. (A)	56. (A)	70. (D)	84. (A)	

Memory for Addresses

1. (D)	14. (B)	27. (D)	40. (E)	53. (C)	66. (D)	79. (E)
2. (C)	15. (B)	28. (E)	41. (C)	54. (C)	67. (B)	80. (A)
3. (D)	16. (A)	29. (A)	42. (A)	55. (A)	68. (B)	81. (B)
4. (D)	17. (A)	30. (A)	43. (B)	56. (D)	69. (D)	82. (D)
5. (A)	18. (C)	31. (D)	44. (E)	57. (E)	70. (C)	83. (C)
6. (C)	19. (E)	32. (C)	45. (B)	58. (A)	71. (E)	84. (E)
7. (E)	20. (B)	33. (B)	46. (B)	59. (B)	72. (E)	85. (A)
8. (B)	21. (B)	34. (E)	47. (A)	60. (B)	73. (A)	86. (B)
9. (D)	22. (A)	35. (A)	48. (E)	61. (D)	74. (A)	87. (D)
10. (A)	23. (D)	36. (B)	49. (D)	62. (A)	75. (B)	88. (D)
11. (E)	24. (C)	37. (C)	50. (A)	63. (A)	76. (C)	
12. (E)	25. (C)	38. (D)	51. (B)	64. (E)	77. (D)	
13. (E)	26. (C)	39. (E)	52. (A)	65. (C)	78. (E)	

Note: There is only an answer key for the "Memory for Addresses" section.

Number Series

1.	(D)	13.	(A)
2.	(A)	14.	(B)
3.	(C)	15.	(D)
4.	(D)	16.	(E)
5.	(E)	17.	(C)
6.	(B)	18.	(A)
7.	(E)	19.	(B)
8.	(A)	20.	(D)
9.	(D)	21.	(E)
10.	(B)	22.	(A)
11.	(C)	23.	(C)
12.	(C)	24.	(D)

Following Oral Directions
(Please see "Detailed Explanations of Answers.")

DETAILED EXPLANATIONS
OF ANSWERS

Test 5

Address Checking

1. alike
2. 2902 Stone**he**dge Rd.   2902 Stone**he**nge Rd.
3. alike
4. alike
5. 37 Water St.   37 Wa**l**ter St.
6. **4B** Thrush Dr.   **43** Thrush Dr.
7. alike
8. 410 Spotswood-Matawan Rd.   4**2**10 Spotswood-Matawan Rd.
9. alike
10. alike
11. 497 St Hwy. No. **27**   497 St Hwy. No. **7**
12. **2**003 US Hwy. 130   **2**03 US Hwy. 130
13. alike
14. 23 **W.** Prospect St.   23 **(E)** Prospect St.
15. alike
16. 3391 Route **516**   3391 Route **561**
17. alike
18. alike
19. A-2 Cornwall **Rd.**   A-2 Cornwall **Dr.**
20. Grove & Livingston Ave.   Grove**n** & Livingston Ave.
21. alike
22. alike
23. alike
24. 3 Progress **Cir.**   3 Progress **Ct.**
25. 1 H**aus**sling Pl.   1 H**ous**ling Pl.
26. alike

27. alike
28. 55**D** Avenue **C**   55**C** Avenue **D**
29. 503 Chest**er** Ct.   503 Chest**nut** Ct.
30. 109**B** Diamond Lane   109**3** Diamond Lane
31. alike
32. 170 Garretson Cir.   170 Garnetson Cir
33. 5 **B**arkley Ct.   5 **B**erkley Ct.
34. alike
35. alike
36. alike
37. 31 (E) 233rd St. Apt. 5D   30 (E) 233rd St. Apt. 5D
38. alike
39. 807 **Old** Raritan Rd.   807 Raritan Rd.
40. 55 Smullen St.   5S Smullen St.
41. 21 Qui**ck** Way   21 Qui**nk** Way
42. alike
43. alike
44. 15B **Red** Oak Lane   15B Oak Lane
45. alike
46. 83**K** Loretta St.   835 Loretta St.
47. alike
48. 15 W. 65th St.   151 W. 65th St.
49. alike
50. alike
51. alike
52. 4603 **N.** Wells Drive   4603-**N** Wells Drive
53. alike
54. 58 Tan**b**ark Dr.   58 Tar**b**ark Dr.
55. alike
56. alike
57. 135D Selwaren Ave.   135D Selvaren Ave.
58. 10 New Jersey Tpke.   110 New Jersey Tpke.
59. 7 Honeysuckle **Ct.**   7 Honeysuckle **St.**
60. 38 Exeter Ave.   38**B** Exeter Ave.
61. alike
62. alike
63. 232 S. First Ave.   2332 S. First Ave.

64.	12 Frandson Ave.	12 Frankson Ave.
65.	32B Amberly Ct.	32D Amberly Ct.
66.	alike	
67.	3664 St. Hwy. No. 18	364 St Hwy. No. 18
68.	10 Peter **Dr.**	10 Peter **Ct.**
69.	alike	
70.	37 Outcalt Rd.	37 Outcalf Rd.
71.	alike	
72.	157 Luke St. Apt. 1A	157 Luke St. Apt. 1D
73.	alike	
74.	9 Clembri Ct.	9 **O**lembri Ct.
75.	alike	
76.	13 Albert Ave.	133 Albert Ave.
77.	alike	
78.	4525 **Peru** Lane	4525 **Pearl** Lane
79.	35 Maple **Ct.**	35 Maple **St.**
80.	alike	
81.	alike	
82.	alike	
83.	2131 Cross Bronx Expwy.	231 Cross Bronx Expwy.
84.	alike	
85.	158 **Norris** Ave.	158 North Ave.
86.	alike	
87.	2 Mount Ct.	2 Mount**ain** Ct.
88.	alike	
89.	alike	
90.	653-A Cranbury Cross Rd.	6537 Cranbury Cross Rd.
91.	alike	
92.	46 Apple Place	461 Apple Place
93.	1 Gourmet Lane	1 Courvet Lane
94.	alike	
95.	alike	

Number Series

1. **(D)** Beginning with the number 1, this series is formed by adding 3 each time, and separating that number with the number 64. The correct answer is (D) 13, 64.

2. **(A)** There are two alternating series here. The first begins with 1 and increases by 1 each time, and the second takes the number from the first series, multiplies it by itself, and adds 2. Therefore, the correct response is (A) 5, 27.

3. **(C)** Beginning with 1, add 4 each time to form this series. The correct response is (C) 33, 37.

4. **(D)** This problem has two alternating series. The first begins with 1 and adds 4 each time, and the second begins with 5 and adds 5 each time. The correct answer is (D) 17, 25.

5. **(E)** Beginning with 2, multiply by 2, add 2 to the new number, and then repeat this process. The correct choice is (E) 62, 124.

6. **(B)** This problem has two alternating series. The first begins with 1 and adds 1 each time, and the second begins with 50 and subtracts 1 each time. Therefore, the correct response is (B) 5, 46.

7. **(E)** A series beginning with 100 and decreasing by 5 each time is separated by the number 4. Therefore, the correct answer is (E) 80, 4.

8. **(A)** This is a series of increasing odd numbers, each repeated twice and separated by the number 100. The correct answer is (A) 100, 7.

9. **(D)** There are two alternating series here. The first begins with 10 and adds 10 each time, and the second divides the number from the first series immediately preceding it by 2 and adds 1. The correct response is (D) 50, 26.

10. **(B)** In these two alternating series, the first begins with 1 and increases by 1 each time. In the second, each odd number from the first series is in-

creased by 6, and each even number is multiplied by 6. The correct answer is (B) 5, 11.

11. **(C)** In these two alternating series, the first begins with 25 and is increased by 25 each time, and the second begins with 5 and is increased by 5 each time. The correct choice is (C) 125, 25.

12. **(C)** This series begins with 1.1 and is increased by 11 each time. The correct response is (C) 89.1, 100.1.

13. **(A)** A series beginning with 1 and increasing by 1 is alternated with each number plus 2 and multiplied by 7. The correct response is (A) 5, 49.

14. **(B)** A series beginning with 1 and increasing by 1 is alternated with the square of each number plus 1, so the correct answer is (B) 9, 100.

15. **(D)** A series beginning with 99 and decreasing by 11 each time is separated by the number 11, so the correct answer is (D) 55, 11.

16. **(E)** A series beginning with 30 and increasing by 30 each time is alternated with each number divided by three, then this number plus 3; so the correct response is (E) 150, 53.

17. **(C)** A series beginning with 1 and increasing by 1 is alternated with each number multiplied by 3 minus 1, so the correct choice is (C) 5,14.

18. **(A)** A series of increasing numbers squared is separated by the number 5. The correct response is (A) 25, 5.

19. **(B)** Beginning with 1, a number is added starting with 5, and increasing by 5 each time. The correct answer is (B) 181, 226.

20. **(D)** The series begins with 1, and 2 is added, followed by an increasing even number each time. The correct response is (D) 73, 91.

21. **(E)**   Beginning with 100, first 1 is subtracted, and then 2, and then 3, and so on—the amount subtracted grows by 1 each time. The correct response is (E) 64, 55.

22. **(A)**   There are two alternating series here. The first begins with 1 and adds 4 each time, and the second begins with 100 and subtracts 5 each time. The correct response is (A) 17, 80.

23. **(C)**   This is a series of increasing odd numbers beginning with 1 and separated by the numbers 21 and 22. Therefore, the correct answer is (C) 22, 7.

24. **(D)**   Beginning with 200, subtract increasing square roots from each preceding number (1, 4, 9, 16, 25, etc.). The correct answer is (D) 109, 60.

Following Oral Directions

This is how your worksheet should look:

1.

2. 23:305 **B**   31:101   46:212   51:108 **B**   26:290

3.
| South St. 78 **D** | Masereel Pl. 89 | Guinness Ave. 64 |

4. 2   3   4   5   7   10
   A   **A**

5. Monday   Wednesday   Tuesday   Sunday   Friday

6. 32/14   44/13   50/19   49/10
   A   **B**   **C**   **D**

7.
   A   B   C   D

8. A _____   C _____   15 __**B**__   16 __**D**__

9. Derkins   Duncan   Dandamyr   Dwight

10. 2<u>4</u>15   6<u>8</u>12   35<u>4</u>2   48<u>80</u>

11. 30   40   50   70   80

In this section, please note that the solution to each problem is preceded by the actual instructions read by the examiner.

Examine sample one. (Pause 2-3 seconds) If the number in the small square is greater than the number in the small circle, write the letter from the large circle inside the small circle and the letter from the large square inside the small square. (Pause 5 seconds) If not, write the letter from the triangle inside both the small square and the small circle. (Pause 2 seconds) Darken the number/letter combination you have chosen. (Pause 5 seconds)

ANSWER: The number in the small square (35) is greater than the number in the small circle (29). Therefore, write the letter from the large circle (E) inside the small circle and the letter from the large square (B) inside the small square; then darken the oval for F for number 29 and darken the oval for B for number 35.

Examine sample one again. (Pause 2-3 seconds) If the letters are arranged alphabetically, write the number 22 inside the largest square and darken the corresponding number/letter combination. (Pause 5 seconds) If not, go to number 24 on your answer sheet and darken the letter A as in "apple." (Pause 5 seconds)

ANSWER: Since the letters are arranged alphabetically, write the number 22 in the largest square and darken the number/letter combination—22 B.

Examine sample two. (Pause 2-3 seconds) The first number represents the number of houses in a certain postal route, and the second, the number of miles. The fewer the number of houses compared with the length of the route, the more rural the route. Using this information, pick the most rural route and the least rural route and write the letter B as in "boy" beside each one. (Pause 7 seconds) Darken the corresponding number/letter combination on your answer sheet. (Pause 5 seconds)

ANSWER: The most rural route is 23; the least rural route is 51. Go to number 23 on your answer sheet and darken the oval for B; then go to 51 on your answer sheet and darken the oval for B.

Examine sample three. (Pause 2-3 seconds) Inside each box is the name of a street on a certain postal route and the number of addresses on that route.

If the number of addresses on Masereel Pl. is greater than that on Guinness Ave. and on South St., go to the number on your answer sheet corresponding with the number of addresses on Masereel Pl., and darken the letter B as in "boy." (Pause 7 seconds) If Masereel has fewer addresses than either of the other streets, go to the same number and darken the letter E as in "elephant." (Pause 5 seconds) If Masereel has more than South St. but less than Guinness Ave., go to the same number and darken the oval for C as in "cat." (Pause 5 seconds)

ANSWER: The number of addresses on Masereel Pl. (89) is greater than the number of addresses on Guinness Ave. (64) and South St. (78). Go to number 89 (the number of addresses on Masereel Pl.) and darken the oval for B.

Examine sample three again. (Pause 2-3 seconds) Write the letter D as in "dog" in the Guinness Ave. box if it has more addresses than the other two streets combined. (Pause 5 seconds) If not, mark the same letter in the South St. box. (Pause 2 seconds) Darken the number/letter combination you have chosen. (Pause 5 seconds)

ANSWER: Guinness Ave. does not have more addresses than the other two streets combined. Mark the letter D in the South St. box. Darken the number/letter combination on your answer sheet—78 D.

Examine sample four. (Pause 2-3 seconds) If these numbers increase by adding 1 to each previous number, write the letter A as in "apple" under the second-to-last number and under the second number. (Pause 7 seconds) If they increase by adding two to each number, write the letter B as in "boy" under the third number and the third from last number. (Pause 7 seconds) If neither of these statements is true, write the letter A as in "apple" under the first and last numbers. (Pause 2 seconds) Darken the number/letter combination you have chosen. (Pause 5 seconds)

ANSWER: The numbers listed do not increase by adding 1 to each previous number or by adding 2 to each number. Therefore, go to numbers 2 (the first number in your list) and 10 (the last number in your list) on your answer sheets and darken the ovals for A.

Examine sample four again. (Pause 2-3 seconds) If there are as many even as odd numbers in the list, go to number 39 on your answer sheet and darken the oval for E as in "elephant." (Pause 5 seconds) If there are more even numbers, go to the same number and darken the same oval. (Pause 2 seconds) If there are more odd numbers, go to number 93 on your answer sheet and darken the oval with the same letter. (Pause 5 seconds)

ANSWER: There are as many even numbers as odd numbers. Go to number 39 on your answer sheet and darken the oval for E.

Examine sample four again. (Pause 2-3 seconds) If the last number is equal to or greater than the sum of the first three numbers, go to the product of the first two numbers on the answer sheet and darken the oval for D as in "dog." (Pause 10 seconds) If it is smaller than the sum of the first three numbers, go to the product of the last two numbers and darken the oval for B as in "boy." (Pause 7 seconds)

ANSWER: Since the last number (10) is greater than the sum of the first three numbers (2 + 3 + 4 = 9), go to 6 (the product of the first two numbers) on the answer sheet and darken the oval for D.

Examine sample five. (Pause 2-3 seconds) If the third day mentioned comes before the fifth day in an actual week, go to number 84 on your answer sheet and darken the oval for D as in "dog." (Pause 5 seconds) If not, go to number 38 and darken the oval for B as in "boy." (Pause 5 seconds)

ANSWER: Since the third day mentioned (Tuesday) comes before the fifth day in an actual week (Thursday), go to number 84 on your answer sheet and darken the oval for D.

Examine sample five again. (Pause 2-3 seconds) If the fourth day has the same number of letters in it as any other two days, go to number 41 on your answer sheet and darken the oval for E as in "elephant." (Pause 5 seconds) If it only has the same number of letters as one other day, go to number 12 and darken the same letter. (Pause 2 seconds) If no other day has the same number of letters, go to number 12 and darken the oval for C as in "cat." (Pause 5 seconds)

ANSWER: The fourth day (Sunday) has six letters in it; so does Friday. Therefore, go to number 41 on your answer sheet and darken the oval for E.

Examine sample six. (Pause 2-3 seconds) These numbers represent the sorting speeds of four different employees at the same post office. The first number represents how many letters they can sort in a certain amount of time, and the second represents the number of magazines. Write the letters A as in "apple" through D as in "dog," one under each pair of numbers. (Pause 5 seconds) Find the employee who sorts the most magazines in a certain amount of time, and, using the letter written under that pair of numbers, darken the corresponding number/letter combination on your answer sheet. (Pause 5 seconds)

ANSWER: The most amount of magazines sorted by an employee is 19. Using the letter written under that pair on numbers, darken the corresponding number/letter combination on your answer sheet—19 C.

Examine sample six again. (Pause 2-3 seconds) Find the employee who sorts the smallest number of magazines in a certain amount of time, and using the same letters you marked for the question above, darken the corresponding number/letter combination on your answer sheet. (Pause 5 seconds)

ANSWER: The smallest amount of magazines sorted by an employee is 10. Using the letter written under that pair of numbers, darken the number/letter combination on your answer sheet—10 D. However, you should have previously darkened 10 A. You have two choices — either darken 10 D and erase 10 A or do not erase 10 A and don't darken 10 D.

Examine sample six again. (Pause 2-3 seconds) If the total sum of all of the magazines sorted is more than the sum of the first two numbers for letters sorted, go to the number on your answer sheet corresponding to the third number of letters sorted, and mark the number/letter combination on your answer sheet. (Pause 10 seconds) If this is not the case, go to the last number of letters sorted and mark this number/letter combination on your answer sheet. (Pause 5 seconds)

ANSWER: The total sum of all of the magazines sorted (14 + 13 + 19 + 10 = 56) is not more than the sum of the first two numbers (32 + 44 = 76). Go to the last number of letters sorted (49) and mark the number/letter combination on your answer sheet—49 D.

Examine sample seven. (Pause 2-3 seconds) If these figures are not arranged in order of increasing number of sides, mark the number 28 in the figure with the second-most sides. (Pause 2 seconds) If they are arranged in this order, go to the figure with the second-least number of sides and write the same number. (Pause 2 seconds) Mark the number/letter combination you have chosen on your answer sheet. (Pause 5 seconds)

ANSWER: The figures are in order of increasing number of sides. Go to the figure with the second-least number of sides (B) and write 28 in the figure. Mark the number/letter combination—28 B—on your answer sheet.

Examine sample seven again. (Pause 2-3 seconds) If the last figure shown has less sides than the sum of the number of sides of the first two figures, write the number 82 in the figure with the second-least number of sides. (Pause 7 seconds) If this statement is not true, find the figure with the most sides and write the number 80. (Pause 2 seconds) Mark the number/letter combination you have chosen. (Pause 5 seconds)

ANSWER: The last figure shown, which has 6 sides, has less sides than the sum of the number of sides of the first two figures (3 + 4 = 7). Mark 82 in the figure with the second-least number of sides (the second figure). Mark the number/letter combination you have chosen on your answer sheet—82 B.

Examine sample eight. (Pause 2-3 seconds) If the second letter chosen is the fourth letter of the alphabet, write it next to the second number shown. (Pause 2 seconds) If not, write the actual fourth letter of the alphabet next to the second number shown. (Pause 2 seconds) Mark this combination on your answer sheet. (Pause 5 seconds)

ANSWER: Since the second letter chosen (C) is not the fourth letter of the alphabet, write D next to the second number shown (16). Go to 16 on your answer sheet and mark the oval for D.

Examine sample eight again. (Pause 2-3 seconds) If there is a letter in the alphabet which comes between the two letters shown in this sample, mark it next to the first number shown. (Pause 2 seconds) If not, write the letter which comes immediately after the last number shown and write this after the first number. (Pause 2 seconds) Darken the number/letter combination you have chosen on your answer sheet. (Pause 5 seconds)

ANSWER: Since there is a letter in the alphabet (B) that comes between the two letters (A and C) in this sample, mark the letter B next to the first number shown (15). Mark the number/letter combination—15 B—on your answer sheet.

Examine sample nine. (Pause 2-3 seconds) These are the names of customers of the same postal substation. If the third name mentioned would come before the first and after the fourth name if they were all arranged alphabetically, go to number 85 on your answer sheet and darken the oval for D as in "dog." (Pause 10 seconds) If this statement is not true, go to number 58 and darken the oval for B as in "boy." (Pause 5 seconds)

ANSWER: The third name mentioned (Dandamyr) would come first before the first name mentioned (Derkins) if they were arranged alphabetically; however, it would not come after the fourth name mentioned (Dwight). Therefore, go to number 58 on your answer sheet and darken the oval for B.

Examine sample nine again. (Pause 2-3 seconds) If the last name mentioned would be the last name if these were all arranged in an alphabetical list, go to number 53 on your answer sheet and darken the oval for C as in "cat." (Pause 7 seconds) If this is not the case, go to the same number and darken the same oval. (Pause 5 seconds)

ANSWER: The last name mentioned (Dwight) would be the last name if these names were all arranged in an alphabetical list. Go to number 53 and darken the oval for C.

Examine sample ten. (Pause 2-3 seconds) Underline the second and fourth digit of each number listed. (Pause 2 seconds) If these are all even numbers, go to the number on your answer sheet that is the sum of the first two numbers you have underlined, and darken the oval for E as in "elephant." (Pause 5 seconds) If they are all odd numbers, go to the same number but darken the oval for B as in "boy." (Pause 2 seconds) If there are some even and some odd numbers, go to the number which is the same as the sum of the last two numbers underlined and darken the oval for E as in "elephant." (Pause 5 seconds)

ANSWER: There are some even and some odd numbers underlined. Therefore, go to the number which is the same as the sum of the last two numbers underlined, which is 8 (8 + 0 = 8) and darken the oval for E.

Examine sample ten again. (Pause 2-3 seconds) If the fourth number you have underlined is greater than or equal to the sixth number that you have underlined, go to number 87 on your answer sheet and darken the oval for C as in "cat." (Pause 2 seconds) If it is less, go to both numbers 88 and 90 and darken the same letter. (Pause 5 seconds)

ANSWER: The fourth number that you underlined (2) is equal to the sixth number that you underlined. Therefore, go to number 87 on your answer sheet and darken the oval for C.

Examine sample eleven. (Pause 2-3 seconds) If the third number is 20 more than the number before it and 20 more than the number after it, go to the fourth number from the sample on your answer sheet and write the letter E as in "elephant." (Pause 5 seconds) If it is 10 more than the number before it and 10 less than the number after it, go to the number 17 on your answer sheet and darken the letter D as in "dog." (Pause 5 seconds) If it is 10 more than the number before it and 20 less than the number after it, go to the first number and write the letter A as in "apple." (Pause 2 seconds) Darken the corresponding number/letter combination on your answer sheet. (Pause 5 seconds)

ANSWER: The third number (50) is 10 more than the number before it (40) and 20 less than the number after it (70). Therefore, go to the first number (30) and write the letter A. Darken the corresponding number/letter combination on your answer sheet—30 A.

Examine sample eleven again. (Pause 2-3 seconds) Find the number which is equal to the sum of the first two numbers. Write the letter D as in "dog" under it. (Pause 2 seconds) Add six to this number, and darken the corresponding number/letter combination on your answer sheet. (Pause 5 seconds)

ANSWER: The sum of the first two numbers is 70. Add 6 to this number (76) and darken the corresponding number/letter combination on your answer sheet—76 D.

Examine sample two again. (Pause 2-3 seconds) Choose the route with the most miles. Go to the number on your answer sheet equivalent to the first two digits of the number you have chosen plus 10. (Pause 5 seconds) Darken the oval for E as in "elephant." (Pause 5 seconds)

ANSWER: The route with the most miles is 305; the first two digits are 30 plus 10 equals 40. Go to number 40 on your answer sheet and darken the oval for E.

POSTAL EXAM
Test 5 - Following Oral Directions
ANSWER KEY

#	Answer
1.	Ⓐ Ⓑ Ⓒ Ⓓ Ⓔ
2.	**●** Ⓑ Ⓒ Ⓓ Ⓔ
3.	Ⓐ Ⓑ Ⓒ Ⓓ Ⓔ
4.	Ⓐ Ⓑ Ⓒ Ⓓ Ⓔ
5.	Ⓐ Ⓑ Ⓒ Ⓓ Ⓔ
6.	Ⓐ Ⓑ Ⓒ Ⓓ Ⓔ
7.	Ⓐ Ⓑ Ⓒ Ⓓ Ⓔ
8.	Ⓐ Ⓑ Ⓒ Ⓓ **●**
9.	Ⓐ Ⓑ Ⓒ Ⓓ Ⓔ
10.	**●** Ⓑ Ⓒ **●** Ⓔ
11.	Ⓐ Ⓑ Ⓒ Ⓓ Ⓔ
12.	Ⓐ Ⓑ Ⓒ Ⓓ Ⓔ
13.	Ⓐ Ⓑ Ⓒ Ⓓ Ⓔ
14.	Ⓐ Ⓑ Ⓒ Ⓓ Ⓔ
15.	Ⓐ **●** Ⓒ Ⓓ Ⓔ
16.	Ⓐ Ⓑ Ⓒ **●** Ⓔ
17.	Ⓐ Ⓑ Ⓒ Ⓓ Ⓔ
18.	Ⓐ Ⓑ Ⓒ Ⓓ Ⓔ
19.	Ⓐ Ⓑ **●** Ⓓ Ⓔ
20.	Ⓐ Ⓑ Ⓒ Ⓓ Ⓔ
21.	Ⓐ Ⓑ Ⓒ Ⓓ Ⓔ
22.	Ⓐ **●** Ⓒ Ⓓ Ⓔ
23.	Ⓐ **●** Ⓒ Ⓓ Ⓔ
24.	Ⓐ Ⓑ Ⓒ Ⓓ Ⓔ
25.	Ⓐ Ⓑ Ⓒ Ⓓ Ⓔ
26.	Ⓐ Ⓑ Ⓒ Ⓓ Ⓔ
27.	Ⓐ Ⓑ Ⓒ Ⓓ Ⓔ
28.	Ⓐ **●** Ⓒ Ⓓ Ⓔ
29.	Ⓐ Ⓑ Ⓒ Ⓓ **●**
30.	**●** Ⓑ Ⓒ Ⓓ Ⓔ
31.	Ⓐ Ⓑ Ⓒ Ⓓ Ⓔ
32.	Ⓐ Ⓑ Ⓒ Ⓓ Ⓔ
33.	Ⓐ Ⓑ Ⓒ Ⓓ Ⓔ
34.	Ⓐ Ⓑ Ⓒ Ⓓ Ⓔ
35.	Ⓐ **●** Ⓒ Ⓓ Ⓔ
36.	Ⓐ Ⓑ Ⓒ Ⓓ Ⓔ
37.	Ⓐ Ⓑ Ⓒ Ⓓ Ⓔ
38.	Ⓐ Ⓑ Ⓒ Ⓓ Ⓔ
39.	Ⓐ Ⓑ Ⓒ Ⓓ **●**
40.	Ⓐ Ⓑ Ⓒ Ⓓ **●**
41.	Ⓐ Ⓑ Ⓒ Ⓓ **●**
42.	Ⓐ Ⓑ Ⓒ Ⓓ Ⓔ
43.	Ⓐ Ⓑ Ⓒ Ⓓ Ⓔ
44.	Ⓐ Ⓑ Ⓒ Ⓓ Ⓔ
45.	Ⓐ Ⓑ Ⓒ Ⓓ Ⓔ
46.	Ⓐ Ⓑ Ⓒ Ⓓ Ⓔ
47.	Ⓐ Ⓑ Ⓒ Ⓓ Ⓔ
48.	Ⓐ Ⓑ Ⓒ Ⓓ Ⓔ
49.	Ⓐ Ⓑ Ⓒ **●** Ⓔ
50.	Ⓐ Ⓑ Ⓒ Ⓓ Ⓔ
51.	Ⓐ **●** Ⓒ Ⓓ Ⓔ
52.	Ⓐ Ⓑ Ⓒ Ⓓ Ⓔ
53.	Ⓐ Ⓑ **●** Ⓓ Ⓔ
54.	Ⓐ Ⓑ Ⓒ Ⓓ Ⓔ
55.	Ⓐ Ⓑ Ⓒ Ⓓ Ⓔ
56.	Ⓐ Ⓑ Ⓒ Ⓓ Ⓔ
57.	Ⓐ Ⓑ Ⓒ Ⓓ Ⓔ
58.	Ⓐ **●** Ⓒ Ⓓ Ⓔ
59.	Ⓐ Ⓑ Ⓒ Ⓓ Ⓔ
60.	Ⓐ Ⓑ Ⓒ Ⓓ Ⓔ
61.	Ⓐ Ⓑ Ⓒ Ⓓ Ⓔ
62.	Ⓐ Ⓑ Ⓒ Ⓓ Ⓔ
63.	Ⓐ Ⓑ Ⓒ Ⓓ Ⓔ
64.	Ⓐ Ⓑ Ⓒ Ⓓ Ⓔ
65.	Ⓐ Ⓑ Ⓒ Ⓓ Ⓔ
66.	Ⓐ Ⓑ Ⓒ Ⓓ Ⓔ
67.	Ⓐ Ⓑ Ⓒ Ⓓ Ⓔ
68.	Ⓐ Ⓑ Ⓒ Ⓓ Ⓔ
69.	Ⓐ Ⓑ Ⓒ Ⓓ Ⓔ
70.	Ⓐ Ⓑ Ⓒ Ⓓ Ⓔ
71.	Ⓐ Ⓑ Ⓒ Ⓓ Ⓔ
72.	Ⓐ Ⓑ Ⓒ Ⓓ Ⓔ
73.	Ⓐ Ⓑ Ⓒ Ⓓ Ⓔ
74.	Ⓐ Ⓑ Ⓒ Ⓓ Ⓔ
75.	Ⓐ Ⓑ Ⓒ Ⓓ Ⓔ
76.	Ⓐ Ⓑ Ⓒ **●** Ⓔ
77.	Ⓐ Ⓑ Ⓒ Ⓓ Ⓔ
78.	Ⓐ Ⓑ Ⓒ **●** Ⓔ
79.	Ⓐ Ⓑ Ⓒ Ⓓ Ⓔ
80.	Ⓐ Ⓑ Ⓒ Ⓓ Ⓔ
81.	Ⓐ Ⓑ Ⓒ Ⓓ Ⓔ
82.	Ⓐ **●** Ⓒ Ⓓ Ⓔ
83.	Ⓐ Ⓑ Ⓒ Ⓓ Ⓔ
84.	Ⓐ Ⓑ Ⓒ **●** Ⓔ
85.	Ⓐ Ⓑ Ⓒ Ⓓ Ⓔ
86.	Ⓐ Ⓑ Ⓒ Ⓓ Ⓔ
87.	Ⓐ Ⓑ **●** Ⓓ Ⓔ
88.	Ⓐ Ⓑ Ⓒ Ⓓ Ⓔ
89.	Ⓐ **●** Ⓒ Ⓓ Ⓔ
90.	Ⓐ Ⓑ Ⓒ Ⓓ Ⓔ
91.	Ⓐ Ⓑ Ⓒ Ⓓ Ⓔ
92.	Ⓐ Ⓑ Ⓒ Ⓓ Ⓔ
93.	Ⓐ Ⓑ Ⓒ Ⓓ Ⓔ
94.	Ⓐ Ⓑ Ⓒ Ⓓ Ⓔ
95.	Ⓐ Ⓑ Ⓒ Ⓓ Ⓔ
96.	Ⓐ Ⓑ Ⓒ Ⓓ Ⓔ
97.	Ⓐ Ⓑ Ⓒ Ⓓ Ⓔ
98.	Ⓐ Ⓑ Ⓒ Ⓓ Ⓔ

Test 6

TEST 6

Address Checking

(Answer sheets appear in the back of this book.)

TIME: 6 Minutes
95 Questions

DIRECTIONS: In this section you will be asked to compare two lists of addresses, deciding if they are alike or different. If the addresses are alike, you will mark oval "A" on your answer sheet; if they are different, you will mark oval "D" on your answer sheet.

---

1. 14 Vineland Terrace   14 Vineland Terrace
2. 26B N. Huston St.   26B N. Huston St.
3. 17 Tulane Ave.   17B Tulane Ave.
4. 231C Osprey Court   23C Osprey Court
5. 955 Madison Drive   955 Madison Avenue
6. 2415 Statue Lane   2415 Statue Lane
7. 2021 Decoy Rd.   2021 Decoy Rd.
8. 2 North Tenth Ave.   2 North Tenth Ave.
9. 78 Desolee Dr.   78 Desiree Dr.
10. 63 Beacon Place   63 Beacon Place
11. 317 McDowell Dr.   317 McDonald Dr.
12. 20 Sine Rd.   20 Sine Rd.
13. 115F Albourne Way   115K Albourne Way
14. 931B Village Dr.   931B Village Dr.
15. 2 N. Wermich Place   2 N. Wermich Place
16. 6 N. Rhoda St.   6N (E) Rhoda St.

17.	5065 St. Hwy. No. 34	5065 St. Hwy. No. 35
18.	32 Cty. Hwy. No. 519	32 Cty. Hwy. No. 519
19.	391C Orington Lane	3910 Orington Lane
20.	4 Sadowski Rd.	4 Sadowski St.
21.	30 Foxwood Dr.	230 Foxwood Dr.
22.	15 Leffert Ct.	15 Leffert Ct.
23.	6 VanHise Court	6 VanHise Court
24.	264 N. Middlebury Lane	264-N Middlebury Lane
25.	86 Major Road	86 Major Road
26.	28 Hadler Dr.	28 Handler Dr.
27.	31 Mariposa Place	31 Mariposa Place
28.	554 McKeon Pkwy.	5554 McKeon Pkwy.
29.	98 Klauser Lane	98 Klauser Lane
30.	15 Grand Blvd.	15 Grand Blvd.
31.	244 State Hwy. No. 31	244 State Hwy. No. 31
32.	1135 Butternut Mall St.	1135 Butternut St.
33.	52B Kossman Terrace	528 Kossman Terrace
34.	4 N. Woodlot Rd.	4 N. Woodlot Rd.
35.	187 Parker St. North	18L Parker St. North
36.	6K Jewel Place	6K Jewel Place
37.	153 Tunison Rd.	152 Tunison Rd.
38.	65 Magiera Terrace	65 Magiera Terrace
39.	3 Windsor Rd.	3 Windsor Rd.
40.	53 Rachel Ct.	53 Rachett Ct.
41.	213B White Birch Rd	213B White Birch Rd
42.	43 Cameo Place	43C Ameo Place
43.	20F Reler Lane	20F Reler Lane

44.	1401 Oval Ave	140 Loval Ave.
45.	6 Stiles Lane	6 Stiles Lane
46.	326A Nantucket St.	326A Nantuckett St.
47.	51 W. Almond Dr.	51 W. Almond Dr.
48.	535 (E) Gay Ct.	53 (E) Gay Ct.
49.	98B Executive Ave.	98B Executive Ave.
50.	197 Correja Ave.	197 Correja Ave.
51.	1050W N. Pekola St.	1050W N. Pekota St.
52.	14 Class Place	14 Class Place
53.	264 (E) Elmer Ct.	264 (E) Elmer Ct.
54.	1240 Cindy St.	124-0 Cindy St.
55.	19 DeBonis Dr.	19 DeBonis Dr.
56.	2 Honeysuckle Lane	22 Honeysuckle Lane
57.	24 Sturgis Rd.	24 Sturges Rd.
58.	640 Shunpike Rd.	640 Shunpike Rd.
59.	George & US Hwy. 18	George & US Hwy. 81
60.	44 (E) Lane Place	44 (E) Lani Place
61.	52 Rainford Rd.	52 Rainford Rd.
62.	13 Lordina Dr.	13 Lordina Dr.
63.	24 DeVoe Ave.	24 DeRoe Ave.
64.	30A Alva Ct.	30A Alva Ct.
65.	88 Boovean Ave.	88 Boorean Ave.
66.	2146 Strawberry Lane	2416 Strawberry Lane
67.	3302 Suloff St.	3302 Suloff St.
68.	112 Josephine Lane	11S Josephine Lane
69.	2500 Menlo Park Mall	2500 Menlo Park Mall
70.	717 Rivendale Way	717 Riverdale Way

71.	1 JFK Blvd.	1 JFK Blvd.
72.	5 Drexel Hill Dr.	51 Drexel Hill Dr.
73.	18B Redfield Village	188 Redfield Village
74.	251 Gregety Way	251 Gregety Way
75.	253C Jernee Dr.	253C Jernee Dr.
76.	41 Victory Bridge Pl.	41 Bridge Pl.
77.	17 Erik Dr.	17 Eric Dr.
78.	1210 Westminster Blvd.	1210 Westminster Blvd.
79.	68F Maxwell Ave.	681 Maxwell Ave.
80.	State Hwy 27 & Vern Ave.	State Hwy 27 & Vern Ave.
81.	829 Harned Terrace	829 Harvard Terrace
82.	96 MacArthur Ave.	96 MacArthur Ave.
83.	12 Civic Center Dr.	12 Civic Center Ct.
84.	85 Wilshire Ct.	85 Wilshire Ct.
85.	83 Coventry Circle	83 Coventry Circle
86.	255D Midwood Way	255D Midwood Way
87.	5125 Beatty Place	5125 Deatty Place
88.	12 Florence St. West	12 Florence St. West
89.	5 Boyard Ct.	5 Bayard Ct.
90.	920 Forest Haven Blvd.	920 Forest Haven Blvd.
91.	100 Mt. Pleasant Ave.	100 Pleasant Ave.
92.	44 Driftwood Dr.	44 Driftwood Dr.
93.	233 (E) 55th St.	233 (E) 55th St.
94.	C11H West End Ave.	211H West End Ave.
95.	22B Plymouth St.	222B Plymouth St.

TEST 6

Memory for Addresses

(Answer sheets appear in the back of this book.)

TIME: Study 5 Minutes, Work 5 Minutes
88 Questions

DIRECTIONS: Below are five boxes labeled A,B,C,D, and E. Each box contains five addresses. You will be given five minutes to memorize the addresses in the boxes and their locations. After five minutes are up, you will have an additional five minutes to answer the following 88 questions and mark on the answer sheet the letter of the box in which the address belongs. You will not be able to refer back to the boxes once you begin answering the questions.

A	B	C	D	E
8100-8799 McMullen	2200-3599 McMullen	1700-2199 McMullen	8200-8899 McMullen	7600-8399 McMullen
Wyoming	Hegel	Neilly	Bonniebrook	Summit
7600-8399 Busch	8200-8899 Busch	8100-8799 Busch	1700-2199 Busch	2200-3599 Busch
Old	International	Wildberry	Lumiere	Mackintosh
2200-3599 Crabapple	1700-2199 Crabapple	8200-8899 Crabapple	7600-8399 Crabapple	8100-8799 Crabapple

1. 8200-8899 Crabapple
2. Wyoming
3. Neilly
4. 7600-8399 Busch
5. 8100-8799 McMullen
6. 8100-8799 Crabapple
7. Mackintosh
8. 7600-8399 Crabapple
9. 1700-2199 Busch
10. Summit
11. 2200-3599 Crabapple
12. 2200-3599 McMullen
13. Bonniebrook
14. 7600-8399 McMullen
15. Hegel
16. 8200-8899 McMullen
17. Old
18. 2200-3599 Busch
19. International
20. Wildberry
21. 8100-8799 Busch
22. Lumiere
23. 8200-8899 Busch
24. 1700-2199 McMullen
25. 1700-2199 Crabapple
26. 8200-8899 Crabapple
27. 7600-8399 Crabapple

28. Bonniebrook

29. Wyoming

30. 2200-3599 McMullen

31. 8100-8799 Crabapple

32. Hegel

33. 8100-8799 McMullen

34. Mackintosh

35. Neilly

36. 1700-2199 Busch

37. International

38. 7600-8399 Busch

39. 8100-8799 Busch

40. 8200-8899 McMullen

41. Wildberry

42. Summit

43. Lumiere

44. 8200-8899 Busch

45. 2200-3599 Crabapple

46. 1700-2199 Crabapple

47. 2200-3599 McMullen

48. Old

49. 7600-8399 Crabapple

50. 7600-8399 McMullen

51. 1700-2199 McMullen

52. Bonniebrook

53. 2200-3599 Busch

54. 8100-8799 McMullen

55. International

56. Wyoming

57. 1700-2199 Busch

58. 8100-8799 Crabapple

59. 8200-8899 Crabapple

60. Neilly

61. 7600-8399 Busch

62. Hegel

63. 8200-8899 McMullen

64. Mackintosh

65. Lumiere

66. 2200-3599 Crabapple

67. Old

68. Summit

69. 1700-2199 Crabapple

70. 8200-8899 Busch

71. 8100-8799 Busch

72. 7600-8399 Crabapple

73. 7600-8399 McMullen

74. Wildberry

75. 8100-8799 McMullen

76. Bonniebrook

77. Wyoming

78. Hegel

79. 2200-3599 McMullen

80. 2200-3599 Busch

81. 8100-8799 Crabapple

82. 1700-2199 Busch

83. 1700-2199 McMullen

84. Mackintosh

85. Neilly

86. International

87. 8100-8799 Busch

88. 1700-2199 Crabapple

TEST 6

Number Series

(Answer sheets appear in the back of this book.)

TIME: 20 Minutes
24 Questions

DIRECTIONS: For each question, there is a series of numbers that follow some definite order. Look at the series of numbers and decide which two numbers will come next in the series. You will be given five answers to choose from.

1. 1   2   3   2   3   5   3   4   _____   _____

   (A) 5, 6

   (B) 7, 4

   (C) 4, 8

   (D) 8, 16

   (E) 6, 8

2. 10   1   9   9   2   7   8   3   _____   _____

   (A) 11, 7

   (B) 5, 6

   (C) 5, 7

   (D) 7, 4

   (E) 6, 5

3. 1   2   2   2   3   6   3   4   _____   _____

    (A) 12, 4

    (B) 7, 9

    (C) 4, 12

    (D) 5, 6

    (E) 12, 24

4. 4   5   12   13   28   29   60   _____   _____

    (A) 120, 240

    (B) 120, 121

    (C) 124, 248

    (D) 61, 124

    (E) 61, 62

5. 144   132   121   110   100   90   81   72   _____
    _____

    (A) 63, 54

    (B) 60, 50

    (C) 63, 54

    (D) 64, 56

    (E) 49, 42

6. 100   88   1   13   76   64   25   37   _____   _____

    (A) 52, 40

    (B) 49, 51

    (C) 21, 19

    (D) 64, 128

    (E) 50, 74

7. 1   2   3   4   10   5   6   7   8   26   _____
    _____

    (A) 28, 30

    (B) 9, 10

    (C) 52, 104

    (D) 9, 18

    (E) 6, 7

8. 2   1   4   3   6   5   8   7   _____   _____

    (A) 8, 9

    (B) 14, 28

    (C) 16, 14

    (D) 11, 8

    (E) 10, 9

9. 1   2   3   6   7   8   9   24   _____   _____

    (A) 25, 50

    (B) 10, 11

    (C) 25, 26

    (D) 48, 96

    (E) 18, 36

10. 1   3   6   8   16   18   36   38   _____   _____

    (A) 40, 42

    (B) 46, 58

    (C) 56, 68

    (D) 76, 78

    (E) 43, 86

11. 1   121   11   2   144   12   3   169   _____   _____

    (A) 13, 4

    (B) 4, 5

    (C) 4, 16

    (D) 16, 32

    (E) 13, 5

12. 2   4   8   6   8   48   10   12   _____   _____

    (A) 14, 16

    (B) 48, 14

    (C) 24, 48

    (D) 24, 26

    (E) 120, 14

13. 5   250   10   255   15   260   20   265   _____
    _____

    (A) 40, 80

    (B) 275, 285

    (C) 25, 270

    (D) 25, 130

    (E) 30, 275

14. 1   10   11   10   21   10   31   10   _____   _____

    (A) 20, 30

    (B) 41, 10

    (C) 62, 124

    (D) 10, 41

    (E) 51, 20

15. 1   1   3   2   5   7   3   9   _____   _____

    (A) 18, 36

    (B) 5, 10

    (C) 4, 5

    (D) 4, 11

    (E) 11, 4

16. 1   23   2   34   3   45   4   56   _____   _____

    (A) 6, 132

    (B) 7, 14

    (C) 5, 65

    (D) 4, 16

    (E) 132, 264

17. 1   31   2   31   3   31   4   31   _____   _____

    (A) 6, 31

    (B) 8, 62

    (C) 8, 31

    (D) 5, 31

    (E) 31, 5

18. 1   100   101   2   99   101   3   98   _____   _____

    (A) 4, 5

    (B) 101, 4

    (C) 5, 7

    (D) 5, 101

    (E) 5, 100

19.   4   10   20   8   30   40   12   50   _____   _____

    (A) 60, 70

    (B) 70, 90

    (C) 12, 60

    (D) 12, 16

    (E) 60, 16

20.   1   1   2   2   2   4   3   3   _____   _____

    (A) 3, 4

    (B) 6, 12

    (C) 6, 4

    (D) 12, 8

    (E) 24, 16

21.   1   3   2   3   5   2   5   7   _____   _____

    (A) 6, 7

    (B) 7, 9

    (C) 2, 5

    (D) 7, 2

    (E) 2, 7

22.   123   223   234   334   345   445   456   556   _____   _____

    (A) 543, 456

    (B) 567, 667

    (C) 432, 345

    (D) 123, 321

    (E) 567, 765

23. 1   4   3   2   5   4   3   6   _____   _____

    (A) 5, 4

    (B) 12, 24

    (C) 6, 18

    (D) 24, 12

    (E) 10, 20

24. 2   20   30   3   30   40   4   40   _____   _____

    (A) 80, 160

    (B) 50, 5

    (C) 50, 50

    (D) 80, 40

    (E) 5, 50

TEST 6

Following Oral Directions - Worksheet

(Answer sheets appear in the back of this book.)

TIME: Instructions will be read at approximately 80 words per minute.

DIRECTIONS: Follow the instructions that are read to you. They will not be repeated during the examination. You are to mark your worksheets according to the instructions that are read to you. After each set of instructions, you will be given time to record your answer on your answer sheet. You should have only one space darkened for each number. If you go to darken a space for a number and you have already darkened another space, either erase the first mark and darken the space for your new choice **or** let the original mark remain.

---

1. 417   320   139   851   729

2. △   ▭   ▭   ◯

3. F   A   H   B   E

4. Wednesday   Friday   Saturday   Monday

5. ◯   ▭   △   ‾E‾

6. ◯   ▭   △   ◯   △

7. C   B   E   A   D
     37   6   23   25   14

8. AZ   CA   DE   BO   NY
     32   8   16   27   9

9. D/11:15   C/9:07   A/10:07   E/8:14

10. 32650   32981   32630   33317   22153

TEST 6

ANSWER KEY

Address Checking

1.	(A)	15.	(A)	29.	(A)	43.	(A)	57.	(D)	71.	(A)	85.	(A)
2.	(A)	16.	(D)	30.	(A)	44.	(D)	58.	(A)	72.	(D)	86.	(A)
3.	(D)	17.	(D)	31.	(A)	45.	(A)	59.	(D)	73.	(D)	87.	(D)
4.	(D)	18.	(A)	32.	(D)	46.	(D)	60.	(D)	74.	(A)	88.	(A)
5.	(D)	19.	(D)	33.	(D)	47.	(A)	61.	(A)	75.	(A)	89.	(D)
6.	(A)	20.	(D)	34.	(A)	48.	(D)	62.	(A)	76.	(D)	90.	(A)
7.	(A)	21.	(D)	35.	(D)	49.	(A)	63.	(D)	77.	(D)	91.	(D)
8.	(A)	22.	(A)	36.	(A)	50.	(A)	64.	(A)	78.	(A)	92.	(A)
9.	(D)	23.	(A)	37.	(D)	51.	(D)	65.	(D)	79.	(D)	93.	(A)
10.	(A)	24.	(D)	38.	(A)	52.	(A)	66.	(D)	80.	(A)	94.	(D)
11.	(D)	25.	(A)	39.	(A)	53.	(A)	67.	(A)	81.	(D)	95.	(D)
12.	(A)	26.	(D)	40.	(D)	54.	(D)	68.	(D)	82.	(A)		
13.	(D)	27.	(A)	41.	(A)	55.	(A)	69.	(A)	83.	(D)		
14.	(A)	28.	(D)	42.	(D)	56.	(D)	70.	(D)	84.	(A)		

Memory for Addresses

1.	(C)	14.	(E)	27.	(D)	40.	(D)	53.	(E)	66.	(A)	79.	(B)
2.	(A)	15.	(B)	28.	(D)	41.	(C)	54.	(A)	67.	(A)	80.	(E)
3.	(C)	16.	(D)	29.	(A)	42.	(E)	55.	(B)	68.	(E)	81.	(E)
4.	(A)	17.	(A)	30.	(B)	43.	(D)	56.	(A)	69.	(B)	82.	(D)
5.	(A)	18.	(E)	31.	(E)	44.	(B)	57.	(D)	70.	(B)	83.	(C)
6.	(E)	19.	(B)	32.	(B)	45.	(A)	58.	(E)	71.	(C)	84.	(E)
7.	(E)	20.	(C)	33.	(A)	46.	(B)	59.	(C)	72.	(D)	85.	(C)
8.	(D)	21.	(C)	34.	(E)	47.	(B)	60.	(C)	73.	(E)	86.	(B)
9.	(D)	22.	(D)	35.	(C)	48.	(A)	61.	(A)	74.	(C)	87.	(C)
10.	(E)	23.	(B)	36.	(D)	49.	(D)	62.	(B)	75.	(A)	88.	(B)
11.	(A)	24.	(C)	37.	(B)	50.	(E)	63.	(D)	76.	(D)		
12.	(B)	25.	(B)	38.	(A)	51.	(C)	64.	(E)	77.	(A)		
13.	(D)	26.	(C)	39.	(C)	52.	(D)	65.	(D)	78.	(B)		

Note: There is only an answer key for the "Memory for Addresses" section.

Number Series

1.	(B)	13.	(C)
2.	(C)	14.	(B)
3.	(A)	15.	(E)
4.	(D)	16.	(C)
5.	(D)	17.	(D)
6.	(A)	18.	(B)
7.	(B)	19.	(E)
8.	(E)	20.	(C)
9.	(C)	21.	(E)
10.	(D)	22.	(B)
11.	(A)	23.	(A)
12.	(E)	24.	(B)

Following Oral Directions

(Please see "Detailed Explanations of Answers.")

DETAILED EXPLANATIONS
OF ANSWERS

Test 6

Address Checking

1. alike
2. alike
3. 17 Tulane Ave.   17B Tulane Ave.
4. 231C Osprey Court   23C Ospey Court
5. 955 Madison **Drive**   955 Madison **Avenue**
6. alike
7. alike
8. alike
9. 78 Desolee Dr.   78 Desiree Dr.
10. alike
11. 317 McDowell Dr.   317 McDonald Dr.
12. alike
13. 115F Albourne Way   115K Albourne Way
14. alike
15. alike
16. 6 N. Rhoda St.   6NE. Rhoda St.
17. 5065 St. Hwy. No. 34   5065 St. Hwy. No. 35
18. alike
19. 391C Orington Lane   3910 Orington Lane
20. 4 Sadowski **Rd.**   4 Sadowski **St.**
21. 30 Foxwood Dr.   230 Foxwood Dr.
22. alike
23. alike
24. 264 **N.** Middlebury Lane   264-N Middlebury Lane
25. alike
26. 28 Hadler Dr.   28 Handler Dr.

27. alike
28. 554 McKeon Pkwy.   5554 McKeon Pkwy.
29. alike
30. alike
31. alike
32. 1135 Butternut **Mall** St.   1135 Butternut St.
33. 52**B** Kossman Terrace   528 Kossman Terrace
34. alike
35. 187 Parker St. North   18L Parker St. North
36. alike
37. 153 Tunison Rd.   152 Tunison Rd.
38. alike
39. alike
40. 53 Rachel Ct.   53 Rachett Ct.
41. alike
42. 43 **Cameo** Place   43C Ameo Place
43. alike
44. 1401 **O**val Ave.   140 **L**oval Ave.
45. alike
46. 326A Nantucket St.   326A Nantuckett St.
47. alike
48. 535 (E) Gay Ct.   53 (E) Gay Ct.
49. alike
50. alike
51. 1050W N. Pekola St.   1050W N. Pekota St.
52. alike
53. alike
54. 1240 Cindy St.   124-0 Cindy St.
55. alike
56. 2 Honeysuckle Lane   22 Honeysuckle Lane
57. 24 Stug**is** Rd.   24 Stug**es** Rd.
58. alike
59. George & US Hwy. **18**   George & US Hwy. **81**
60. 44 (E) Lane Place   44 (E) Lani Place
61. alike
62. alike
63. 24 DeVoe Ave.   24 DeRoe Ave.

64. alike
65. 88 Boovean Ave.   88 Boorean Ave.
66. 2146 Strawberry Lane   2416 Strawberry Lane
67. alike
68. 112 Josephine Lane   11S Josephine Lane
69. alike
70. 717 Rivendale Way   717 Riverdale Way
71. alike
72. 5 Drexel Hill Dr.   51 Drexel Hill Dr.
73. 18B Redfield Village   188 Redfield Village
74. alike
75. alike
76. 41 **Victory** Bridge Pl.   41 Bridge Pl.
77. 17 Erik Dr.   17 Eric Dr.
78. alike
79. 68F Maxwell Ave.   681 Maxwell Ave.
80. alike
81. 829 **Harned** Terrace   829 **Harvard** Terrace
82. alike
83. 12 Civic Center **Dr.**   12 Civic Center **Ct.**
84. alike
85. alike
86. alike
87. 5125 **Beatty** Place   5125 **Deatty** Place
88. alike
89. 5 Boyard Ct.   5 Bayard Ct.
90. alike
91. 100 **Mt.** Pleasant Ave.   100 Pleasant Ave.
92. alike
93. alike
94. **C**11H West End Ave.   **2**11H West End Ave.
95. 22B Plymouth St.   222B Plymouth St.

Number Series

1. **(B)** In this series, a pattern beginning with 1 and increasing by 1 is followed each time by the number plus 1, and then by both of these digits added together. The correct response is (B) 7, 4.

2. **(C)** This has three alternating series. The first begins with 10 and decreases by 1 each time, the second begins with 1 and increases by 1 each time, and the third is always the difference between these two numbers. Therefore, the correct response is (C) 5, 7.

3. **(A)** Once again there are three alternating series. The first begins with 1 and increases by 1 each time, the second adds 1 to the first number, and the third is the product of the first two numbers. The correct response is (A) 12, 4.

4. **(D)** Beginning with 4, first add 1, then add 1 to the new number and multiply by 2, then repeat the process. The correct choice is (D) 61, 124.

5. **(D)** This shows two series. The first, beginning with 144, shows decreasing squares of numbers. This is alternated with the second series, which is the difference between each number and the square root of that number. The correct response is (D) 64, 56.

6. **(A)** This problem has two series, alternating two at a time. The first begins with 100 and subtracts 12 each time, and the second begins with 1 and adds 12 each time. The correct response is (A) 52, 40.

7. **(B)** This series begins with 1 and increases by 1 each time, but after each set of four numbers, insert the sum of those numbers. The correct response is (B) 9, 10.

8. **(E)** This has two alternating series. The first begins with 2 and increases by 2, and the second begins with 1 and increases by 2. The correct answer is (E) 10, 9.

9. **(C)** This is a series of numbers beginning with 1 and increasing by 1, but after every set of three numbers, insert the sum of those numbers. The correct choice is (C) 25, 26.

10. **(D)** To form this series, begin with 1, and alternately add 2 and multiply by 2. Therefore, the correct response is (D) 76, 78.

11. **(A)** This problem has three alternating series. The first begins with 1 and increases by 1 each time. The second takes the number from the first series, adds 10, and then squares the new number. The third takes the preceding number from the second series and derives its square root. The correct choice is (A) 13, 4.

12. **(E)** This has a series of numbers beginning with 2 and increasing by 2, and after each set of two numbers, the product of those numbers is inserted. The correct answer is (E) 120, 14.

13. **(C)** Beginning with 5, a series that adds 5 each time is alternated with the sum of each number in the first series and 245. Therefore, the correct answer is (C) 25, 270.

14. **(B)** A series beginning with 1 and adding 10 each time is separated by the repeated number 10. The correct response is (B) 41, 10.

15. **(E)** Two series are alternated, with one digit of the first being followed by two digits of the second. The first begins with 1 and adds 1 each time, and the second begins with 1 and adds 2 each time. The correct choice is (E) 11, 4.

16. **(C)** A series beginning with 1 and increasing by 1 each time is alternated with a series that begins with the sum of the number from the first series plus 22, and then for each proceeding number adds an extra 10 each time (1 + 22, 2 + 32, 3 + 42, etc.). The correct answer is (C) 5, 65.

17. **(D)** A series beginning with 1 and adding 1 each time is separated by the number 31. Therefore, the correct response is (D) 5, 31.

18. **(B)**   There are three alternating series in this problem. The first begins with 1 and adds 1 each time, the second begins with 100 and subtracts 1 each time, and the third simply repeats the number 101. So the correct answer is (B) 101, 4.

19. **(E)**   There are two series alternated here. The first begins with 4 and proceeds by 4. The second, which occurs twice for each single occurrence of the first series, begins with 10 and adds 10 each time. The correct answer is (E) 60, 16.

20. **(C)**   This series, beginning with 1, is formed by adding a number to itself, the sum of which makes the third number, then adding 1 to the original number, and repeating the pattern. The correct answer is (C) 6, 4.

21. **(E)**   There are three alternating series in this problem. The first begins with 1 and adds 2 each time, the second begins with 3 and adds 2 each time, and the third is simply the number 2 repeated. The correct answer is (E) 2, 7.

22. **(B)**   Beginning with the number 123, first add 100 to the first number to get the second number, then add 1 to the second number to get the third number. Then, beginning with the third number, first add 100 to the previous number and then 1, then repeat the pattern. The correct answer is (B) 567, 667.

23. **(A)**   To make this series, beginning with 1, first add 3 and then subtract 1. Repeat this pattern with 2, and then 3, and so on. The correct answer is (A) 5, 4.

24. **(B)**   To make this series, beginning with 2, first multiply the first number by 10, and then add 10 to the product. Repeat this pattern with 3, and then 4, and so on. The correct response is (B) 50, 5.

Following Oral Directions

This is how your worksheet should look:

	A	**B**	**C**	**D**	**E**
1.	417	320	139	851	729

2.

3. F   A   H   B   **42**
       63   E

12	**9**	**8**	**11**
4. Wednesday	Friday	Saturday	Monday

5.

6.

7.	C	B	E	A	D
	37	6	23	25	14

8.	Ⓐ Z	Ⓒ A	Ⓓ E	Ⓑ O	Ⓝ Y
	32	8	16	27	9

9. D/11:15   C/9:07   A/10:07   E/8:14

10. 32⑥50   32⑨81   32⑥30   33③17   22①53

In this section, please note that the solution to each problem is preceded by the actual instructions read by the examiner.

Examine sample one. (Pause 2-3 seconds) If any of the numbers listed are odd, go to number 46 on the answer sheet and darken the oval for E as in "elephant." (Pause 2-3 seconds) Then add the digits in the first number together. Go to this number on the answer sheet and darken the oval for A as in "apple." (Pause 5 seconds)

ANSWER: Since some of the numbers listed are odd, darken the oval for 46 E. Then add the first number together (4 + 1 + 7 = 12). Then go to number 12 on the answer sheet and darken the oval for A.

Examine sample one again. (Pause 2-3 seconds) Write the letter A as in "apple" through E as in "elephant" in alphabetical order over each number. (Pause 2-3 seconds) If the sum of the number under D as in "dog" plus 10 is less than 500, go to number 17 on the answer sheet and darken the oval for B as in "boy." (Pause 2-3 seconds) Otherwise, go to number 18 on the answer sheet and darken the oval for C as in "cat." (Pause 5 seconds)

ANSWER: The sum of the number under D plus 10 is 861. 861 is not less than 500. Therefore, go to number 18 on the answer sheet and darken the oval for C.

Examine sample two. (Pause 2-3 seconds) Write the number 17 in the circle. (Pause) Then write the number equivalent to 2 times 8 in the triangle. (Pause) If there are no numbers in any of the squares, then go to number 61 on the answer sheet and darken the oval for E as in "elephant." (Pause 2-3 seconds) If the number in the triangle is less than half of the number in the circle, go to number 24 on the answer sheet and darken the oval for the letter B as in "boy." (Pause 5 seconds)

ANSWER: There are no numbers in the squares so go to number 61 on the answer sheet and darken the oval for E. The number in the triangle (16) is not less than half of the number in the circle (half the number in the circle would be 8.5).

Examine sample two again. (Pause 2-3 seconds) Go to the number written in the circle on the answer sheet and darken the oval for B as in "boy." (Pause 2-3 seconds) Then add the number in the triangle together with the number in the circle. Go to this number on the answer sheet and darken the oval for A as in "apple." (Pause 7 seconds)

ANSWER: Go to the number 17 (the number in the circle) on your answer sheet and darken the oval for B. Then add the numbers in the triangle and the square (16 + 17 = 33). Go to number 33 on the answer sheet and darken the oval for A.

Examine sample three. (Pause 2-3 seconds) Find the fifth letter of the alphabet and write the number 42 over it. Find the first letter of the alphabet and write the number 63 under it. Find letter E as in "elephant," and go to the number listed by this letter on the answer sheet and darken that number/letter combination. (Pause 2-3 seconds) If any of the letters listed are in the word "house," go to number 10 on the answer sheet and darken the oval for D as in "dog." (Pause 5 seconds)

ANSWER: Go to number 42 on the answer sheet and darken the oval for E. The letters "h" and "e" are in the word "house"; therefore, go to the number 10 on your answer sheet and darken the oval for D.

Examine sample three again. (Pause 2-3 seconds) If the first letter listed in this sample comes before the third letter in the alphabet, go to number 35 on the answer sheet and darken the oval for B as in "boy." (Pause 2-3 seconds) Otherwise, go to number 16 on the answer sheet and darken the oval for A as in "apple." (Pause 5 seconds)

ANSWER: The first letter listed (F) does not come before C, the third letter in the alphabet. Go to number 16 on the answer sheet and darken the oval for A.

Examine sample four. (Pause 2-3 seconds) If the last day listed in the sample falls on a weekend, go to number 33 on the answer sheet and darken the space for C as in "cat." (Pause 2-3 seconds) If the last day listed does not fall on a weekend, go to number 52 on the answer sheet and darken the oval for D as in "dog." (Pause 5 seconds)

ANSWER: The last day listed, Monday, does not fall on a weekend. Therefore, go to number 52 on your answer sheet and darken the oval for D.

Examine sample four again. (Pause 2-3 seconds) Write the numbers 12, 9, 8, and 11, in that order, over the days listed in the sample. Go to the number on the answer sheet that is listed over Friday and darken the oval for B as in "boy." (Pause 2-3 seconds) If any of the words have more than 6 but less than 9 letters, go to number 23 on the answer sheet and darken the oval for A as in "apple." (Pause 5 seconds)

ANSWER: Go to the number on the answer sheet that is listed over Friday (9) and darken the oval for B. The word "Wednesday" has exactly 9 letters; the word "Friday" has 6 letters. Therefore, do not fill in number 23 D on your answer sheet.

Examine sample five. (Pause 2-3 seconds) Write the number 6 in the rectangle, the number 11 in the triangle, and the number 1 in the circle. If the numbers in the circle and in the rectangle add up to the number in the triangle, then go to number 16 on the answer sheet and darken the oval for A as in "apple." (Pause 2-3 seconds) If the number in the triangle plus 12 is less than half of the number in the rectangle, go to number 28 on the answer sheet and darken the oval for D as in "dog." (Pause 5 seconds)

ANSWER: The numbers in the circle and rectangle add up to 7, which is not the number in the triangle (11). The number in the triangle plus 12 is 33, which is not half the number in the rectangle.

Examine sample five again. (Pause 2-3 seconds) Write the letter E over the line. Go to the number listed in the triangle on the answer sheet and darken the letter for B as in "boy." (Pause 2-3 seconds) Then go to the answer sheet to the number listed under the line and darken the oval for the letter listed above the line. (Pause 5 seconds)

ANSWER: Go to the number listed in the triangle (11) and darken the letter for B. Then go to the number listed under the line (65) on your answer sheet and darken the oval for the letter listed above the line (E).

Examine sample six. (Pause 2-3 seconds) If there are more triangles than squares in this sample, go to number 68 on the answer sheet and darken the oval for C as in "cat." (Pause 2-3 seconds) Otherwise, go to number 12 on the answer sheet and darken the same oval. (Pause 2-3 seconds) Now go to number 13 on the answer sheet and darken the ovals for A as in "apple" and B as in "boy." (Pause 5 seconds)

ANSWER: There are more triangles than squares in the sample; therefore, go to number 68 on your answer sheet and darken the oval for C. The instructions tell you to go to darken the ovals for A and B on your answer sheet for number 13 on your answer sheet. This is meant to trick you. You must fill in either A or B.

Examine sample six again. (Pause 2-3 seconds) Write the number 32 in the largest figure in the sample. If the number 32 is in the circle, go to number 50 on the answer sheet and darken the oval for D as in "dog." (Pause 2-3 seconds) If the number 32 is in a triangle, go to the same number and darken the oval for B as in "boy." (Pause 2-3 seconds) If the number is in a square, go to the number 21 on the answer sheet and darken the same oval. (Pause 5 seconds)

ANSWER: Number 32 is in the square. Go to number 21 on your answer sheet and darken the oval for B

Example sample seven. (Pause 2-3 seconds) If the number under A as in "apple" is 2 more than the number under E as in "elephant," then go to number 40 on the answer sheet and darken the oval for the letter listed over number 37 in the sample. (Pause 2-3 seconds) Otherwise, go to number 35 on the answer sheet and darken the same oval. (Pause 5 seconds)

ANSWER: The number under A (25) is two more than the number under E (25). Therefore, go to number 40 on your answer sheet and darken the oval for C (C is the letter listed over 37 in the sample).

Examine sample seven again. (Pause 2-3 seconds) Find the second largest number listed in the sample. Multiply this number by two. Go to this number on the answer sheet, and darken the oval for the letter listed over the lowest number of the sample. (Pause 2-3 seconds) Then go to number 56 on the answer sheet and darken the oval for the letter E as in "elephant." (Pause 5 seconds)

ANSWER: The second largest number in the sample is 25; multiply 25 by 2 which equals 50. Go to 50 on your answer sheet and darken the oval for B (this is the letter listed over the lowest number of the sample, 6). Then go to number 56 on your answer sheet and darken the oval for E.

Examine sample eight. (Pause 2-3 seconds) If any of the letter combinations are state abbreviations, go to number 30 on the answer sheet and darken the oval for C as in "cat." (Pause 2-3 seconds) If there is a letter combination that is not a state abbreviation, go to the number under that letter combination and darken the oval for A as in "apple." (Pause 2-3 seconds) Otherwise, go to number 2 on the answer sheet and darken the oval for D as in "dog." (Pause 5 seconds)

ANSWER: Four of the five letter combinations are state abbreviations. Therefore, go to number 30 on your answer sheet and darken the oval for C. There is one letter combination that is not a state abbreviation (BO). Go to the number under this combination (27) on your answer sheet and darken the oval for A.

Examine sample eight again. (Pause 2-3 seconds) Circle the first letter in each letter combination. Look at the second letter circled. Go to the number listed under this letter on the answer sheet and darken the letter circled. (Pause 2-3 seconds) Then go to the highest number listed in this sample, and darken the oval for the letter listed above the number. (Pause 5 seconds)

ANSWER: The second letter circled is "C". Go to the number listed under this letter (8) on your answer sheet and darken the oval for C. Then go to the highest number listed in this sample (32) and darken the oval for the letter listed above the number (A) on your answer sheet.

Examine sample nine. (Pause 2-3 seconds) Each letter represents a mailbox on the same route, and the number next to it represents what time the mail was picked up. Circle the letter of the mailbox with the earliest pick-up. Then go to number 44 on the answer sheet and darken the oval of the letter next to the latest pickup time. (Pause 5 seconds)

ANSWER: Go to number 44 on your answer sheet and darken the oval for D (the letter next to the latest pickup time).

Examine sample nine again. (Pause 2-3 seconds) If the first two digits of the time next to the letter A as in "apple" form an even number, then go to number 20 on the answer sheet and darken the oval for B as in "boy." (Pause 2-3 seconds) Otherwise, go to the same number and darken the oval for D as in "dog." (Pause 5 seconds)

ANSWER: The first two digits of the time next to the letter A (10) form an even number; therefore, go to number 20 on your answer sheet and darken the oval for B.

Examine sample ten. (Pause 2-3 seconds) Circle the second and third numbers of each zip code shown. Then go on the answer sheet to the highest number circled and darken the oval for the letter C as in "cat." (Pause 2-3 seconds) Then go to the lowest number circled and fill in the letter for D as in "dog." (Pause 2-3 seconds) Then go to number 3 on the answer sheet and darken the letter for B as in "boy." (Pause 5 seconds)

ANSWER: Go to number 33 (the highest number circled) on your answer sheet and you can darken the oval for C. However, the oval for A on your answer sheet for number 33 should already be darkened. You can erase A and darken oval C or leave A darkened and do not darken C. Then go to number 21 (the lowest number circled) on your answer sheet and darken the oval for D. However, the oval for B on your answer sheet for number 21 should already be darkened. You can erase B and darken oval D or leave B darkened and do not darken D. Then go to number 3 on your answer sheet and darken the oval for B.

Examine sample ten again. (Pause 2-3 seconds) If the last zip code ends in a 0, 2, or 4, then go to number 5 on the answer sheet and darken the oval for the letter E as in "elephant." (Pause 2-3 seconds) If the last zip code ends in a 1, 3, or 5, go to number 4 and darken the oval for D as in "dog." Otherwise, go to number 16 on the answer sheet and darken the oval for A as in "apple." (Pause 5 seconds)

ANSWER: The last zip code ends in 3. Go to number 4 on your answer sheet and darken the oval for D.

POSTAL EXAM
Test 6 - Following Oral Directions
ANSWER KEY

#	Answer
1.	Ⓐ Ⓑ Ⓒ Ⓓ Ⓔ
2.	Ⓐ Ⓑ Ⓒ Ⓓ Ⓔ
3.	Ⓐ **●** Ⓒ Ⓓ Ⓔ
4.	Ⓐ Ⓑ Ⓒ **●** Ⓔ
5.	Ⓐ Ⓑ Ⓒ Ⓓ Ⓔ
6.	Ⓐ Ⓑ Ⓒ Ⓓ Ⓔ
7.	Ⓐ Ⓑ Ⓒ Ⓓ Ⓔ
8.	Ⓐ Ⓑ **●** Ⓓ Ⓔ
9.	Ⓐ **●** Ⓒ Ⓓ Ⓔ
10.	Ⓐ Ⓑ Ⓒ **●** Ⓔ
11.	Ⓐ **●** Ⓒ Ⓓ Ⓔ
12.	**●** Ⓑ Ⓒ Ⓓ Ⓔ
13.	**●** **●** Ⓒ Ⓓ Ⓔ
14.	Ⓐ Ⓑ Ⓒ Ⓓ Ⓔ
15.	Ⓐ Ⓑ Ⓒ Ⓓ Ⓔ
16.	**●** Ⓑ Ⓒ Ⓓ Ⓔ
17.	Ⓐ **●** Ⓒ Ⓓ Ⓔ
18.	Ⓐ Ⓑ **●** Ⓓ Ⓔ
19.	Ⓐ Ⓑ Ⓒ Ⓓ Ⓔ
20.	Ⓐ **●** Ⓒ Ⓓ Ⓔ
21.	Ⓐ **●** Ⓒ **●** Ⓔ
22.	Ⓐ Ⓑ Ⓒ Ⓓ Ⓔ
23.	**●** Ⓑ Ⓒ Ⓓ Ⓔ
24.	Ⓐ Ⓑ Ⓒ Ⓓ Ⓔ
25.	Ⓐ Ⓑ Ⓒ Ⓓ **●**
26.	Ⓐ Ⓑ Ⓒ Ⓓ Ⓔ
27.	**●** Ⓑ Ⓒ Ⓓ Ⓔ
28.	Ⓐ Ⓑ Ⓒ Ⓓ Ⓔ
29.	Ⓐ Ⓑ **●** Ⓓ Ⓔ
30.	Ⓐ Ⓑ **●** Ⓓ Ⓔ
31.	Ⓐ Ⓑ Ⓒ Ⓓ Ⓔ
32.	**●** Ⓑ Ⓒ Ⓓ Ⓔ
33.	**●** Ⓑ **●** Ⓓ Ⓔ
34.	Ⓐ Ⓑ Ⓒ Ⓓ Ⓔ
35.	Ⓐ Ⓑ Ⓒ Ⓓ Ⓔ
36.	Ⓐ Ⓑ Ⓒ Ⓓ Ⓔ
37.	Ⓐ Ⓑ Ⓒ Ⓓ Ⓔ
38.	Ⓐ Ⓑ Ⓒ Ⓓ Ⓔ
39.	Ⓐ Ⓑ Ⓒ Ⓓ Ⓔ
40.	Ⓐ Ⓑ **●** Ⓓ Ⓔ
41.	Ⓐ Ⓑ Ⓒ Ⓓ Ⓔ
42.	Ⓐ Ⓑ Ⓒ Ⓓ **●**
43.	Ⓐ Ⓑ Ⓒ Ⓓ Ⓔ
44.	Ⓐ Ⓑ Ⓒ **●** Ⓔ
45.	Ⓐ Ⓑ Ⓒ Ⓓ Ⓔ
46.	Ⓐ Ⓑ Ⓒ Ⓓ **●**
47.	Ⓐ Ⓑ Ⓒ Ⓓ Ⓔ
48.	Ⓐ Ⓑ Ⓒ Ⓓ Ⓔ
49.	Ⓐ Ⓑ Ⓒ Ⓓ Ⓔ
50.	Ⓐ **●** Ⓒ Ⓓ Ⓔ
51.	Ⓐ Ⓑ Ⓒ Ⓓ Ⓔ
52.	Ⓐ Ⓑ Ⓒ **●** Ⓔ
53.	Ⓐ Ⓑ Ⓒ Ⓓ Ⓔ
54.	Ⓐ Ⓑ Ⓒ Ⓓ Ⓔ
55.	Ⓐ Ⓑ Ⓒ Ⓓ Ⓔ
56.	Ⓐ Ⓑ Ⓒ Ⓓ **●**
57.	Ⓐ Ⓑ Ⓒ Ⓓ Ⓔ
58.	Ⓐ Ⓑ Ⓒ Ⓓ Ⓔ
59.	Ⓐ Ⓑ Ⓒ Ⓓ Ⓔ
60.	Ⓐ Ⓑ Ⓒ Ⓓ Ⓔ
61.	Ⓐ Ⓑ Ⓒ Ⓓ **●**
62.	Ⓐ Ⓑ Ⓒ Ⓓ Ⓔ
63.	Ⓐ Ⓑ Ⓒ Ⓓ Ⓔ
64.	Ⓐ Ⓑ Ⓒ Ⓓ Ⓔ
65.	Ⓐ Ⓑ Ⓒ Ⓓ **●**
66.	Ⓐ Ⓑ Ⓒ Ⓓ Ⓔ
67.	Ⓐ Ⓑ Ⓒ Ⓓ Ⓔ
68.	Ⓐ Ⓑ **●** Ⓓ Ⓔ
69.	Ⓐ Ⓑ Ⓒ Ⓓ Ⓔ
70.	Ⓐ Ⓑ Ⓒ Ⓓ Ⓔ
71.	Ⓐ Ⓑ Ⓒ Ⓓ Ⓔ
72.	Ⓐ Ⓑ Ⓒ Ⓓ Ⓔ
73.	Ⓐ Ⓑ Ⓒ Ⓓ Ⓔ
74.	Ⓐ Ⓑ Ⓒ Ⓓ Ⓔ
75.	Ⓐ Ⓑ Ⓒ Ⓓ Ⓔ
76.	Ⓐ Ⓑ Ⓒ Ⓓ Ⓔ
77.	Ⓐ Ⓑ Ⓒ Ⓓ Ⓔ
78.	Ⓐ Ⓑ Ⓒ Ⓓ Ⓔ
79.	Ⓐ Ⓑ Ⓒ Ⓓ Ⓔ
80.	Ⓐ Ⓑ Ⓒ Ⓓ Ⓔ
81.	Ⓐ Ⓑ Ⓒ Ⓓ Ⓔ
82.	Ⓐ Ⓑ Ⓒ Ⓓ Ⓔ
83.	Ⓐ Ⓑ Ⓒ Ⓓ Ⓔ
84.	Ⓐ Ⓑ Ⓒ Ⓓ Ⓔ
85.	Ⓐ Ⓑ Ⓒ Ⓓ Ⓔ
86.	Ⓐ Ⓑ Ⓒ Ⓓ Ⓔ
87.	Ⓐ Ⓑ Ⓒ Ⓓ Ⓔ
88.	Ⓐ Ⓑ Ⓒ Ⓓ Ⓔ
89.	Ⓐ Ⓑ Ⓒ Ⓓ Ⓔ
90.	Ⓐ Ⓑ Ⓒ Ⓓ Ⓔ
91.	Ⓐ Ⓑ Ⓒ Ⓓ Ⓔ
92.	Ⓐ Ⓑ Ⓒ Ⓓ Ⓔ
93.	Ⓐ Ⓑ Ⓒ Ⓓ Ⓔ
94.	Ⓐ Ⓑ Ⓒ Ⓓ Ⓔ
95.	Ⓐ Ⓑ Ⓒ Ⓓ Ⓔ

Answer Sheets

POSTAL EXAM
Diagnostic Test
ANSWER SHEET
Address Checking

1. Ⓐ Ⓓ
2. Ⓐ Ⓓ
3. Ⓐ Ⓓ
4. Ⓐ Ⓓ
5. Ⓐ Ⓓ
6. Ⓐ Ⓓ
7. Ⓐ Ⓓ
8. Ⓐ Ⓓ
9. Ⓐ Ⓓ
10. Ⓐ Ⓓ
11. Ⓐ Ⓓ
12. Ⓐ Ⓓ
13. Ⓐ Ⓓ
14. Ⓐ Ⓓ
15. Ⓐ Ⓓ
16. Ⓐ Ⓓ
17. Ⓐ Ⓓ
18. Ⓐ Ⓓ
19. Ⓐ Ⓓ
20. Ⓐ Ⓓ
21. Ⓐ Ⓓ
22. Ⓐ Ⓓ
23. Ⓐ Ⓓ
24. Ⓐ Ⓓ
25. Ⓐ Ⓓ
26. Ⓐ Ⓓ
27. Ⓐ Ⓓ
28. Ⓐ Ⓓ
29. Ⓐ Ⓓ
30. Ⓐ Ⓓ
31. Ⓐ Ⓓ
32. Ⓐ Ⓓ
33. Ⓐ Ⓓ

34. Ⓐ Ⓓ
35. Ⓐ Ⓓ
36. Ⓐ Ⓓ
37. Ⓐ Ⓓ
38. Ⓐ Ⓓ
39. Ⓐ Ⓓ
40. Ⓐ Ⓓ
41. Ⓐ Ⓓ
42. Ⓐ Ⓓ
43. Ⓐ Ⓓ
44. Ⓐ Ⓓ
45. Ⓐ Ⓓ
46. Ⓐ Ⓓ
47. Ⓐ Ⓓ
48. Ⓐ Ⓓ
49. Ⓐ Ⓓ
50. Ⓐ Ⓓ
51. Ⓐ Ⓓ
52. Ⓐ Ⓓ
53. Ⓐ Ⓓ
54. Ⓐ Ⓓ
55. Ⓐ Ⓓ
56. Ⓐ Ⓓ
57. Ⓐ Ⓓ
58. Ⓐ Ⓓ
59. Ⓐ Ⓓ
60. Ⓐ Ⓓ
61. Ⓐ Ⓓ
62. Ⓐ Ⓓ
63. Ⓐ Ⓓ
64. Ⓐ Ⓓ
65. Ⓐ Ⓓ
66. Ⓐ Ⓓ

67. Ⓐ Ⓓ
68. Ⓐ Ⓓ
69. Ⓐ Ⓓ
70. Ⓐ Ⓓ
71. Ⓐ Ⓓ
72. Ⓐ Ⓓ
73. Ⓐ Ⓓ
74. Ⓐ Ⓓ
75. Ⓐ Ⓓ
76. Ⓐ Ⓓ
77. Ⓐ Ⓓ
78. Ⓐ Ⓓ
79. Ⓐ Ⓓ
80. Ⓐ Ⓓ
81. Ⓐ Ⓓ
82. Ⓐ Ⓓ
83. Ⓐ Ⓓ
84. Ⓐ Ⓓ
85. Ⓐ Ⓓ
86. Ⓐ Ⓓ
87. Ⓐ Ⓓ
88. Ⓐ Ⓓ
89. Ⓐ Ⓓ
90. Ⓐ Ⓓ
91. Ⓐ Ⓓ
92. Ⓐ Ⓓ
93. Ⓐ Ⓓ
94. Ⓐ Ⓓ
95. Ⓐ Ⓓ

POSTAL EXAM
Diagnostic Test
ANSWER SHEET
Memory for Addresses

1. (A) (B) (C) (D) (E)
2. (A) (B) (C) (D) (E)
3. (A) (B) (C) (D) (E)
4. (A) (B) (C) (D) (E)
5. (A) (B) (C) (D) (E)
6. (A) (B) (C) (D) (E)
7. (A) (B) (C) (D) (E)
8. (A) (B) (C) (D) (E)
9. (A) (B) (C) (D) (E)
10. (A) (B) (C) (D) (E)
11. (A) (B) (C) (D) (E)
12. (A) (B) (C) (D) (E)
13. (A) (B) (C) (D) (E)
14. (A) (B) (C) (D) (E)
15. (A) (B) (C) (D) (E)
16. (A) (B) (C) (D) (E)
17. (A) (B) (C) (D) (E)
18. (A) (B) (C) (D) (E)
19. (A) (B) (C) (D) (E)
20. (A) (B) (C) (D) (E)
21. (A) (B) (C) (D) (E)
22. (A) (B) (C) (D) (E)
23. (A) (B) (C) (D) (E)
24. (A) (B) (C) (D) (E)
25. (A) (B) (C) (D) (E)
26. (A) (B) (C) (D) (E)
27. (A) (B) (C) (D) (E)
28. (A) (B) (C) (D) (E)
29. (A) (B) (C) (D) (E)
30. (A) (B) (C) (D) (E)
31. (A) (B) (C) (D) (E)
32. (A) (B) (C) (D) (E)
33. (A) (B) (C) (D) (E)

34. (A) (B) (C) (D) (E)
35. (A) (B) (C) (D) (E)
36. (A) (B) (C) (D) (E)
37. (A) (B) (C) (D) (E)
38. (A) (B) (C) (D) (E)
39. (A) (B) (C) (D) (E)
40. (A) (B) (C) (D) (E)
41. (A) (B) (C) (D) (E)
42. (A) (B) (C) (D) (E)
43. (A) (B) (C) (D) (E)
44. (A) (B) (C) (D) (E)
45. (A) (B) (C) (D) (F)
46. (A) (B) (C) (D) (E)
47. (A) (B) (C) (D) (E)
48. (A) (B) (C) (D) (E)
49. (A) (B) (C) (D) (E)
50. (A) (B) (C) (D) (E)
51. (A) (B) (C) (D) (E)
52. (A) (B) (C) (D) (E)
53. (A) (B) (C) (D) (E)
54. (A) (B) (C) (D) (E)
55. (A) (B) (C) (D) (E)
56. (A) (B) (C) (D) (E)
57. (A) (B) (C) (D) (E)
58. (A) (B) (C) (D) (E)
59. (A) (B) (C) (D) (E)
60. (A) (B) (C) (D) (E)
61. (A) (B) (C) (D) (E)
62. (A) (B) (C) (D) (E)
63. (A) (B) (C) (D) (E)
64. (A) (B) (C) (D) (E)
65. (A) (B) (C) (D) (E)
66. (A) (B) (C) (D) (E)

67. (A) (B) (C) (D) (E)
68. (A) (B) (C) (D) (E)
69. (A) (B) (C) (D) (E)
70. (A) (B) (C) (D) (E)
71. (A) (B) (C) (D) (E)
72. (A) (B) (C) (D) (E)
73. (A) (B) (C) (D) (E)
74. (A) (B) (C) (D) (E)
75. (A) (B) (C) (D) (E)
76. (A) (B) (C) (D) (E)
77. (A) (B) (C) (D) (E)
78. (A) (B) (C) (D) (E)
79. (A) (B) (C) (D) (E)
80. (A) (B) (C) (D) (E)
81. (A) (B) (C) (D) (E)
82. (A) (B) (C) (D) (E)
83. (A) (B) (C) (D) (E)
84. (A) (B) (C) (D) (E)
85. (A) (B) (C) (D) (E)
86. (A) (B) (C) (D) (E)
87. (A) (B) (C) (D) (E)
88. (A) (B) (C) (D) (E)

POSTAL EXAM
Diagnostic Test
ANSWER SHEET
Number Series

1. (A) (B) (C) (D) (E)
2. (A) (B) (C) (D) (E)
3. (A) (B) (C) (D) (E)
4. (A) (B) (C) (D) (E)
5. (A) (B) (C) (D) (E)
6. (A) (B) (C) (D) (E)
7. (A) (B) (C) (D) (E)
8. (A) (B) (C) (D) (E)
9. (A) (B) (C) (D) (E)
10. (A) (B) (C) (D) (E)
11. (A) (B) (C) (D) (E)
12. (A) (B) (C) (D) (E)

13. (A) (B) (C) (D) (E)
14. (A) (B) (C) (D) (E)
15. (A) (B) (C) (D) (E)
16. (A) (B) (C) (D) (E)
17. (A) (B) (C) (D) (E)
18. (A) (B) (C) (D) (E)
19. (A) (B) (C) (D) (E)
20. (A) (B) (C) (D) (E)
21. (A) (B) (C) (D) (E)
22. (A) (B) (C) (D) (E)
23. (A) (B) (C) (D) (E)
24. (A) (B) (C) (D) (E)

POSTAL EXAM
Diagnostic Test
ANSWER SHEET
Following Oral Directions

1. Ⓐ Ⓑ Ⓒ Ⓓ Ⓔ
2. Ⓐ Ⓑ Ⓒ Ⓓ Ⓔ
3. Ⓐ Ⓑ Ⓒ Ⓓ Ⓔ
4. Ⓐ Ⓑ Ⓒ Ⓓ Ⓔ
5. Ⓐ Ⓑ Ⓒ Ⓓ Ⓔ
6. Ⓐ Ⓑ Ⓒ Ⓓ Ⓔ
7. Ⓐ Ⓑ Ⓒ Ⓓ Ⓔ
8. Ⓐ Ⓑ Ⓒ Ⓓ Ⓔ
9. Ⓐ Ⓑ Ⓒ Ⓓ Ⓔ
10. Ⓐ Ⓑ Ⓒ Ⓓ Ⓔ
11. Ⓐ Ⓑ Ⓒ Ⓓ Ⓔ
12. Ⓐ Ⓑ Ⓒ Ⓓ Ⓔ
13. Ⓐ Ⓑ Ⓒ Ⓓ Ⓔ
14. Ⓐ Ⓑ Ⓒ Ⓓ Ⓔ
15. Ⓐ Ⓑ Ⓒ Ⓓ Ⓔ
16. Ⓐ Ⓑ Ⓒ Ⓓ Ⓔ
17. Ⓐ Ⓑ Ⓒ Ⓓ Ⓔ
18. Ⓐ Ⓑ Ⓒ Ⓓ Ⓔ
19. Ⓐ Ⓑ Ⓒ Ⓓ Ⓔ
20. Ⓐ Ⓑ Ⓒ Ⓓ Ⓔ
21. Ⓐ Ⓑ Ⓒ Ⓓ Ⓔ
22. Ⓐ Ⓑ Ⓒ Ⓓ Ⓔ
23. Ⓐ Ⓑ Ⓒ Ⓓ Ⓔ
24. Ⓐ Ⓑ Ⓒ Ⓓ Ⓔ
25. Ⓐ Ⓑ Ⓒ Ⓓ Ⓔ
26. Ⓐ Ⓑ Ⓒ Ⓓ Ⓔ
27. Ⓐ Ⓑ Ⓒ Ⓓ Ⓔ
28. Ⓐ Ⓑ Ⓒ Ⓓ Ⓔ
29. Ⓐ Ⓑ Ⓒ Ⓓ Ⓔ
30. Ⓐ Ⓑ Ⓒ Ⓓ Ⓔ
31. Ⓐ Ⓑ Ⓒ Ⓓ Ⓔ
32. Ⓐ Ⓑ Ⓒ Ⓓ Ⓔ
33. Ⓐ Ⓑ Ⓒ Ⓓ Ⓔ

34. Ⓐ Ⓑ Ⓒ Ⓓ Ⓔ
35. Ⓐ Ⓑ Ⓒ Ⓓ Ⓔ
36. Ⓐ Ⓑ Ⓒ Ⓓ Ⓔ
37. Ⓐ Ⓑ Ⓒ Ⓓ Ⓔ
38. Ⓐ Ⓑ Ⓒ Ⓓ Ⓔ
39. Ⓐ Ⓑ Ⓒ Ⓓ Ⓔ
40. Ⓐ Ⓑ Ⓒ Ⓓ Ⓔ
41. Ⓐ Ⓑ Ⓒ Ⓓ Ⓔ
42. Ⓐ Ⓑ Ⓒ Ⓓ Ⓔ
43. Ⓐ Ⓑ Ⓒ Ⓓ Ⓔ
44. Ⓐ Ⓑ Ⓒ Ⓓ Ⓔ
45. Ⓐ Ⓑ Ⓒ Ⓓ Ⓔ
46. Ⓐ Ⓑ Ⓒ Ⓓ Ⓔ
47. Ⓐ Ⓑ Ⓒ Ⓓ Ⓔ
48. Ⓐ Ⓑ Ⓒ Ⓓ Ⓔ
49. Ⓐ Ⓑ Ⓒ Ⓓ Ⓔ
50. Ⓐ Ⓑ Ⓒ Ⓓ Ⓔ
51. Ⓐ Ⓑ Ⓒ Ⓓ Ⓔ
52. Ⓐ Ⓑ Ⓒ Ⓓ Ⓔ
53. Ⓐ Ⓑ Ⓒ Ⓓ Ⓔ
54. Ⓐ Ⓑ Ⓒ Ⓓ Ⓔ
55. Ⓐ Ⓑ Ⓒ Ⓓ Ⓔ
56. Ⓐ Ⓑ Ⓒ Ⓓ Ⓔ
57. Ⓐ Ⓑ Ⓒ Ⓓ Ⓔ
58. Ⓐ Ⓑ Ⓒ Ⓓ Ⓔ
59. Ⓐ Ⓑ Ⓒ Ⓓ Ⓔ
60. Ⓐ Ⓑ Ⓒ Ⓓ Ⓔ
61. Ⓐ Ⓑ Ⓒ Ⓓ Ⓔ
62. Ⓐ Ⓑ Ⓒ Ⓓ Ⓔ
63. Ⓐ Ⓑ Ⓒ Ⓓ Ⓔ
64. Ⓐ Ⓑ Ⓒ Ⓓ Ⓔ
65. Ⓐ Ⓑ Ⓒ Ⓓ Ⓔ
66. Ⓐ Ⓑ Ⓒ Ⓓ Ⓔ

67. Ⓐ Ⓑ Ⓒ Ⓓ Ⓔ
68. Ⓐ Ⓑ Ⓒ Ⓓ Ⓔ
69. Ⓐ Ⓑ Ⓒ Ⓓ Ⓔ
70. Ⓐ Ⓑ Ⓒ Ⓓ Ⓔ
71. Ⓐ Ⓑ Ⓒ Ⓓ Ⓔ
72. Ⓐ Ⓑ Ⓒ Ⓓ Ⓔ
73. Ⓐ Ⓑ Ⓒ Ⓓ Ⓔ
74. Ⓐ Ⓑ Ⓒ Ⓓ Ⓔ
75. Ⓐ Ⓑ Ⓒ Ⓓ Ⓔ
76. Ⓐ Ⓑ Ⓒ Ⓓ Ⓔ
77. Ⓐ Ⓑ Ⓒ Ⓓ Ⓔ
78. Ⓐ Ⓑ Ⓒ Ⓓ Ⓔ
79. Ⓐ Ⓑ Ⓒ Ⓓ Ⓔ
80. Ⓐ Ⓑ Ⓒ Ⓓ Ⓔ
81. Ⓐ Ⓑ Ⓒ Ⓓ Ⓔ
82. Ⓐ Ⓑ Ⓒ Ⓓ Ⓔ
83. Ⓐ Ⓑ Ⓒ Ⓓ Ⓔ
84. Ⓐ Ⓑ Ⓒ Ⓓ Ⓔ
85. Ⓐ Ⓑ Ⓒ Ⓓ Ⓔ
86. Ⓐ Ⓑ Ⓒ Ⓓ Ⓔ
87. Ⓐ Ⓑ Ⓒ Ⓓ Ⓔ
88. Ⓐ Ⓑ Ⓒ Ⓓ Ⓔ
89. Ⓐ Ⓑ Ⓒ Ⓓ Ⓔ
90. Ⓐ Ⓑ Ⓒ Ⓓ Ⓔ
91. Ⓐ Ⓑ Ⓒ Ⓓ Ⓔ
92. Ⓐ Ⓑ Ⓒ Ⓓ Ⓔ
93. Ⓐ Ⓑ Ⓒ Ⓓ Ⓔ
94. Ⓐ Ⓑ Ⓒ Ⓓ Ⓔ
95. Ⓐ Ⓑ Ⓒ Ⓓ Ⓔ
96. Ⓐ Ⓑ Ⓒ Ⓓ Ⓔ
97. Ⓐ Ⓑ Ⓒ Ⓓ Ⓔ
98. Ⓐ Ⓑ Ⓒ Ⓓ Ⓔ

POSTAL EXAM
Test 1
ANSWER SHEET
Address Checking

1. Ⓐ Ⓓ
2. Ⓐ Ⓓ
3. Ⓐ Ⓓ
4. Ⓐ Ⓓ
5. Ⓐ Ⓓ
6. Ⓐ Ⓓ
7. Ⓐ Ⓓ
8. Ⓐ Ⓓ
9. Ⓐ Ⓓ
10. Ⓐ Ⓓ
11. Ⓐ Ⓓ
12. Ⓐ Ⓓ
13. Ⓐ Ⓓ
14. Ⓐ Ⓓ
15. Ⓐ Ⓓ
16. Ⓐ Ⓓ
17. Ⓐ Ⓓ
18. Ⓐ Ⓓ
19. Ⓐ Ⓓ
20. Ⓐ Ⓓ
21. Ⓐ Ⓓ
22. Ⓐ Ⓓ
23. Ⓐ Ⓓ
24. Ⓐ Ⓓ
25. Ⓐ Ⓓ
26. Ⓐ Ⓓ
27. Ⓐ Ⓓ
28. Ⓐ Ⓓ
29. Ⓐ Ⓓ
30. Ⓐ Ⓓ
31. Ⓐ Ⓓ
32. Ⓐ Ⓓ
33. Ⓐ Ⓓ

34. Ⓐ Ⓓ
35. Ⓐ Ⓓ
36. Ⓐ Ⓓ
37. Ⓐ Ⓓ
38. Ⓐ Ⓓ
39. Ⓐ Ⓓ
40. Ⓐ Ⓓ
41. Ⓐ Ⓓ
42. Ⓐ Ⓓ
43. Ⓐ Ⓓ
44. Ⓐ Ⓓ
45. Ⓐ Ⓓ
46. Ⓐ Ⓓ
47. Ⓐ Ⓓ
48. Ⓐ Ⓓ
49. Ⓐ Ⓓ
50. Ⓐ Ⓓ
51. Ⓐ Ⓓ
52. Ⓐ Ⓓ
53. Ⓐ Ⓓ
54. Ⓐ Ⓓ
55. Ⓐ Ⓓ
56. Ⓐ Ⓓ
57. Ⓐ Ⓓ
58. Ⓐ Ⓓ
59. Ⓐ Ⓓ
60. Ⓐ Ⓓ
61. Ⓐ Ⓓ
62. Ⓐ Ⓓ
63. Ⓐ Ⓓ
64. Ⓐ Ⓓ
65. Ⓐ Ⓓ
66. Ⓐ Ⓓ

67. Ⓐ Ⓓ
68. Ⓐ Ⓓ
69. Ⓐ Ⓓ
70. Ⓐ Ⓓ
71. Ⓐ Ⓓ
72. Ⓐ Ⓓ
73. Ⓐ Ⓓ
74. Ⓐ Ⓓ
75. Ⓐ Ⓓ
76. Ⓐ Ⓓ
77. Ⓐ Ⓓ
78. Ⓐ Ⓓ
79. Ⓐ Ⓓ
80. Ⓐ Ⓓ
81. Ⓐ Ⓓ
82. Ⓐ Ⓓ
83. Ⓐ Ⓓ
84. Ⓐ Ⓓ
85. Ⓐ Ⓓ
86. Ⓐ Ⓓ
87. Ⓐ Ⓓ
88. Ⓐ Ⓓ
89. Ⓐ Ⓓ
90. Ⓐ Ⓓ
91. Ⓐ Ⓓ
92. Ⓐ Ⓓ
93. Ⓐ Ⓓ
94. Ⓐ Ⓓ
95. Ⓐ Ⓓ

POSTAL EXAM
Test 1
ANSWER SHEET
Memory for Addresses

1. Ⓐ Ⓑ Ⓒ Ⓓ Ⓔ
2. Ⓐ Ⓑ Ⓒ Ⓓ Ⓔ
3. Ⓐ Ⓑ Ⓒ Ⓓ Ⓔ
4. Ⓐ Ⓑ Ⓒ Ⓓ Ⓔ
5. Ⓐ Ⓑ Ⓒ Ⓓ Ⓔ
6. Ⓐ Ⓑ Ⓒ Ⓓ Ⓔ
7. Ⓐ Ⓑ Ⓒ Ⓓ Ⓔ
8. Ⓐ Ⓑ Ⓒ Ⓓ Ⓔ
9   Ⓐ Ⓑ Ⓒ Ⓓ Ⓔ
10. Ⓐ Ⓑ Ⓒ Ⓓ Ⓔ
11. Ⓐ Ⓑ Ⓒ Ⓓ Ⓔ
12. Ⓐ Ⓑ Ⓒ Ⓓ Ⓔ
13. Ⓐ Ⓑ Ⓒ Ⓓ Ⓔ
14. Ⓐ Ⓑ Ⓒ Ⓓ Ⓔ
15. Ⓐ Ⓑ Ⓒ Ⓓ Ⓔ
16. Ⓐ Ⓑ Ⓒ Ⓓ Ⓔ
17. Ⓐ Ⓑ Ⓒ Ⓓ Ⓔ
18. Ⓐ Ⓑ Ⓒ Ⓓ Ⓔ
19. Ⓐ Ⓑ Ⓒ Ⓓ Ⓔ
20. Ⓐ Ⓑ Ⓒ Ⓓ Ⓔ
21. Ⓐ Ⓑ Ⓒ Ⓓ Ⓔ
22. Ⓐ Ⓑ Ⓒ Ⓓ Ⓔ
23. Ⓐ Ⓑ Ⓒ Ⓓ Ⓔ
24. Ⓐ Ⓑ Ⓒ Ⓓ Ⓔ
25. Ⓐ Ⓑ Ⓒ Ⓓ Ⓔ
26. Ⓐ Ⓑ Ⓒ Ⓓ Ⓔ
27. Ⓐ Ⓑ Ⓒ Ⓓ Ⓔ
28. Ⓐ Ⓑ Ⓒ Ⓓ Ⓔ
29. Ⓐ Ⓑ Ⓒ Ⓓ Ⓔ
30. Ⓐ Ⓑ Ⓒ Ⓓ Ⓔ
31. Ⓐ Ⓑ Ⓒ Ⓓ Ⓔ
32. Ⓐ Ⓑ Ⓒ Ⓓ Ⓔ
33. Ⓐ Ⓑ Ⓒ Ⓓ Ⓔ

34. Ⓐ Ⓑ Ⓒ Ⓓ Ⓔ
35. Ⓐ Ⓑ Ⓒ Ⓓ Ⓔ
36. Ⓐ Ⓑ Ⓒ Ⓓ Ⓔ
37. Ⓐ Ⓑ Ⓒ Ⓓ Ⓔ
38. Ⓐ Ⓑ Ⓒ Ⓓ Ⓔ
39. Ⓐ Ⓑ Ⓒ Ⓓ Ⓔ
40. Ⓐ Ⓑ Ⓒ Ⓓ Ⓔ
41. Ⓐ Ⓑ Ⓒ Ⓓ Ⓔ
42. Ⓐ Ⓑ Ⓒ Ⓓ Ⓔ
43. Ⓐ Ⓑ Ⓒ Ⓓ Ⓔ
44. Ⓐ Ⓑ Ⓒ Ⓓ Ⓔ
45. Ⓐ Ⓑ Ⓒ Ⓓ Ⓔ
46. Ⓐ Ⓑ Ⓒ Ⓓ Ⓔ
47. Ⓐ Ⓑ Ⓒ Ⓓ Ⓔ
48. Ⓐ Ⓑ Ⓒ Ⓓ Ⓔ
49. Ⓐ Ⓑ Ⓒ Ⓓ Ⓔ
50. Ⓐ Ⓑ Ⓒ Ⓓ Ⓔ
51. Ⓐ Ⓑ Ⓒ Ⓓ Ⓔ
52. Ⓐ Ⓑ Ⓒ Ⓓ Ⓔ
53. Ⓐ Ⓑ Ⓒ Ⓓ Ⓔ
54. Ⓐ Ⓑ Ⓒ Ⓓ Ⓔ
55. Ⓐ Ⓑ Ⓒ Ⓓ Ⓔ
56. Ⓐ Ⓑ Ⓒ Ⓓ Ⓔ
57. Ⓐ Ⓑ Ⓒ Ⓓ Ⓔ
58. Ⓐ Ⓑ Ⓒ Ⓓ Ⓔ
59. Ⓐ Ⓑ Ⓒ Ⓓ Ⓔ
60. Ⓐ Ⓑ Ⓒ Ⓓ Ⓔ
61. Ⓐ Ⓑ Ⓒ Ⓓ Ⓔ
62. Ⓐ Ⓑ Ⓒ Ⓓ Ⓔ
63. Ⓐ Ⓑ Ⓒ Ⓓ Ⓔ
64. Ⓐ Ⓑ Ⓒ Ⓓ Ⓔ
65. Ⓐ Ⓑ Ⓒ Ⓓ Ⓔ
66. Ⓐ Ⓑ Ⓒ Ⓓ Ⓔ

67. Ⓐ Ⓑ Ⓒ Ⓓ Ⓔ
68. Ⓐ Ⓑ Ⓒ Ⓓ Ⓔ
69. Ⓐ Ⓑ Ⓒ Ⓓ Ⓔ
70. Ⓐ Ⓑ Ⓒ Ⓓ Ⓔ
71. Ⓐ Ⓑ Ⓒ Ⓓ Ⓔ
72. Ⓐ Ⓑ Ⓒ Ⓓ Ⓔ
73. Ⓐ Ⓑ Ⓒ Ⓓ Ⓔ
74. Ⓐ Ⓑ Ⓒ Ⓓ Ⓔ
75. Ⓐ Ⓑ Ⓒ Ⓓ Ⓔ
76. Ⓐ Ⓑ Ⓒ Ⓓ Ⓔ
77. Ⓐ Ⓑ Ⓒ Ⓓ Ⓔ
78. Ⓐ Ⓑ Ⓒ Ⓓ Ⓔ
79. Ⓐ Ⓑ Ⓒ Ⓓ Ⓔ
80. Ⓐ Ⓑ Ⓒ Ⓓ Ⓔ
81. Ⓐ Ⓑ Ⓒ Ⓓ Ⓔ
82. Ⓐ Ⓑ Ⓒ Ⓓ Ⓔ
83. Ⓐ Ⓑ Ⓒ Ⓓ Ⓔ
84. Ⓐ Ⓑ Ⓒ Ⓓ Ⓔ
85. Ⓐ Ⓑ Ⓒ Ⓓ Ⓔ
86. Ⓐ Ⓑ Ⓒ Ⓓ Ⓔ
87. Ⓐ Ⓑ Ⓒ Ⓓ Ⓔ
88. Ⓐ Ⓑ Ⓒ Ⓓ Ⓔ

POSTAL EXAM
Test 1
ANSWER SHEET
Number Series

1. Ⓐ Ⓑ Ⓒ Ⓓ Ⓔ
2. Ⓐ Ⓑ Ⓒ Ⓓ Ⓔ
3. Ⓐ Ⓑ Ⓒ Ⓓ Ⓔ
4. Ⓐ Ⓑ Ⓒ Ⓓ Ⓔ
5. Ⓐ Ⓑ Ⓒ Ⓓ Ⓔ
6. Ⓐ Ⓑ Ⓒ Ⓓ Ⓔ
7. Ⓐ Ⓑ Ⓒ Ⓓ Ⓔ
8. Ⓐ Ⓑ Ⓒ Ⓓ Ⓔ
9. Ⓐ Ⓑ Ⓒ Ⓓ Ⓔ
10. Ⓐ Ⓑ Ⓒ Ⓓ Ⓔ
11. Ⓐ Ⓑ Ⓒ Ⓓ Ⓔ
12. Ⓐ Ⓑ Ⓒ Ⓓ Ⓔ

13. Ⓐ Ⓑ Ⓒ Ⓓ Ⓔ
14. Ⓐ Ⓑ Ⓒ Ⓓ Ⓔ
15. Ⓐ Ⓑ Ⓒ Ⓓ Ⓔ
16. Ⓐ Ⓑ Ⓒ Ⓓ Ⓔ
17. Ⓐ Ⓑ Ⓒ Ⓓ Ⓔ
18. Ⓐ Ⓑ Ⓒ Ⓓ Ⓔ
19. Ⓐ Ⓑ Ⓒ Ⓓ Ⓔ
20. Ⓐ Ⓑ Ⓒ Ⓓ Ⓔ
21. Ⓐ Ⓑ Ⓒ Ⓓ Ⓔ
22. Ⓐ Ⓑ Ⓒ Ⓓ Ⓔ
23. Ⓐ Ⓑ Ⓒ Ⓓ Ⓔ
24. Ⓐ Ⓑ Ⓒ Ⓓ Ⓔ

POSTAL EXAM
Test 1
ANSWER SHEET
Following Oral Directions

1. Ⓐ Ⓑ Ⓒ Ⓓ Ⓔ
2. Ⓐ Ⓑ Ⓒ Ⓓ Ⓔ
3. Ⓐ Ⓑ Ⓒ Ⓓ Ⓔ
4. Ⓐ Ⓑ Ⓒ Ⓓ Ⓔ
5. Ⓐ Ⓑ Ⓒ Ⓓ Ⓔ
6. Ⓐ Ⓑ Ⓒ Ⓓ Ⓔ
7. Ⓐ Ⓑ Ⓒ Ⓓ Ⓔ
8. Ⓐ Ⓑ Ⓒ Ⓓ Ⓔ
9. Ⓐ Ⓑ Ⓒ Ⓓ Ⓔ
10. Ⓐ Ⓑ Ⓒ Ⓓ Ⓔ
11. Ⓐ Ⓑ Ⓒ Ⓓ Ⓔ
12. Ⓐ Ⓑ Ⓒ Ⓓ Ⓔ
13. Ⓐ Ⓑ Ⓒ Ⓓ Ⓔ
14. Ⓐ Ⓑ Ⓒ Ⓓ Ⓔ
15. Ⓐ Ⓑ Ⓒ Ⓓ Ⓔ
16. Ⓐ Ⓑ Ⓒ Ⓓ Ⓔ
17. Ⓐ Ⓑ Ⓒ Ⓓ Ⓔ
18. Ⓐ Ⓑ Ⓒ Ⓓ Ⓔ
19. Ⓐ Ⓑ Ⓒ Ⓓ Ⓔ
20. Ⓐ Ⓑ Ⓒ Ⓓ Ⓔ
21. Ⓐ Ⓑ Ⓒ Ⓓ Ⓔ
22. Ⓐ Ⓑ Ⓒ Ⓓ Ⓔ
23. Ⓐ Ⓑ Ⓒ Ⓓ Ⓔ
24. Ⓐ Ⓑ Ⓒ Ⓓ Ⓔ
25. Ⓐ Ⓑ Ⓒ Ⓓ Ⓔ
26. Ⓐ Ⓑ Ⓒ Ⓓ Ⓔ
27. Ⓐ Ⓑ Ⓒ Ⓓ Ⓔ
28. Ⓐ Ⓑ Ⓒ Ⓓ Ⓔ
29. Ⓐ Ⓑ Ⓒ Ⓓ Ⓔ
30. Ⓐ Ⓑ Ⓒ Ⓓ Ⓔ
31. Ⓐ Ⓑ Ⓒ Ⓓ Ⓔ
32. Ⓐ Ⓑ Ⓒ Ⓓ Ⓔ
33. Ⓐ Ⓑ Ⓒ Ⓓ Ⓔ

34. Ⓐ Ⓑ Ⓒ Ⓓ Ⓔ
35. Ⓐ Ⓑ Ⓒ Ⓓ Ⓔ
36. Ⓐ Ⓑ Ⓒ Ⓓ Ⓔ
37. Ⓐ Ⓑ Ⓒ Ⓓ Ⓔ
38. Ⓐ Ⓑ Ⓒ Ⓓ Ⓔ
39. Ⓐ Ⓑ Ⓒ Ⓓ Ⓔ
40. Ⓐ Ⓑ Ⓒ Ⓓ Ⓔ
41. Ⓐ Ⓑ Ⓒ Ⓓ Ⓔ
42. Ⓐ Ⓑ Ⓒ Ⓓ Ⓔ
43. Ⓐ Ⓑ Ⓒ Ⓓ Ⓔ
44. Ⓐ Ⓑ Ⓒ Ⓓ Ⓔ
45. Ⓐ Ⓑ Ⓒ Ⓓ Ⓔ
46. Ⓐ Ⓑ Ⓒ Ⓓ Ⓔ
47. Ⓐ Ⓑ Ⓒ Ⓓ Ⓔ
48. Ⓐ Ⓑ Ⓒ Ⓓ Ⓔ
49. Ⓐ Ⓑ Ⓒ Ⓓ Ⓔ
50. Ⓐ Ⓑ Ⓒ Ⓓ Ⓔ
51. Ⓐ Ⓑ Ⓒ Ⓓ Ⓔ
52. Ⓐ Ⓑ Ⓒ Ⓓ Ⓔ
53. Ⓐ Ⓑ Ⓒ Ⓓ Ⓔ
54. Ⓐ Ⓑ Ⓒ Ⓓ Ⓔ
55. Ⓐ Ⓑ Ⓒ Ⓓ Ⓔ
56. Ⓐ Ⓑ Ⓒ Ⓓ Ⓔ
57. Ⓐ Ⓑ Ⓒ Ⓓ Ⓔ
58. Ⓐ Ⓑ Ⓒ Ⓓ Ⓔ
59. Ⓐ Ⓑ Ⓒ Ⓓ Ⓔ
60. Ⓐ Ⓑ Ⓒ Ⓓ Ⓔ
61. Ⓐ Ⓑ Ⓒ Ⓓ Ⓔ
62. Ⓐ Ⓑ Ⓒ Ⓓ Ⓔ
63. Ⓐ Ⓑ Ⓒ Ⓓ Ⓔ
64. Ⓐ Ⓑ Ⓒ Ⓓ Ⓔ
65. Ⓐ Ⓑ Ⓒ Ⓓ Ⓔ
66. Ⓐ Ⓑ Ⓒ Ⓓ Ⓔ

67. Ⓐ Ⓑ Ⓒ Ⓓ Ⓔ
68. Ⓐ Ⓑ Ⓒ Ⓓ Ⓔ
69. Ⓐ Ⓑ Ⓒ Ⓓ Ⓔ
70. Ⓐ Ⓑ Ⓒ Ⓓ Ⓔ
71. Ⓐ Ⓑ Ⓒ Ⓓ Ⓔ
72. Ⓐ Ⓑ Ⓒ Ⓓ Ⓔ
73. Ⓐ Ⓑ Ⓒ Ⓓ Ⓔ
74. Ⓐ Ⓑ Ⓒ Ⓓ Ⓔ
75. Ⓐ Ⓑ Ⓒ Ⓓ Ⓔ
76. Ⓐ Ⓑ Ⓒ Ⓓ Ⓔ
77. Ⓐ Ⓑ Ⓒ Ⓓ Ⓔ
78. Ⓐ Ⓑ Ⓒ Ⓓ Ⓔ
79. Ⓐ Ⓑ Ⓒ Ⓓ Ⓔ
80. Ⓐ Ⓑ Ⓒ Ⓓ Ⓔ
81. Ⓐ Ⓑ Ⓒ Ⓓ Ⓔ
82. Ⓐ Ⓑ Ⓒ Ⓓ Ⓔ
83. Ⓐ Ⓑ Ⓒ Ⓓ Ⓔ
84. Ⓐ Ⓑ Ⓒ Ⓓ Ⓔ
85. Ⓐ Ⓑ Ⓒ Ⓓ Ⓔ
86. Ⓐ Ⓑ Ⓒ Ⓓ Ⓔ
87. Ⓐ Ⓑ Ⓒ Ⓓ Ⓔ
88. Ⓐ Ⓑ Ⓒ Ⓓ Ⓔ
89. Ⓐ Ⓑ Ⓒ Ⓓ Ⓔ
90. Ⓐ Ⓑ Ⓒ Ⓓ Ⓔ
91. Ⓐ Ⓑ Ⓒ Ⓓ Ⓔ
92. Ⓐ Ⓑ Ⓒ Ⓓ Ⓔ
93. Ⓐ Ⓑ Ⓒ Ⓓ Ⓔ
94. Ⓐ Ⓑ Ⓒ Ⓓ Ⓔ
95. Ⓐ Ⓑ Ⓒ Ⓓ Ⓔ
96. Ⓐ Ⓑ Ⓒ Ⓓ Ⓔ
97. Ⓐ Ⓑ Ⓒ Ⓓ Ⓔ
98. Ⓐ Ⓑ Ⓒ Ⓓ Ⓔ

POSTAL EXAM
Test 2
ANSWER SHEET
Address Checking

1. Ⓐ Ⓓ
2. Ⓐ Ⓓ
3. Ⓐ Ⓓ
4. Ⓐ Ⓓ
5. Ⓐ Ⓓ
6. Ⓐ Ⓓ
7. Ⓐ Ⓓ
8. Ⓐ Ⓓ
9. Ⓐ Ⓓ
10. Ⓐ Ⓓ
11. Ⓐ Ⓓ
12. Ⓐ Ⓓ
13. Ⓐ Ⓓ
14. Ⓐ Ⓓ
15. Ⓐ Ⓓ
16. Ⓐ Ⓓ
17. Ⓐ Ⓓ
18. Ⓐ Ⓓ
19. Ⓐ Ⓓ
20. Ⓐ Ⓓ
21. Ⓐ Ⓓ
22. Ⓐ Ⓓ
23. Ⓐ Ⓓ
24. Ⓐ Ⓓ
25. Ⓐ Ⓓ
26. Ⓐ Ⓓ
27. Ⓐ Ⓓ
28. Ⓐ Ⓓ
29. Ⓐ Ⓓ
30. Ⓐ Ⓓ
31. Ⓐ Ⓓ
32. Ⓐ Ⓓ
33. Ⓐ Ⓓ

34. Ⓐ Ⓓ
35. Ⓐ Ⓓ
36. Ⓐ Ⓓ
37. Ⓐ Ⓓ
38. Ⓐ Ⓓ
39. Ⓐ Ⓓ
40. Ⓐ Ⓓ
41. Ⓐ Ⓓ
42. Ⓐ Ⓓ
43. Ⓐ Ⓓ
44. Ⓐ Ⓓ
45. Ⓐ Ⓓ
46. Ⓐ Ⓓ
47. Ⓐ Ⓓ
48. Ⓐ Ⓓ
49. Ⓐ Ⓓ
50. Ⓐ Ⓓ
51. Ⓐ Ⓓ
52. Ⓐ Ⓓ
53. Ⓐ Ⓓ
54. Ⓐ Ⓓ
55. Ⓐ Ⓓ
56. Ⓐ Ⓓ
57. Ⓐ Ⓓ
58. Ⓐ Ⓓ
59. Ⓐ Ⓓ
60. Ⓐ Ⓓ
61. Ⓐ Ⓓ
62. Ⓐ Ⓓ
63. Ⓐ Ⓓ
64. Ⓐ Ⓓ
65. Ⓐ Ⓓ
66. Ⓐ Ⓓ

67. Ⓐ Ⓓ
68. Ⓐ Ⓓ
69. Ⓐ Ⓓ
70. Ⓐ Ⓓ
71. Ⓐ Ⓓ
72. Ⓐ Ⓓ
73. Ⓐ Ⓓ
74. Ⓐ Ⓓ
75. Ⓐ Ⓓ
76. Ⓐ Ⓓ
77. Ⓐ Ⓓ
78. Ⓐ Ⓓ
79. Ⓐ Ⓓ
80. Ⓐ Ⓓ
81. Ⓐ Ⓓ
82. Ⓐ Ⓓ
83. Ⓐ Ⓓ
84. Ⓐ Ⓓ
85. Ⓐ Ⓓ
86. Ⓐ Ⓓ
87. Ⓐ Ⓓ
88. Ⓐ Ⓓ
89. Ⓐ Ⓓ
90. Ⓐ Ⓓ
91. Ⓐ Ⓓ
92. Ⓐ Ⓓ
93. Ⓐ Ⓓ
94. Ⓐ Ⓓ
95. Ⓐ Ⓓ

POSTAL EXAM
Test 2
ANSWER SHEET
Memory for Addresses

1. Ⓐ Ⓑ Ⓒ Ⓓ Ⓔ
2. Ⓐ Ⓑ Ⓒ Ⓓ Ⓔ
3. Ⓐ Ⓑ Ⓒ Ⓓ Ⓔ
4. Ⓐ Ⓑ Ⓒ Ⓓ Ⓔ
5. Ⓐ Ⓑ Ⓒ Ⓓ Ⓔ
6. Ⓐ Ⓑ Ⓒ Ⓓ Ⓔ
7. Ⓐ Ⓑ Ⓒ Ⓓ Ⓔ
8. Ⓐ Ⓑ Ⓒ Ⓓ Ⓔ
9. Ⓐ Ⓑ Ⓒ Ⓓ Ⓔ
10. Ⓐ Ⓑ Ⓒ Ⓓ Ⓔ
11. Ⓐ Ⓑ Ⓒ Ⓓ Ⓔ
12. Ⓐ Ⓑ Ⓒ Ⓓ Ⓔ
13. Ⓐ Ⓑ Ⓒ Ⓓ Ⓔ
14. Ⓐ Ⓑ Ⓒ Ⓓ Ⓔ
15. Ⓐ Ⓑ Ⓒ Ⓓ Ⓔ
16. Ⓐ Ⓑ Ⓒ Ⓓ Ⓔ
17. Ⓐ Ⓑ Ⓒ Ⓓ Ⓔ
18. Ⓐ Ⓑ Ⓒ Ⓓ Ⓔ
19. Ⓐ Ⓑ Ⓒ Ⓓ Ⓔ
20. Ⓐ Ⓑ Ⓒ Ⓓ Ⓔ
21. Ⓐ Ⓑ Ⓒ Ⓓ Ⓔ
22. Ⓐ Ⓑ Ⓒ Ⓓ Ⓔ
23. Ⓐ Ⓑ Ⓒ Ⓓ Ⓔ
24. Ⓐ Ⓑ Ⓒ Ⓓ Ⓔ
25. Ⓐ Ⓑ Ⓒ Ⓓ Ⓔ
26. Ⓐ Ⓑ Ⓒ Ⓓ Ⓔ
27. Ⓐ Ⓑ Ⓒ Ⓓ Ⓔ
28. Ⓐ Ⓑ Ⓒ Ⓓ Ⓔ
29. Ⓐ Ⓑ Ⓒ Ⓓ Ⓔ
30. Ⓐ Ⓑ Ⓒ Ⓓ Ⓔ
31. Ⓐ Ⓑ Ⓒ Ⓓ Ⓔ
32. Ⓐ Ⓑ Ⓒ Ⓓ Ⓔ
33. Ⓐ Ⓑ Ⓒ Ⓓ Ⓔ

34. Ⓐ Ⓑ Ⓒ Ⓓ Ⓔ
35. Ⓐ Ⓑ Ⓒ Ⓓ Ⓔ
36. Ⓐ Ⓑ Ⓒ Ⓓ Ⓔ
37. Ⓐ Ⓑ Ⓒ Ⓓ Ⓔ
38. Ⓐ Ⓑ Ⓒ Ⓓ Ⓔ
39. Ⓐ Ⓑ Ⓒ Ⓓ Ⓔ
40. Ⓐ Ⓑ Ⓒ Ⓓ Ⓔ
41. Ⓐ Ⓑ Ⓒ Ⓓ Ⓔ
42. Ⓐ Ⓑ Ⓒ Ⓓ Ⓔ
43. Ⓐ Ⓑ Ⓒ Ⓓ Ⓔ
44. Ⓐ Ⓑ Ⓒ Ⓓ Ⓔ
45. Ⓐ Ⓑ Ⓒ Ⓓ Ⓔ
46. Ⓐ Ⓑ Ⓒ Ⓓ Ⓔ
47. Ⓐ Ⓑ Ⓒ Ⓓ Ⓔ
48. Ⓐ Ⓑ Ⓒ Ⓓ Ⓔ
49. Ⓐ Ⓑ Ⓒ Ⓓ Ⓔ
50. Ⓐ Ⓑ Ⓒ Ⓓ Ⓔ
51. Ⓐ Ⓑ Ⓒ Ⓓ Ⓔ
52. Ⓐ Ⓑ Ⓒ Ⓓ Ⓔ
53. Ⓐ Ⓑ Ⓒ Ⓓ Ⓔ
54. Ⓐ Ⓑ Ⓒ Ⓓ Ⓔ
55. Ⓐ Ⓑ Ⓒ Ⓓ Ⓔ
56. Ⓐ Ⓑ Ⓒ Ⓓ Ⓔ
57. Ⓐ Ⓑ Ⓒ Ⓓ Ⓔ
58. Ⓐ Ⓑ Ⓒ Ⓓ Ⓔ
59. Ⓐ Ⓑ Ⓒ Ⓓ Ⓔ
60. Ⓐ Ⓑ Ⓒ Ⓓ Ⓔ
61. Ⓐ Ⓑ Ⓒ Ⓓ Ⓔ
62. Ⓐ Ⓑ Ⓒ Ⓓ Ⓔ
63. Ⓐ Ⓑ Ⓒ Ⓓ Ⓔ
64. Ⓐ Ⓑ Ⓒ Ⓓ Ⓔ
65. Ⓐ Ⓑ Ⓒ Ⓓ Ⓔ
66. Ⓐ Ⓑ Ⓒ Ⓓ Ⓔ

67. Ⓐ Ⓑ Ⓒ Ⓓ Ⓔ
68. Ⓐ Ⓑ Ⓒ Ⓓ Ⓔ
69. Ⓐ Ⓑ Ⓒ Ⓓ Ⓔ
70. Ⓐ Ⓑ Ⓒ Ⓓ Ⓔ
71. Ⓐ Ⓑ Ⓒ Ⓓ Ⓔ
72. Ⓐ Ⓑ Ⓒ Ⓓ Ⓔ
73. Ⓐ Ⓑ Ⓒ Ⓓ Ⓔ
74. Ⓐ Ⓑ Ⓒ Ⓓ Ⓔ
75. Ⓐ Ⓑ Ⓒ Ⓓ Ⓔ
76. Ⓐ Ⓑ Ⓒ Ⓓ Ⓔ
77. Ⓐ Ⓑ Ⓒ Ⓓ Ⓔ
78. Ⓐ Ⓑ Ⓒ Ⓓ Ⓔ
79. Ⓐ Ⓑ Ⓒ Ⓓ Ⓔ
80. Ⓐ Ⓑ Ⓒ Ⓓ Ⓔ
81. Ⓐ Ⓑ Ⓒ Ⓓ Ⓔ
82. Ⓐ Ⓑ Ⓒ Ⓓ Ⓔ
83. Ⓐ Ⓑ Ⓒ Ⓓ Ⓔ
84. Ⓐ Ⓑ Ⓒ Ⓓ Ⓔ
85. Ⓐ Ⓑ Ⓒ Ⓓ Ⓔ
86. Ⓐ Ⓑ Ⓒ Ⓓ Ⓔ
87. Ⓐ Ⓑ Ⓒ Ⓓ Ⓔ
88. Ⓐ Ⓑ Ⓒ Ⓓ Ⓔ

POSTAL EXAM
Test 2
ANSWER SHEET
Number Series

1. Ⓐ Ⓑ Ⓒ Ⓓ Ⓔ
2. Ⓐ Ⓑ Ⓒ Ⓓ Ⓔ
3. Ⓐ Ⓑ Ⓒ Ⓓ Ⓔ
4. Ⓐ Ⓑ Ⓒ Ⓓ Ⓔ
5. Ⓐ Ⓑ Ⓒ Ⓓ Ⓔ
6. Ⓐ Ⓑ Ⓒ Ⓓ Ⓔ
7. Ⓐ Ⓑ Ⓒ Ⓓ Ⓔ
8. Ⓐ Ⓑ Ⓒ Ⓓ Ⓔ
9. Ⓐ Ⓑ Ⓒ Ⓓ Ⓔ
10. Ⓐ Ⓑ Ⓒ Ⓓ Ⓔ
11. Ⓐ Ⓑ Ⓒ Ⓓ Ⓔ
12. Ⓐ Ⓑ Ⓒ Ⓓ Ⓔ

13. Ⓐ Ⓑ Ⓒ Ⓓ Ⓔ
14. Ⓐ Ⓑ Ⓒ Ⓓ Ⓔ
15. Ⓐ Ⓑ Ⓒ Ⓓ Ⓔ
16. Ⓐ Ⓑ Ⓒ Ⓓ Ⓔ
17. Ⓐ Ⓑ Ⓒ Ⓓ Ⓔ
18. Ⓐ Ⓑ Ⓒ Ⓓ Ⓔ
19. Ⓐ Ⓑ Ⓒ Ⓓ Ⓔ
20. Ⓐ Ⓑ Ⓒ Ⓓ Ⓔ
21. Ⓐ Ⓑ Ⓒ Ⓓ Ⓔ
22. Ⓐ Ⓑ Ⓒ Ⓓ Ⓔ
23. Ⓐ Ⓑ Ⓒ Ⓓ Ⓔ
24. Ⓐ Ⓑ Ⓒ Ⓓ Ⓔ

POSTAL EXAM
Test 2
ANSWER SHEET
Following Oral Directions

1. Ⓐ Ⓑ Ⓒ Ⓓ Ⓔ	34. Ⓐ Ⓑ Ⓒ Ⓓ Ⓔ	67. Ⓐ Ⓑ Ⓒ Ⓓ Ⓔ
2. Ⓐ Ⓑ Ⓒ Ⓓ Ⓔ	35. Ⓐ Ⓑ Ⓒ Ⓓ Ⓔ	68. Ⓐ Ⓑ Ⓒ Ⓓ Ⓔ
3. Ⓐ Ⓑ Ⓒ Ⓓ Ⓔ	36. Ⓐ Ⓑ Ⓒ Ⓓ Ⓔ	69. Ⓐ Ⓑ Ⓒ Ⓓ Ⓔ
4. Ⓐ Ⓑ Ⓒ Ⓓ Ⓔ	37. Ⓐ Ⓑ Ⓒ Ⓓ Ⓔ	70. Ⓐ Ⓑ Ⓒ Ⓓ Ⓔ
5. Ⓐ Ⓑ Ⓒ Ⓓ Ⓔ	38. Ⓐ Ⓑ Ⓒ Ⓓ Ⓔ	71. Ⓐ Ⓑ Ⓒ Ⓓ Ⓔ
6. Ⓐ Ⓑ Ⓒ Ⓓ Ⓔ	39. Ⓐ Ⓑ Ⓒ Ⓓ Ⓔ	72. Ⓐ Ⓑ Ⓒ Ⓓ Ⓔ
7. Ⓐ Ⓑ Ⓒ Ⓓ Ⓔ	40. Ⓐ Ⓑ Ⓒ Ⓓ Ⓔ	73. Ⓐ Ⓑ Ⓒ Ⓓ Ⓔ
8. Ⓐ Ⓑ Ⓒ Ⓓ Ⓔ	41. Ⓐ Ⓑ Ⓒ Ⓓ Ⓔ	74. Ⓐ Ⓑ Ⓒ Ⓓ Ⓔ
9. Ⓐ Ⓑ Ⓒ Ⓓ Ⓔ	42. Ⓐ Ⓑ Ⓒ Ⓓ Ⓔ	75. Ⓐ Ⓑ Ⓒ Ⓓ Ⓔ
10. Ⓐ Ⓑ Ⓒ Ⓓ Ⓔ	43. Ⓐ Ⓑ Ⓒ Ⓓ Ⓔ	76. Ⓐ Ⓑ Ⓒ Ⓓ Ⓔ
11. Ⓐ Ⓑ Ⓒ Ⓓ Ⓔ	44. Ⓐ Ⓑ Ⓒ Ⓓ Ⓔ	77. Ⓐ Ⓑ Ⓒ Ⓓ Ⓔ
12. Ⓐ Ⓑ Ⓒ Ⓓ Ⓔ	45. Ⓐ Ⓑ Ⓒ Ⓓ Ⓔ	78. Ⓐ Ⓑ Ⓒ Ⓓ Ⓔ
13. Ⓐ Ⓑ Ⓒ Ⓓ Ⓔ	46. Ⓐ Ⓑ Ⓒ Ⓓ Ⓔ	79. Ⓐ Ⓑ Ⓒ Ⓓ Ⓔ
14. Ⓐ Ⓑ Ⓒ Ⓓ Ⓔ	47. Ⓐ Ⓑ Ⓒ Ⓓ Ⓔ	80. Ⓐ Ⓑ Ⓒ Ⓓ Ⓔ
15. Ⓐ Ⓑ Ⓒ Ⓓ Ⓔ	48. Ⓐ Ⓑ Ⓒ Ⓓ Ⓔ	81. Ⓐ Ⓑ Ⓒ Ⓓ Ⓔ
16. Ⓐ Ⓑ Ⓒ Ⓓ Ⓔ	49. Ⓐ Ⓑ Ⓒ Ⓓ Ⓔ	82. Ⓐ Ⓑ Ⓒ Ⓓ Ⓔ
17. Ⓐ Ⓑ Ⓒ Ⓓ Ⓔ	50. Ⓐ Ⓑ Ⓒ Ⓓ Ⓔ	83. Ⓐ Ⓑ Ⓒ Ⓓ Ⓔ
18. Ⓐ Ⓑ Ⓒ Ⓓ Ⓔ	51. Ⓐ Ⓑ Ⓒ Ⓓ Ⓔ	84. Ⓐ Ⓑ Ⓒ Ⓓ Ⓔ
19. Ⓐ Ⓑ Ⓒ Ⓓ Ⓔ	52. Ⓐ Ⓑ Ⓒ Ⓓ Ⓔ	85. Ⓐ Ⓑ Ⓒ Ⓓ Ⓔ
20. Ⓐ Ⓑ Ⓒ Ⓓ Ⓔ	53. Ⓐ Ⓑ Ⓒ Ⓓ Ⓔ	86. Ⓐ Ⓑ Ⓒ Ⓓ Ⓔ
21. Ⓐ Ⓑ Ⓒ Ⓓ Ⓔ	54. Ⓐ Ⓑ Ⓒ Ⓓ Ⓔ	87. Ⓐ Ⓑ Ⓒ Ⓓ Ⓔ
22. Ⓐ Ⓑ Ⓒ Ⓓ Ⓔ	55. Ⓐ Ⓑ Ⓒ Ⓓ Ⓔ	88. Ⓐ Ⓑ Ⓒ Ⓓ Ⓔ
23. Ⓐ Ⓑ Ⓒ Ⓓ Ⓔ	56. Ⓐ Ⓑ Ⓒ Ⓓ Ⓔ	89. Ⓐ Ⓑ Ⓒ Ⓓ Ⓔ
24. Ⓐ Ⓑ Ⓒ Ⓓ Ⓔ	57. Ⓐ Ⓑ Ⓒ Ⓓ Ⓔ	90. Ⓐ Ⓑ Ⓒ Ⓓ Ⓔ
25. Ⓐ Ⓑ Ⓒ Ⓓ Ⓔ	58. Ⓐ Ⓑ Ⓒ Ⓓ Ⓔ	91. Ⓐ Ⓑ Ⓒ Ⓓ Ⓔ
26. Ⓐ Ⓑ Ⓒ Ⓓ Ⓔ	59. Ⓐ Ⓑ Ⓒ Ⓓ Ⓔ	92. Ⓐ Ⓑ Ⓒ Ⓓ Ⓔ
27. Ⓐ Ⓑ Ⓒ Ⓓ Ⓔ	60. Ⓐ Ⓑ Ⓒ Ⓓ Ⓔ	93. Ⓐ Ⓑ Ⓒ Ⓓ Ⓔ
28. Ⓐ Ⓑ Ⓒ Ⓓ Ⓔ	61. Ⓐ Ⓑ Ⓒ Ⓓ Ⓔ	94. Ⓐ Ⓑ Ⓒ Ⓓ Ⓔ
29. Ⓐ Ⓑ Ⓒ Ⓓ Ⓔ	62. Ⓐ Ⓑ Ⓒ Ⓓ Ⓔ	95. Ⓐ Ⓑ Ⓒ Ⓓ Ⓔ
30. Ⓐ Ⓑ Ⓒ Ⓓ Ⓔ	63. Ⓐ Ⓑ Ⓒ Ⓓ Ⓔ	96. Ⓐ Ⓑ Ⓒ Ⓓ Ⓔ
31. Ⓐ Ⓑ Ⓒ Ⓓ Ⓔ	64. Ⓐ Ⓑ Ⓒ Ⓓ Ⓔ	97. Ⓐ Ⓑ Ⓒ Ⓓ Ⓔ
32. Ⓐ Ⓑ Ⓒ Ⓓ Ⓔ	65. Ⓐ Ⓑ Ⓒ Ⓓ Ⓔ	98. Ⓐ Ⓑ Ⓒ Ⓓ Ⓔ
33. Ⓐ Ⓑ Ⓒ Ⓓ Ⓔ	66. Ⓐ Ⓑ Ⓒ Ⓓ Ⓔ	

POSTAL EXAM
Test 3
ANSWER SHEET
Address Checking

1. Ⓐ Ⓓ
2. Ⓐ Ⓓ
3. Ⓐ Ⓓ
4. Ⓐ Ⓓ
5. Ⓐ Ⓓ
6. Ⓐ Ⓓ
7. Ⓐ Ⓓ
8. Ⓐ Ⓓ
9. Ⓐ Ⓓ
10. Ⓐ Ⓓ
11. Ⓐ Ⓓ
12. Ⓐ Ⓓ
13. Ⓐ Ⓓ
14. Ⓐ Ⓓ
15. Ⓐ Ⓓ
16. Ⓐ Ⓓ
17. Ⓐ Ⓓ
18. Ⓐ Ⓓ
19. Ⓐ Ⓓ
20. Ⓐ Ⓓ
21. Ⓐ Ⓓ
22. Ⓐ Ⓓ
23. Ⓐ Ⓓ
24. Ⓐ Ⓓ
25. Ⓐ Ⓓ
26. Ⓐ Ⓓ
27. Ⓐ Ⓓ
28. Ⓐ Ⓓ
29. Ⓐ Ⓓ
30. Ⓐ Ⓓ
31. Ⓐ Ⓓ
32. Ⓐ Ⓓ
33. Ⓐ Ⓓ

34. Ⓐ Ⓓ
35. Ⓐ Ⓓ
36. Ⓐ Ⓓ
37. Ⓐ Ⓓ
38. Ⓐ Ⓓ
39. Ⓐ Ⓓ
40. Ⓐ Ⓓ
41. Ⓐ Ⓓ
42. Ⓐ Ⓓ
43. Ⓐ Ⓓ
44. Ⓐ Ⓓ
45. Ⓐ Ⓓ
46. Ⓐ Ⓓ
47. Ⓐ Ⓓ
48. Ⓐ Ⓓ
49. Ⓐ Ⓓ
50. Ⓐ Ⓓ
51. Ⓐ Ⓓ
52. Ⓐ Ⓓ
53. Ⓐ Ⓓ
54. Ⓐ Ⓓ
55. Ⓐ Ⓓ
56. Ⓐ Ⓓ
57. Ⓐ Ⓓ
58. Ⓐ Ⓓ
59. Ⓐ Ⓓ
60. Ⓐ Ⓓ
61. Ⓐ Ⓓ
62. Ⓐ Ⓓ
63. Ⓐ Ⓓ
64. Ⓐ Ⓓ
65. Ⓐ Ⓓ
66. Ⓐ Ⓓ

67. Ⓐ Ⓓ
68. Ⓐ Ⓓ
69. Ⓐ Ⓓ
70. Ⓐ Ⓓ
71. Ⓐ Ⓓ
72. Ⓐ Ⓓ
73. Ⓐ Ⓓ
74. Ⓐ Ⓓ
75. Ⓐ Ⓓ
76. Ⓐ Ⓓ
77. Ⓐ Ⓓ
78. Ⓐ Ⓓ
79. Ⓐ Ⓓ
80. Ⓐ Ⓓ
81. Ⓐ Ⓓ
82. Ⓐ Ⓓ
83. Ⓐ Ⓓ
84. Ⓐ Ⓓ
85. Ⓐ Ⓓ
86. Ⓐ Ⓓ
87. Ⓐ Ⓓ
88. Ⓐ Ⓓ
89. Ⓐ Ⓓ
90. Ⓐ Ⓓ
91. Ⓐ Ⓓ
92. Ⓐ Ⓓ
93. Ⓐ Ⓓ
94. Ⓐ Ⓓ
95. Ⓐ Ⓓ

POSTAL EXAM
Test 3
ANSWER SHEET
Memory for Addresses

1. Ⓐ Ⓑ Ⓒ Ⓓ Ⓔ
2. Ⓐ Ⓑ Ⓒ Ⓓ Ⓔ
3. Ⓐ Ⓑ Ⓒ Ⓓ Ⓔ
4. Ⓐ Ⓑ Ⓒ Ⓓ Ⓔ
5. Ⓐ Ⓑ Ⓒ Ⓓ Ⓔ
6. Ⓐ Ⓑ Ⓒ Ⓓ Ⓔ
7. Ⓐ Ⓑ Ⓒ Ⓓ Ⓔ
8. Ⓐ Ⓑ Ⓒ Ⓓ Ⓔ
9. Ⓐ Ⓑ Ⓒ Ⓓ Ⓔ
10. Ⓐ Ⓑ Ⓒ Ⓓ Ⓔ
11. Ⓐ Ⓑ Ⓒ Ⓓ Ⓔ
12. Ⓐ Ⓑ Ⓒ Ⓓ Ⓔ
13. Ⓐ Ⓑ Ⓒ Ⓓ Ⓔ
14. Ⓐ Ⓑ Ⓒ Ⓓ Ⓔ
15. Ⓐ Ⓑ Ⓒ Ⓓ Ⓔ
16. Ⓐ Ⓑ Ⓒ Ⓓ Ⓔ
17. Ⓐ Ⓑ Ⓒ Ⓓ Ⓔ
18. Ⓐ Ⓑ Ⓒ Ⓓ Ⓔ
19. Ⓐ Ⓑ Ⓒ Ⓓ Ⓔ
20. Ⓐ Ⓑ Ⓒ Ⓓ Ⓔ
21. Ⓐ Ⓑ Ⓒ Ⓓ Ⓔ
22. Ⓐ Ⓑ Ⓒ Ⓓ Ⓔ
23. Ⓐ Ⓑ Ⓒ Ⓓ Ⓔ
24. Ⓐ Ⓑ Ⓒ Ⓓ Ⓔ
25. Ⓐ Ⓑ Ⓒ Ⓓ Ⓔ
26. Ⓐ Ⓑ Ⓒ Ⓓ Ⓔ
27. Ⓐ Ⓑ Ⓒ Ⓓ Ⓔ
28. Ⓐ Ⓑ Ⓒ Ⓓ Ⓔ
29. Ⓐ Ⓑ Ⓒ Ⓓ Ⓔ
30. Ⓐ Ⓑ Ⓒ Ⓓ Ⓔ
31. Ⓐ Ⓑ Ⓒ Ⓓ Ⓔ
32. Ⓐ Ⓑ Ⓒ Ⓓ Ⓔ
33. Ⓐ Ⓑ Ⓒ Ⓓ Ⓔ

34. Ⓐ Ⓑ Ⓒ Ⓓ Ⓔ
35. Ⓐ Ⓑ Ⓒ Ⓓ Ⓔ
36. Ⓐ Ⓑ Ⓒ Ⓓ Ⓔ
37. Ⓐ Ⓑ Ⓒ Ⓓ Ⓔ
38. Ⓐ Ⓑ Ⓒ Ⓓ Ⓔ
39. Ⓐ Ⓑ Ⓒ Ⓓ Ⓔ
40. Ⓐ Ⓑ Ⓒ Ⓓ Ⓔ
41. Ⓐ Ⓑ Ⓒ Ⓓ Ⓔ
42. Ⓐ Ⓑ Ⓒ Ⓓ Ⓔ
43. Ⓐ Ⓑ Ⓒ Ⓓ Ⓔ
44. Ⓐ Ⓑ Ⓒ Ⓓ Ⓔ
45. Ⓐ Ⓑ Ⓒ Ⓓ Ⓔ
46. Ⓐ Ⓑ Ⓒ Ⓓ Ⓔ
47. Ⓐ Ⓑ Ⓒ Ⓓ Ⓔ
48. Ⓐ Ⓑ Ⓒ Ⓓ Ⓔ
49. Ⓐ Ⓑ Ⓒ Ⓓ Ⓔ
50. Ⓐ Ⓑ Ⓒ Ⓓ Ⓔ
51. Ⓐ Ⓑ Ⓒ Ⓓ Ⓔ
52. Ⓐ Ⓑ Ⓒ Ⓓ Ⓔ
53. Ⓐ Ⓑ Ⓒ Ⓓ Ⓔ
54. Ⓐ Ⓑ Ⓒ Ⓓ Ⓔ
55. Ⓐ Ⓑ Ⓒ Ⓓ Ⓔ
56. Ⓐ Ⓑ Ⓒ Ⓓ Ⓔ
57. Ⓐ Ⓑ Ⓒ Ⓓ Ⓔ
58. Ⓐ Ⓑ Ⓒ Ⓓ Ⓔ
59. Ⓐ Ⓑ Ⓒ Ⓓ Ⓔ
60. Ⓐ Ⓑ Ⓒ Ⓓ Ⓔ
61. Ⓐ Ⓑ Ⓒ Ⓓ Ⓔ
62. Ⓐ Ⓑ Ⓒ Ⓓ Ⓔ
63. Ⓐ Ⓑ Ⓒ Ⓓ Ⓔ
64. Ⓐ Ⓑ Ⓒ Ⓓ Ⓔ
65. Ⓐ Ⓑ Ⓒ Ⓓ Ⓔ
66. Ⓐ Ⓑ Ⓒ Ⓓ Ⓔ

67. Ⓐ Ⓑ Ⓒ Ⓓ Ⓔ
68. Ⓐ Ⓑ Ⓒ Ⓓ Ⓔ
69. Ⓐ Ⓑ Ⓒ Ⓓ Ⓔ
70. Ⓐ Ⓑ Ⓒ Ⓓ Ⓔ
71. Ⓐ Ⓑ Ⓒ Ⓓ Ⓔ
72. Ⓐ Ⓑ Ⓒ Ⓓ Ⓔ
73. Ⓐ Ⓑ Ⓒ Ⓓ Ⓔ
74. Ⓐ Ⓑ Ⓒ Ⓓ Ⓔ
75. Ⓐ Ⓑ Ⓒ Ⓓ Ⓔ
76. Ⓐ Ⓑ Ⓒ Ⓓ Ⓔ
77. Ⓐ Ⓑ Ⓒ Ⓓ Ⓔ
78. Ⓐ Ⓑ Ⓒ Ⓓ Ⓔ
79. Ⓐ Ⓑ Ⓒ Ⓓ Ⓔ
80. Ⓐ Ⓑ Ⓒ Ⓓ Ⓔ
81. Ⓐ Ⓑ Ⓒ Ⓓ Ⓔ
82. Ⓐ Ⓑ Ⓒ Ⓓ Ⓔ
83. Ⓐ Ⓑ Ⓒ Ⓓ Ⓔ
84. Ⓐ Ⓑ Ⓒ Ⓓ Ⓔ
85. Ⓐ Ⓑ Ⓒ Ⓓ Ⓔ
86. Ⓐ Ⓑ Ⓒ Ⓓ Ⓔ
87. Ⓐ Ⓑ Ⓒ Ⓓ Ⓔ
88. Ⓐ Ⓑ Ⓒ Ⓓ Ⓔ

POSTAL EXAM
Test 3
ANSWER SHEET
Number Series

1. Ⓐ Ⓑ Ⓒ Ⓓ Ⓔ
2. Ⓐ Ⓑ Ⓒ Ⓓ Ⓔ
3. Ⓐ Ⓑ Ⓒ Ⓓ Ⓔ
4. Ⓐ Ⓑ Ⓒ Ⓓ Ⓔ
5. Ⓐ Ⓑ Ⓒ Ⓓ Ⓔ
6. Ⓐ Ⓑ Ⓒ Ⓓ Ⓔ
7. Ⓐ Ⓑ Ⓒ Ⓓ Ⓔ
8. Ⓐ Ⓑ Ⓒ Ⓓ Ⓔ
9. Ⓐ Ⓑ Ⓒ Ⓓ Ⓔ
10. Ⓐ Ⓑ Ⓒ Ⓓ Ⓔ
11. Ⓐ Ⓑ Ⓒ Ⓓ Ⓔ
12. Ⓐ Ⓑ Ⓒ Ⓓ Ⓔ

13. Ⓐ Ⓑ Ⓒ Ⓓ Ⓔ
14. Ⓐ Ⓑ Ⓒ Ⓓ Ⓔ
15. Ⓐ Ⓑ Ⓒ Ⓓ Ⓔ
16. Ⓐ Ⓑ Ⓒ Ⓓ Ⓔ
17. Ⓐ Ⓑ Ⓒ Ⓓ Ⓔ
18. Ⓐ Ⓑ Ⓒ Ⓓ Ⓔ
19. Ⓐ Ⓑ Ⓒ Ⓓ Ⓔ
20. Ⓐ Ⓑ Ⓒ Ⓓ Ⓔ
21. Ⓐ Ⓑ Ⓒ Ⓓ Ⓔ
22. Ⓐ Ⓑ Ⓒ Ⓓ Ⓔ
23. Ⓐ Ⓑ Ⓒ Ⓓ Ⓔ
24. Ⓐ Ⓑ Ⓒ Ⓓ Ⓔ

POSTAL EXAM
Test 3
ANSWER SHEET
Following Oral Directions

1. Ⓐ Ⓑ Ⓒ Ⓓ Ⓔ	34. Ⓐ Ⓑ Ⓒ Ⓓ Ⓔ	67. Ⓐ Ⓑ Ⓒ Ⓓ Ⓔ
2. Ⓐ Ⓑ Ⓒ Ⓓ Ⓔ	35. Ⓐ Ⓑ Ⓒ Ⓓ Ⓔ	68. Ⓐ Ⓑ Ⓒ Ⓓ Ⓔ
3. Ⓐ Ⓑ Ⓒ Ⓓ Ⓔ	36. Ⓐ Ⓑ Ⓒ Ⓓ Ⓔ	69. Ⓐ Ⓑ Ⓒ Ⓓ Ⓔ
4. Ⓐ Ⓑ Ⓒ Ⓓ Ⓔ	37. Ⓐ Ⓑ Ⓒ Ⓓ Ⓔ	70. Ⓐ Ⓑ Ⓒ Ⓓ Ⓔ
5. Ⓐ Ⓑ Ⓒ Ⓓ Ⓔ	38. Ⓐ Ⓑ Ⓒ Ⓓ Ⓔ	71. Ⓐ Ⓑ Ⓒ Ⓓ Ⓔ
6. Ⓐ Ⓑ Ⓒ Ⓓ Ⓔ	39. Ⓐ Ⓑ Ⓒ Ⓓ Ⓔ	72. Ⓐ Ⓑ Ⓒ Ⓓ Ⓔ
7. Ⓐ Ⓑ Ⓒ Ⓓ Ⓔ	40. Ⓐ Ⓑ Ⓒ Ⓓ Ⓔ	73. Ⓐ Ⓑ Ⓒ Ⓓ Ⓔ
8. Ⓐ Ⓑ Ⓒ Ⓓ Ⓔ	41. Ⓐ Ⓑ Ⓒ Ⓓ Ⓔ	74. Ⓐ Ⓑ Ⓒ Ⓓ Ⓔ
9. Ⓐ Ⓑ Ⓒ Ⓓ Ⓔ	42. Ⓐ Ⓑ Ⓒ Ⓓ Ⓔ	75. Ⓐ Ⓑ Ⓒ Ⓓ Ⓔ
10. Ⓐ Ⓑ Ⓒ Ⓓ Ⓔ	43. Ⓐ Ⓑ Ⓒ Ⓓ Ⓔ	76. Ⓐ Ⓑ Ⓒ Ⓓ Ⓔ
11. Ⓐ Ⓑ Ⓒ Ⓓ Ⓔ	44. Ⓐ Ⓑ Ⓒ Ⓓ Ⓔ	77. Ⓐ Ⓑ Ⓒ Ⓓ Ⓔ
12. Ⓐ Ⓑ Ⓒ Ⓓ Ⓔ	45. Ⓐ Ⓑ Ⓒ Ⓓ Ⓔ	78. Ⓐ Ⓑ Ⓒ Ⓓ Ⓔ
13. Ⓐ Ⓑ Ⓒ Ⓓ Ⓔ	46. Ⓐ Ⓑ Ⓒ Ⓓ Ⓔ	79. Ⓐ Ⓑ Ⓒ Ⓓ Ⓔ
14. Ⓐ Ⓑ Ⓒ Ⓓ Ⓔ	47. Ⓐ Ⓑ Ⓒ Ⓓ Ⓔ	80. Ⓐ Ⓑ Ⓒ Ⓓ Ⓔ
15. Ⓐ Ⓑ Ⓒ Ⓓ Ⓔ	48. Ⓐ Ⓑ Ⓒ Ⓓ Ⓔ	81. Ⓐ Ⓑ Ⓒ Ⓓ Ⓔ
16. Ⓐ Ⓑ Ⓒ Ⓓ Ⓔ	49. Ⓐ Ⓑ Ⓒ Ⓓ Ⓔ	82. Ⓐ Ⓑ Ⓒ Ⓓ Ⓔ
17. Ⓐ Ⓑ Ⓒ Ⓓ Ⓔ	50. Ⓐ Ⓑ Ⓒ Ⓓ Ⓔ	83. Ⓐ Ⓑ Ⓒ Ⓓ Ⓔ
18. Ⓐ Ⓑ Ⓒ Ⓓ Ⓔ	51. Ⓐ Ⓑ Ⓒ Ⓓ Ⓔ	84. Ⓐ Ⓑ Ⓒ Ⓓ Ⓔ
19. Ⓐ Ⓑ Ⓒ Ⓓ Ⓔ	52. Ⓐ Ⓑ Ⓒ Ⓓ Ⓔ	85. Ⓐ Ⓑ Ⓒ Ⓓ Ⓔ
20. Ⓐ Ⓑ Ⓒ Ⓓ Ⓔ	53. Ⓐ Ⓑ Ⓒ Ⓓ Ⓔ	86. Ⓐ Ⓑ Ⓒ Ⓓ Ⓔ
21. Ⓐ Ⓑ Ⓒ Ⓓ Ⓔ	54. Ⓐ Ⓑ Ⓒ Ⓓ Ⓔ	87. Ⓐ Ⓑ Ⓒ Ⓓ Ⓔ
22. Ⓐ Ⓑ Ⓒ Ⓓ Ⓔ	55. Ⓐ Ⓑ Ⓒ Ⓓ Ⓔ	88. Ⓐ Ⓑ Ⓒ Ⓓ Ⓔ
23. Ⓐ Ⓑ Ⓒ Ⓓ Ⓔ	56. Ⓐ Ⓑ Ⓒ Ⓓ Ⓔ	89. Ⓐ Ⓑ Ⓒ Ⓓ Ⓔ
24. Ⓐ Ⓑ Ⓒ Ⓓ Ⓔ	57. Ⓐ Ⓑ Ⓒ Ⓓ Ⓔ	90. Ⓐ Ⓑ Ⓒ Ⓓ Ⓔ
25. Ⓐ Ⓑ Ⓒ Ⓓ Ⓔ	58. Ⓐ Ⓑ Ⓒ Ⓓ Ⓔ	91. Ⓐ Ⓑ Ⓒ Ⓓ Ⓔ
26. Ⓐ Ⓑ Ⓒ Ⓓ Ⓔ	59. Ⓐ Ⓑ Ⓒ Ⓓ Ⓔ	92. Ⓐ Ⓑ Ⓒ Ⓓ Ⓔ
27. Ⓐ Ⓑ Ⓒ Ⓓ Ⓔ	60. Ⓐ Ⓑ Ⓒ Ⓓ Ⓔ	93. Ⓐ Ⓑ Ⓒ Ⓓ Ⓔ
28. Ⓐ Ⓑ Ⓒ Ⓓ Ⓔ	61. Ⓐ Ⓑ Ⓒ Ⓓ Ⓔ	94. Ⓐ Ⓑ Ⓒ Ⓓ Ⓔ
29. Ⓐ Ⓑ Ⓒ Ⓓ Ⓔ	62. Ⓐ Ⓑ Ⓒ Ⓓ Ⓔ	95. Ⓐ Ⓑ Ⓒ Ⓓ Ⓔ
30. Ⓐ Ⓑ Ⓒ Ⓓ Ⓔ	63. Ⓐ Ⓑ Ⓒ Ⓓ Ⓔ	96. Ⓐ Ⓑ Ⓒ Ⓓ Ⓔ
31. Ⓐ Ⓑ Ⓒ Ⓓ Ⓔ	64. Ⓐ Ⓑ Ⓒ Ⓓ Ⓔ	97. Ⓐ Ⓑ Ⓒ Ⓓ Ⓔ
32. Ⓐ Ⓑ Ⓒ Ⓓ Ⓔ	65. Ⓐ Ⓑ Ⓒ Ⓓ Ⓔ	98. Ⓐ Ⓑ Ⓒ Ⓓ Ⓔ
33. Ⓐ Ⓑ Ⓒ Ⓓ Ⓔ	66. Ⓐ Ⓑ Ⓒ Ⓓ Ⓔ	

POSTAL EXAM
Test 4
ANSWER SHEET
Address Checking

1. Ⓐ Ⓓ
2. Ⓐ Ⓓ
3. Ⓐ Ⓓ
4. Ⓐ Ⓓ
5. Ⓐ Ⓓ
6. Ⓐ Ⓓ
7. Ⓐ Ⓓ
8. Ⓐ Ⓓ
9. Ⓐ Ⓓ
10. Ⓐ Ⓓ
11. Ⓐ Ⓓ
12. Ⓐ Ⓓ
13. Ⓐ Ⓓ
14. Ⓐ Ⓓ
15. Ⓐ Ⓓ
16. Ⓐ Ⓓ
17. Ⓐ Ⓓ
18. Ⓐ Ⓓ
19. Ⓐ Ⓓ
20. Ⓐ Ⓓ
21. Ⓐ Ⓓ
22. Ⓐ Ⓓ
23. Ⓐ Ⓓ
24. Ⓐ Ⓓ
25. Ⓐ Ⓓ
26. Ⓐ Ⓓ
27. Ⓐ Ⓓ
28. Ⓐ Ⓓ
29. Ⓐ Ⓓ
30. Ⓐ Ⓓ
31. Ⓐ Ⓓ
32. Ⓐ Ⓓ
33. Ⓐ Ⓓ

34. Ⓐ Ⓓ
35. Ⓐ Ⓓ
36. Ⓐ Ⓓ
37. Ⓐ Ⓓ
38. Ⓐ Ⓓ
39. Ⓐ Ⓓ
40. Ⓐ Ⓓ
41. Ⓐ Ⓓ
42. Ⓐ Ⓓ
43. Ⓐ Ⓓ
44. Ⓐ Ⓓ
45. Ⓐ Ⓓ
46. Ⓐ Ⓓ
47. Ⓐ Ⓓ
48. Ⓐ Ⓓ
49. Ⓐ Ⓓ
50. Ⓐ Ⓓ
51. Ⓐ Ⓓ
52. Ⓐ Ⓓ
53. Ⓐ Ⓓ
54. Ⓐ Ⓓ
55. Ⓐ Ⓓ
56. Ⓐ Ⓓ
57. Ⓐ Ⓓ
58. Ⓐ Ⓓ
59. Ⓐ Ⓓ
60. Ⓐ Ⓓ
61. Ⓐ Ⓓ
62. Ⓐ Ⓓ
63. Ⓐ Ⓓ
64. Ⓐ Ⓓ
65. Ⓐ Ⓓ
66. Ⓐ Ⓓ

67. Ⓐ Ⓓ
68. Ⓐ Ⓓ
69. Ⓐ Ⓓ
70. Ⓐ Ⓓ
71. Ⓐ Ⓓ
72. Ⓐ Ⓓ
73. Ⓐ Ⓓ
74. Ⓐ Ⓓ
75. Ⓐ Ⓓ
76. Ⓐ Ⓓ
77. Ⓐ Ⓓ
78. Ⓐ Ⓓ
79. Ⓐ Ⓓ
80. Ⓐ Ⓓ
81. Ⓐ Ⓓ
82. Ⓐ Ⓓ
83. Ⓐ Ⓓ
84. Ⓐ Ⓓ
85. Ⓐ Ⓓ
86. Ⓐ Ⓓ
87. Ⓐ Ⓓ
88. Ⓐ Ⓓ
89. Ⓐ Ⓓ
90. Ⓐ Ⓓ
91. Ⓐ Ⓓ
92. Ⓐ Ⓓ
93. Ⓐ Ⓓ
94. Ⓐ Ⓓ
95. Ⓐ Ⓓ

POSTAL EXAM
Test 4
ANSWER SHEET
Memory for Addresses

1. Ⓐ Ⓑ Ⓒ Ⓓ Ⓔ
2. Ⓐ Ⓑ Ⓒ Ⓓ Ⓔ
3. Ⓐ Ⓑ Ⓒ Ⓓ Ⓔ
4. Ⓐ Ⓑ Ⓒ Ⓓ Ⓔ
5. Ⓐ Ⓑ Ⓒ Ⓓ Ⓔ
6. Ⓐ Ⓑ Ⓒ Ⓓ Ⓔ
7. Ⓐ Ⓑ Ⓒ Ⓓ Ⓔ
8. Ⓐ Ⓑ Ⓒ Ⓓ Ⓔ
9. Ⓐ Ⓑ Ⓒ Ⓓ Ⓔ
10. Ⓐ Ⓑ Ⓒ Ⓓ Ⓔ
11. Ⓐ Ⓑ Ⓒ Ⓓ Ⓔ
12. Ⓐ Ⓑ Ⓒ Ⓓ Ⓔ
13. Ⓐ Ⓑ Ⓒ Ⓓ Ⓔ
14. Ⓐ Ⓑ Ⓒ Ⓓ Ⓔ
15. Ⓐ Ⓑ Ⓒ Ⓓ Ⓔ
16. Ⓐ Ⓑ Ⓒ Ⓓ Ⓔ
17. Ⓐ Ⓑ Ⓒ Ⓓ Ⓔ
18. Ⓐ Ⓑ Ⓒ Ⓓ Ⓔ
19. Ⓐ Ⓑ Ⓒ Ⓓ Ⓔ
20. Ⓐ Ⓑ Ⓒ Ⓓ Ⓔ
21. Ⓐ Ⓑ Ⓒ Ⓓ Ⓔ
22. Ⓐ Ⓑ Ⓒ Ⓓ Ⓔ
23. Ⓐ Ⓑ Ⓒ Ⓓ Ⓔ
24. Ⓐ Ⓑ Ⓒ Ⓓ Ⓔ
25. Ⓐ Ⓑ Ⓒ Ⓓ Ⓔ
26. Ⓐ Ⓑ Ⓒ Ⓓ Ⓔ
27. Ⓐ Ⓑ Ⓒ Ⓓ Ⓔ
28. Ⓐ Ⓑ Ⓒ Ⓓ Ⓔ
29. Ⓐ Ⓑ Ⓒ Ⓓ Ⓔ
30. Ⓐ Ⓑ Ⓒ Ⓓ Ⓔ
31. Ⓐ Ⓑ Ⓒ Ⓓ Ⓔ
32. Ⓐ Ⓑ Ⓒ Ⓓ Ⓔ
33. Ⓐ Ⓑ Ⓒ Ⓓ Ⓔ

34. Ⓐ Ⓑ Ⓒ Ⓓ Ⓔ
35. Ⓐ Ⓑ Ⓒ Ⓓ Ⓔ
36. Ⓐ Ⓑ Ⓒ Ⓓ Ⓔ
37. Ⓐ Ⓑ Ⓒ Ⓓ Ⓔ
38. Ⓐ Ⓑ Ⓒ Ⓓ Ⓔ
39. Ⓐ Ⓑ Ⓒ Ⓓ Ⓔ
40. Ⓐ Ⓑ Ⓒ Ⓓ Ⓔ
41. Ⓐ Ⓑ Ⓒ Ⓓ Ⓔ
42. Ⓐ Ⓑ Ⓒ Ⓓ Ⓔ
43. Ⓐ Ⓑ Ⓒ Ⓓ Ⓔ
44. Ⓐ Ⓑ Ⓒ Ⓓ Ⓔ
45. Ⓐ Ⓑ Ⓒ Ⓓ Ⓔ
46. Ⓐ Ⓑ Ⓒ Ⓓ Ⓔ
47. Ⓐ Ⓑ Ⓒ Ⓓ Ⓔ
48. Ⓐ Ⓑ Ⓒ Ⓓ Ⓔ
49. Ⓐ Ⓑ Ⓒ Ⓓ Ⓔ
50. Ⓐ Ⓑ Ⓒ Ⓓ Ⓔ
51. Ⓐ Ⓑ Ⓒ Ⓓ Ⓔ
52. Ⓐ Ⓑ Ⓒ Ⓓ Ⓔ
53. Ⓐ Ⓑ Ⓒ Ⓓ Ⓔ
54. Ⓐ Ⓑ Ⓒ Ⓓ Ⓔ
55. Ⓐ Ⓑ Ⓒ Ⓓ Ⓔ
56. Ⓐ Ⓑ Ⓒ Ⓓ Ⓔ
57. Ⓐ Ⓑ Ⓒ Ⓓ Ⓔ
58. Ⓐ Ⓑ Ⓒ Ⓓ Ⓔ
59. Ⓐ Ⓑ Ⓒ Ⓓ Ⓔ
60. Ⓐ Ⓑ Ⓒ Ⓓ Ⓔ
61. Ⓐ Ⓑ Ⓒ Ⓓ Ⓔ
62. Ⓐ Ⓑ Ⓒ Ⓓ Ⓔ
63. Ⓐ Ⓑ Ⓒ Ⓓ Ⓔ
64. Ⓐ Ⓑ Ⓒ Ⓓ Ⓔ
65. Ⓐ Ⓑ Ⓒ Ⓓ Ⓔ
66. Ⓐ Ⓑ Ⓒ Ⓓ Ⓔ

67. Ⓐ Ⓑ Ⓒ Ⓓ Ⓔ
68. Ⓐ Ⓑ Ⓒ Ⓓ Ⓔ
69. Ⓐ Ⓑ Ⓒ Ⓓ Ⓔ
70. Ⓐ Ⓑ Ⓒ Ⓓ Ⓔ
71. Ⓐ Ⓑ Ⓒ Ⓓ Ⓔ
72. Ⓐ Ⓑ Ⓒ Ⓓ Ⓔ
73. Ⓐ Ⓑ Ⓒ Ⓓ Ⓔ
74. Ⓐ Ⓑ Ⓒ Ⓓ Ⓔ
75. Ⓐ Ⓑ Ⓒ Ⓓ Ⓔ
76. Ⓐ Ⓑ Ⓒ Ⓓ Ⓔ
77. Ⓐ Ⓑ Ⓒ Ⓓ Ⓔ
78. Ⓐ Ⓑ Ⓒ Ⓓ Ⓔ
79. Ⓐ Ⓑ Ⓒ Ⓓ Ⓔ
80. Ⓐ Ⓑ Ⓒ Ⓓ Ⓔ
81. Ⓐ Ⓑ Ⓒ Ⓓ Ⓔ
82. Ⓐ Ⓑ Ⓒ Ⓓ Ⓔ
83. Ⓐ Ⓑ Ⓒ Ⓓ Ⓔ
84. Ⓐ Ⓑ Ⓒ Ⓓ Ⓔ
85. Ⓐ Ⓑ Ⓒ Ⓓ Ⓔ
86. Ⓐ Ⓑ Ⓒ Ⓓ Ⓔ
87. Ⓐ Ⓑ Ⓒ Ⓓ Ⓔ
88. Ⓐ Ⓑ Ⓒ Ⓓ Ⓔ

POSTAL EXAM
Test 4
ANSWER SHEET
Number Series

1. Ⓐ Ⓑ Ⓒ Ⓓ Ⓔ
2. Ⓐ Ⓑ Ⓒ Ⓓ Ⓔ
3. Ⓐ Ⓑ Ⓒ Ⓓ Ⓔ
4. Ⓐ Ⓑ Ⓒ Ⓓ Ⓔ
5. Ⓐ Ⓑ Ⓒ Ⓓ Ⓔ
6. Ⓐ Ⓑ Ⓒ Ⓓ Ⓔ
7. Ⓐ Ⓑ Ⓒ Ⓓ Ⓔ
8. Ⓐ Ⓑ Ⓒ Ⓓ Ⓔ
9. Ⓐ Ⓑ Ⓒ Ⓓ Ⓔ
10. Ⓐ Ⓑ Ⓒ Ⓓ Ⓔ
11. Ⓐ Ⓑ Ⓒ Ⓓ Ⓔ
12. Ⓐ Ⓑ Ⓒ Ⓓ Ⓔ

13. Ⓐ Ⓑ Ⓒ Ⓓ Ⓔ
14. Ⓐ Ⓑ Ⓒ Ⓓ Ⓔ
15. Ⓐ Ⓑ Ⓒ Ⓓ Ⓔ
16. Ⓐ Ⓑ Ⓒ Ⓓ Ⓔ
17. Ⓐ Ⓑ Ⓒ Ⓓ Ⓔ
18. Ⓐ Ⓑ Ⓒ Ⓓ Ⓔ
19. Ⓐ Ⓑ Ⓒ Ⓓ Ⓔ
20. Ⓐ Ⓑ Ⓒ Ⓓ Ⓔ
21. Ⓐ Ⓑ Ⓒ Ⓓ Ⓔ
22. Ⓐ Ⓑ Ⓒ Ⓓ Ⓔ
23. Ⓐ Ⓑ Ⓒ Ⓓ Ⓔ
24. Ⓐ Ⓑ Ⓒ Ⓓ Ⓔ

POSTAL EXAM
Test 4
ANSWER SHEET
Following Oral Directions

1. Ⓐ Ⓑ Ⓒ Ⓓ Ⓔ	34. Ⓐ Ⓑ Ⓒ Ⓓ Ⓔ	67. Ⓐ Ⓑ Ⓒ Ⓓ Ⓔ
2. Ⓐ Ⓑ Ⓒ Ⓓ Ⓔ	35. Ⓐ Ⓑ Ⓒ Ⓓ Ⓔ	68. Ⓐ Ⓑ Ⓒ Ⓓ Ⓔ
3. Ⓐ Ⓑ Ⓒ Ⓓ Ⓔ	36. Ⓐ Ⓑ Ⓒ Ⓓ Ⓔ	69. Ⓐ Ⓑ Ⓒ Ⓓ Ⓔ
4. Ⓐ Ⓑ Ⓒ Ⓓ Ⓔ	37. Ⓐ Ⓑ Ⓒ Ⓓ Ⓔ	70. Ⓐ Ⓑ Ⓒ Ⓓ Ⓔ
5. Ⓐ Ⓑ Ⓒ Ⓓ Ⓔ	38. Ⓐ Ⓑ Ⓒ Ⓓ Ⓔ	71. Ⓐ Ⓑ Ⓒ Ⓓ Ⓔ
6. Ⓐ Ⓑ Ⓒ Ⓓ Ⓔ	39. Ⓐ Ⓑ Ⓒ Ⓓ Ⓔ	72. Ⓐ Ⓑ Ⓒ Ⓓ Ⓔ
7. Ⓐ Ⓑ Ⓒ Ⓓ Ⓔ	40. Ⓐ Ⓑ Ⓒ Ⓓ Ⓔ	73. Ⓐ Ⓑ Ⓒ Ⓓ Ⓔ
8. Ⓐ Ⓑ Ⓒ Ⓓ Ⓔ	41. Ⓐ Ⓑ Ⓒ Ⓓ Ⓔ	74. Ⓐ Ⓑ Ⓒ Ⓓ Ⓔ
9. Ⓐ Ⓑ Ⓒ Ⓓ Ⓔ	42. Ⓐ Ⓑ Ⓒ Ⓓ Ⓔ	75. Ⓐ Ⓑ Ⓒ Ⓓ Ⓔ
10. Ⓐ Ⓑ Ⓒ Ⓓ Ⓔ	43. Ⓐ Ⓑ Ⓒ Ⓓ Ⓔ	76. Ⓐ Ⓑ Ⓒ Ⓓ Ⓔ
11. Ⓐ Ⓑ Ⓒ Ⓓ Ⓔ	44. Ⓐ Ⓑ Ⓒ Ⓓ Ⓔ	77. Ⓐ Ⓑ Ⓒ Ⓓ Ⓔ
12. Ⓐ Ⓑ Ⓒ Ⓓ Ⓔ	45. Ⓐ Ⓑ Ⓒ Ⓓ Ⓔ	78. Ⓐ Ⓑ Ⓒ Ⓓ Ⓔ
13. Ⓐ Ⓑ Ⓒ Ⓓ Ⓔ	46. Ⓐ Ⓑ Ⓒ Ⓓ Ⓔ	79. Ⓐ Ⓑ Ⓒ Ⓓ Ⓔ
14. Ⓐ Ⓑ Ⓒ Ⓓ Ⓔ	47. Ⓐ Ⓑ Ⓒ Ⓓ Ⓔ	80. Ⓐ Ⓑ Ⓒ Ⓓ Ⓔ
15. Ⓐ Ⓑ Ⓒ Ⓓ Ⓔ	48. Ⓐ Ⓑ Ⓒ Ⓓ Ⓔ	81. Ⓐ Ⓑ Ⓒ Ⓓ Ⓔ
16. Ⓐ Ⓑ Ⓒ Ⓓ Ⓔ	49. Ⓐ Ⓑ Ⓒ Ⓓ Ⓔ	82. Ⓐ Ⓑ Ⓒ Ⓓ Ⓔ
17. Ⓐ Ⓑ Ⓒ Ⓓ Ⓔ	50. Ⓐ Ⓑ Ⓒ Ⓓ Ⓔ	83. Ⓐ Ⓑ Ⓒ Ⓓ Ⓔ
18. Ⓐ Ⓑ Ⓒ Ⓓ Ⓔ	51. Ⓐ Ⓑ Ⓒ Ⓓ Ⓔ	84. Ⓐ Ⓑ Ⓒ Ⓓ Ⓔ
19. Ⓐ Ⓑ Ⓒ Ⓓ Ⓔ	52. Ⓐ Ⓑ Ⓒ Ⓓ Ⓔ	85. Ⓐ Ⓑ Ⓒ Ⓓ Ⓔ
20. Ⓐ Ⓑ Ⓒ Ⓓ Ⓔ	53. Ⓐ Ⓑ Ⓒ Ⓓ Ⓔ	86. Ⓐ Ⓑ Ⓒ Ⓓ Ⓔ
21. Ⓐ Ⓑ Ⓒ Ⓓ Ⓔ	54. Ⓐ Ⓑ Ⓒ Ⓓ Ⓔ	87. Ⓐ Ⓑ Ⓒ Ⓓ Ⓔ
22. Ⓐ Ⓑ Ⓒ Ⓓ Ⓔ	55. Ⓐ Ⓑ Ⓒ Ⓓ Ⓔ	88. Ⓐ Ⓑ Ⓒ Ⓓ Ⓔ
23. Ⓐ Ⓑ Ⓒ Ⓓ Ⓔ	56. Ⓐ Ⓑ Ⓒ Ⓓ Ⓔ	89. Ⓐ Ⓑ Ⓒ Ⓓ Ⓔ
24. Ⓐ Ⓑ Ⓒ Ⓓ Ⓔ	57. Ⓐ Ⓑ Ⓒ Ⓓ Ⓔ	90. Ⓐ Ⓑ Ⓒ Ⓓ Ⓔ
25. Ⓐ Ⓑ Ⓒ Ⓓ Ⓔ	58. Ⓐ Ⓑ Ⓒ Ⓓ Ⓔ	91. Ⓐ Ⓑ Ⓒ Ⓓ Ⓔ
26. Ⓐ Ⓑ Ⓒ Ⓓ Ⓔ	59. Ⓐ Ⓑ Ⓒ Ⓓ Ⓔ	92. Ⓐ Ⓑ Ⓒ Ⓓ Ⓔ
27. Ⓐ Ⓑ Ⓒ Ⓓ Ⓔ	60. Ⓐ Ⓑ Ⓒ Ⓓ Ⓔ	93. Ⓐ Ⓑ Ⓒ Ⓓ Ⓔ
28. Ⓐ Ⓑ Ⓒ Ⓓ Ⓔ	61. Ⓐ Ⓑ Ⓒ Ⓓ Ⓔ	94. Ⓐ Ⓑ Ⓒ Ⓓ Ⓔ
29. Ⓐ Ⓑ Ⓒ Ⓓ Ⓔ	62. Ⓐ Ⓑ Ⓒ Ⓓ Ⓔ	95. Ⓐ Ⓑ Ⓒ Ⓓ Ⓔ
30. Ⓐ Ⓑ Ⓒ Ⓓ Ⓔ	63. Ⓐ Ⓑ Ⓒ Ⓓ Ⓔ	96. Ⓐ Ⓑ Ⓒ Ⓓ Ⓔ
31. Ⓐ Ⓑ Ⓒ Ⓓ Ⓔ	64. Ⓐ Ⓑ Ⓒ Ⓓ Ⓔ	97. Ⓐ Ⓑ Ⓒ Ⓓ Ⓔ
32. Ⓐ Ⓑ Ⓒ Ⓓ Ⓔ	65. Ⓐ Ⓑ Ⓒ Ⓓ Ⓔ	98. Ⓐ Ⓑ Ⓒ Ⓓ Ⓔ
33. Ⓐ Ⓑ Ⓒ Ⓓ Ⓔ	66. Ⓐ Ⓑ Ⓒ Ⓓ Ⓔ	

POSTAL EXAM
Test 5
ANSWER SHEET
Address Checking

1. Ⓐ Ⓓ
2. Ⓐ Ⓓ
3. Ⓐ Ⓓ
4. Ⓐ Ⓓ
5. Ⓐ Ⓓ
6. Ⓐ Ⓓ
7. Ⓐ Ⓓ
8. Ⓐ Ⓓ
9. Ⓐ Ⓓ
10. Ⓐ Ⓓ
11. Ⓐ Ⓓ
12. Ⓐ Ⓓ
13. Ⓐ Ⓓ
14. Ⓐ Ⓓ
15. Ⓐ Ⓓ
16. Ⓐ Ⓓ
17. Ⓐ Ⓓ
18. Ⓐ Ⓓ
19. Ⓐ Ⓓ
20. Ⓐ Ⓓ
21. Ⓐ Ⓓ
22. Ⓐ Ⓓ
23. Ⓐ Ⓓ
24. Ⓐ Ⓓ
25. Ⓐ Ⓓ
26. Ⓐ Ⓓ
27. Ⓐ Ⓓ
28. Ⓐ Ⓓ
29. Ⓐ Ⓓ
30. Ⓐ Ⓓ
31. Ⓐ Ⓓ
32. Ⓐ Ⓓ
33. Ⓐ Ⓓ

34. Ⓐ Ⓓ
35. Ⓐ Ⓓ
36. Ⓐ Ⓓ
37. Ⓐ Ⓓ
38. Ⓐ Ⓓ
39. Ⓐ Ⓓ
40. Ⓐ Ⓓ
41. Ⓐ Ⓓ
42. Ⓐ Ⓓ
43. Ⓐ Ⓓ
44. Ⓐ Ⓓ
45. Ⓐ Ⓓ
46. Ⓐ Ⓓ
47. Ⓐ Ⓓ
48. Ⓐ Ⓓ
49. Ⓐ Ⓓ
50. Ⓐ Ⓓ
51. Ⓐ Ⓓ
52. Ⓐ Ⓓ
53. Ⓐ Ⓓ
54. Ⓐ Ⓓ
55. Ⓐ Ⓓ
56. Ⓐ Ⓓ
57. Ⓐ Ⓓ
58. Ⓐ Ⓓ
59. Ⓐ Ⓓ
60. Ⓐ Ⓓ
61. Ⓐ Ⓓ
62. Ⓐ Ⓓ
63. Ⓐ Ⓓ
64. Ⓐ Ⓓ
65. Ⓐ Ⓓ
66. Ⓐ Ⓓ

67. Ⓐ Ⓓ
68. Ⓐ Ⓓ
69. Ⓐ Ⓓ
70. Ⓐ Ⓓ
71. Ⓐ Ⓓ
72. Ⓐ Ⓓ
73. Ⓐ Ⓓ
74. Ⓐ Ⓓ
75. Ⓐ Ⓓ
76. Ⓐ Ⓓ
77. Ⓐ Ⓓ
78. Ⓐ Ⓓ
79. Ⓐ Ⓓ
80. Ⓐ Ⓓ
81. Ⓐ Ⓓ
82. Ⓐ Ⓓ
83. Ⓐ Ⓓ
84. Ⓐ Ⓓ
85. Ⓐ Ⓓ
86. Ⓐ Ⓓ
87. Ⓐ Ⓓ
88. Ⓐ Ⓓ
89. Ⓐ Ⓓ
90. Ⓐ Ⓓ
91. Ⓐ Ⓓ
92. Ⓐ Ⓓ
93. Ⓐ Ⓓ
94. Ⓐ Ⓓ
95. Ⓐ Ⓓ

POSTAL EXAM
Test 5
ANSWER SHEET
Memory for Addresses

1. Ⓐ Ⓑ Ⓒ Ⓓ Ⓔ
2. Ⓐ Ⓑ Ⓒ Ⓓ Ⓔ
3. Ⓐ Ⓑ Ⓒ Ⓓ Ⓔ
4. Ⓐ Ⓑ Ⓒ Ⓓ Ⓔ
5. Ⓐ Ⓑ Ⓒ Ⓓ Ⓔ
6. Ⓐ Ⓑ Ⓒ Ⓓ Ⓔ
7. Ⓐ Ⓑ Ⓒ Ⓓ Ⓔ
8. Ⓐ Ⓑ Ⓒ Ⓓ Ⓔ
9. Ⓐ Ⓑ Ⓒ Ⓓ Ⓔ
10. Ⓐ Ⓑ Ⓒ Ⓓ Ⓔ
11. Ⓐ Ⓑ Ⓒ Ⓓ Ⓔ
12. Ⓐ Ⓑ Ⓒ Ⓓ Ⓔ
13. Ⓐ Ⓑ Ⓒ Ⓓ Ⓔ
14. Ⓐ Ⓑ Ⓒ Ⓓ Ⓔ
15. Ⓐ Ⓑ Ⓒ Ⓓ Ⓔ
16. Ⓐ Ⓑ Ⓒ Ⓓ Ⓔ
17. Ⓐ Ⓑ Ⓒ Ⓓ Ⓔ
18. Ⓐ Ⓑ Ⓒ Ⓓ Ⓔ
19. Ⓐ Ⓑ Ⓒ Ⓓ Ⓔ
20. Ⓐ Ⓑ Ⓒ Ⓓ Ⓔ
21. Ⓐ Ⓑ Ⓒ Ⓓ Ⓔ
22. Ⓐ Ⓑ Ⓒ Ⓓ Ⓔ
23. Ⓐ Ⓑ Ⓒ Ⓓ Ⓔ
24. Ⓐ Ⓑ Ⓒ Ⓓ Ⓔ
25. Ⓐ Ⓑ Ⓒ Ⓓ Ⓔ
26. Ⓐ Ⓑ Ⓒ Ⓓ Ⓔ
27. Ⓐ Ⓑ Ⓒ Ⓓ Ⓔ
28. Ⓐ Ⓑ Ⓒ Ⓓ Ⓔ
29. Ⓐ Ⓑ Ⓒ Ⓓ Ⓔ
30. Ⓐ Ⓑ Ⓒ Ⓓ Ⓔ
31. Ⓐ Ⓑ Ⓒ Ⓓ Ⓔ
32. Ⓐ Ⓑ Ⓒ Ⓓ Ⓔ
33. Ⓐ Ⓑ Ⓒ Ⓓ Ⓔ

34. Ⓐ Ⓑ Ⓒ Ⓓ Ⓔ
35. Ⓐ Ⓑ Ⓒ Ⓓ Ⓔ
36. Ⓐ Ⓑ Ⓒ Ⓓ Ⓔ
37. Ⓐ Ⓑ Ⓒ Ⓓ Ⓔ
38. Ⓐ Ⓑ Ⓒ Ⓓ Ⓔ
39. Ⓐ Ⓑ Ⓒ Ⓓ Ⓔ
40. Ⓐ Ⓑ Ⓒ Ⓓ Ⓔ
41. Ⓐ Ⓑ Ⓒ Ⓓ Ⓔ
42. Ⓐ Ⓑ Ⓒ Ⓓ Ⓔ
43. Ⓐ Ⓑ Ⓒ Ⓓ Ⓔ
44. Ⓐ Ⓑ Ⓒ Ⓓ Ⓔ
45. Ⓐ Ⓑ Ⓒ Ⓓ Ⓔ
46. Ⓐ Ⓑ Ⓒ Ⓓ Ⓔ
47. Ⓐ Ⓑ Ⓒ Ⓓ Ⓔ
48. Ⓐ Ⓑ Ⓒ Ⓓ Ⓔ
49. Ⓐ Ⓑ Ⓒ Ⓓ Ⓔ
50. Ⓐ Ⓑ Ⓒ Ⓓ Ⓔ
51. Ⓐ Ⓑ Ⓒ Ⓓ Ⓔ
52. Ⓐ Ⓑ Ⓒ Ⓓ Ⓔ
53. Ⓐ Ⓑ Ⓒ Ⓓ Ⓔ
54. Ⓐ Ⓑ Ⓒ Ⓓ Ⓔ
55. Ⓐ Ⓑ Ⓒ Ⓓ Ⓔ
56. Ⓐ Ⓑ Ⓒ Ⓓ Ⓔ
57. Ⓐ Ⓑ Ⓒ Ⓓ Ⓔ
58. Ⓐ Ⓑ Ⓒ Ⓓ Ⓔ
59. Ⓐ Ⓑ Ⓒ Ⓓ Ⓔ
60. Ⓐ Ⓑ Ⓒ Ⓓ Ⓔ
61. Ⓐ Ⓑ Ⓒ Ⓓ Ⓔ
62. Ⓐ Ⓑ Ⓒ Ⓓ Ⓔ
63. Ⓐ Ⓑ Ⓒ Ⓓ Ⓔ
64. Ⓐ Ⓑ Ⓒ Ⓓ Ⓔ
65. Ⓐ Ⓑ Ⓒ Ⓓ Ⓔ
66. Ⓐ Ⓑ Ⓒ Ⓓ Ⓔ

67. Ⓐ Ⓑ Ⓒ Ⓓ Ⓔ
68. Ⓐ Ⓑ Ⓒ Ⓓ Ⓔ
69. Ⓐ Ⓑ Ⓒ Ⓓ Ⓔ
70. Ⓐ Ⓑ Ⓒ Ⓓ Ⓔ
71. Ⓐ Ⓑ Ⓒ Ⓓ Ⓔ
72. Ⓐ Ⓑ Ⓒ Ⓓ Ⓔ
73. Ⓐ Ⓑ Ⓒ Ⓓ Ⓔ
74. Ⓐ Ⓑ Ⓒ Ⓓ Ⓔ
75. Ⓐ Ⓑ Ⓒ Ⓓ Ⓔ
76. Ⓐ Ⓑ Ⓒ Ⓓ Ⓔ
77. Ⓐ Ⓑ Ⓒ Ⓓ Ⓔ
78. Ⓐ Ⓑ Ⓒ Ⓓ Ⓔ
79. Ⓐ Ⓑ Ⓒ Ⓓ Ⓔ
80. Ⓐ Ⓑ Ⓒ Ⓓ Ⓔ
81. Ⓐ Ⓑ Ⓒ Ⓓ Ⓔ
82. Ⓐ Ⓑ Ⓒ Ⓓ Ⓔ
83. Ⓐ Ⓑ Ⓒ Ⓓ Ⓔ
84. Ⓐ Ⓑ Ⓒ Ⓓ Ⓔ
85. Ⓐ Ⓑ Ⓒ Ⓓ Ⓔ
86. Ⓐ Ⓑ Ⓒ Ⓓ Ⓔ
87. Ⓐ Ⓑ Ⓒ Ⓓ Ⓔ
88. Ⓐ Ⓑ Ⓒ Ⓓ Ⓔ

POSTAL EXAM
Test 5
ANSWER SHEET
Number Series

1. Ⓐ Ⓑ Ⓒ Ⓓ Ⓔ
2. Ⓐ Ⓑ Ⓒ Ⓓ Ⓔ
3. Ⓐ Ⓑ Ⓒ Ⓓ Ⓔ
4. Ⓐ Ⓑ Ⓒ Ⓓ Ⓔ
5. Ⓐ Ⓑ Ⓒ Ⓓ Ⓔ
6. Ⓐ Ⓑ Ⓒ Ⓓ Ⓔ
7. Ⓐ Ⓑ Ⓒ Ⓓ Ⓔ
8. Ⓐ Ⓑ Ⓒ Ⓓ Ⓔ
9. Ⓐ Ⓑ Ⓒ Ⓓ Ⓔ
10. Ⓐ Ⓑ Ⓒ Ⓓ Ⓔ
11. Ⓐ Ⓑ Ⓒ Ⓓ Ⓔ
12. Ⓐ Ⓑ Ⓒ Ⓓ Ⓔ

13. Ⓐ Ⓑ Ⓒ Ⓓ Ⓔ
14. Ⓐ Ⓑ Ⓒ Ⓓ Ⓔ
15. Ⓐ Ⓑ Ⓒ Ⓓ Ⓔ
16. Ⓐ Ⓑ Ⓒ Ⓓ Ⓔ
17. Ⓐ Ⓑ Ⓒ Ⓓ Ⓔ
18. Ⓐ Ⓑ Ⓒ Ⓓ Ⓔ
19. Ⓐ Ⓑ Ⓒ Ⓓ Ⓔ
20. Ⓐ Ⓑ Ⓒ Ⓓ Ⓔ
21. Ⓐ Ⓑ Ⓒ Ⓓ Ⓔ
22. Ⓐ Ⓑ Ⓒ Ⓓ Ⓔ
23. Ⓐ Ⓑ Ⓒ Ⓓ Ⓔ
24. Ⓐ Ⓑ Ⓒ Ⓓ Ⓔ

POSTAL EXAM
Test 5
ANSWER SHEET
Following Oral Directions

1. Ⓐ Ⓑ Ⓒ Ⓓ Ⓔ
2. Ⓐ Ⓑ Ⓒ Ⓓ Ⓔ
3. Ⓐ Ⓑ Ⓒ Ⓓ Ⓔ
4. Ⓐ Ⓑ Ⓒ Ⓓ Ⓔ
5. Ⓐ Ⓑ Ⓒ Ⓓ Ⓔ
6. Ⓐ Ⓑ Ⓒ Ⓓ Ⓔ
7. Ⓐ Ⓑ Ⓒ Ⓓ Ⓔ
8. Ⓐ Ⓑ Ⓒ Ⓓ Ⓔ
9. Ⓐ Ⓑ Ⓒ Ⓓ Ⓔ
10. Ⓐ Ⓑ Ⓒ Ⓓ Ⓔ
11. Ⓐ Ⓑ Ⓒ Ⓓ Ⓔ
12. Ⓐ Ⓑ Ⓒ Ⓓ Ⓔ
13. Ⓐ Ⓑ Ⓒ Ⓓ Ⓔ
14. Ⓐ Ⓑ Ⓒ Ⓓ Ⓔ
15. Ⓐ Ⓑ Ⓒ Ⓓ Ⓔ
16. Ⓐ Ⓑ Ⓒ Ⓓ Ⓔ
17. Ⓐ Ⓑ Ⓒ Ⓓ Ⓔ
18. Ⓐ Ⓑ Ⓒ Ⓓ Ⓔ
19. Ⓐ Ⓑ Ⓒ Ⓓ Ⓔ
20. Ⓐ Ⓑ Ⓒ Ⓓ Ⓔ
21. Ⓐ Ⓑ Ⓒ Ⓓ Ⓔ
22. Ⓐ Ⓑ Ⓒ Ⓓ Ⓔ
23. Ⓐ Ⓑ Ⓒ Ⓓ Ⓔ
24. Ⓐ Ⓑ Ⓒ Ⓓ Ⓔ
25. Ⓐ Ⓑ Ⓒ Ⓓ Ⓔ
26. Ⓐ Ⓑ Ⓒ Ⓓ Ⓔ
27. Ⓐ Ⓑ Ⓒ Ⓓ Ⓔ
28. Ⓐ Ⓑ Ⓒ Ⓓ Ⓔ
29. Ⓐ Ⓑ Ⓒ Ⓓ Ⓔ
30. Ⓐ Ⓑ Ⓒ Ⓓ Ⓔ
31. Ⓐ Ⓑ Ⓒ Ⓓ Ⓔ
32. Ⓐ Ⓑ Ⓒ Ⓓ Ⓔ
33. Ⓐ Ⓑ Ⓒ Ⓓ Ⓔ

34. Ⓐ Ⓑ Ⓒ Ⓓ Ⓔ
35. Ⓐ Ⓑ Ⓒ Ⓓ Ⓔ
36. Ⓐ Ⓑ Ⓒ Ⓓ Ⓔ
37. Ⓐ Ⓑ Ⓒ Ⓓ Ⓔ
38. Ⓐ Ⓑ Ⓒ Ⓓ Ⓔ
39. Ⓐ Ⓑ Ⓒ Ⓓ Ⓔ
40. Ⓐ Ⓑ Ⓒ Ⓓ Ⓔ
41. Ⓐ Ⓑ Ⓒ Ⓓ Ⓔ
42. Ⓐ Ⓑ Ⓒ Ⓓ Ⓔ
43. Ⓐ Ⓑ Ⓒ Ⓓ Ⓔ
44. Ⓐ Ⓑ Ⓒ Ⓓ Ⓔ
45. Ⓐ Ⓑ Ⓒ Ⓓ Ⓔ
46. Ⓐ Ⓑ Ⓒ Ⓓ Ⓔ
47. Ⓐ Ⓑ Ⓒ Ⓓ Ⓔ
48. Ⓐ Ⓑ Ⓒ Ⓓ Ⓔ
49. Ⓐ Ⓑ Ⓒ Ⓓ Ⓔ
50. Ⓐ Ⓑ Ⓒ Ⓓ Ⓔ
51. Ⓐ Ⓑ Ⓒ Ⓓ Ⓔ
52. Ⓐ Ⓑ Ⓒ Ⓓ Ⓔ
53. Ⓐ Ⓑ Ⓒ Ⓓ Ⓔ
54. Ⓐ Ⓑ Ⓒ Ⓓ Ⓔ
55. Ⓐ Ⓑ Ⓒ Ⓓ Ⓔ
56. Ⓐ Ⓑ Ⓒ Ⓓ Ⓔ
57. Ⓐ Ⓑ Ⓒ Ⓓ Ⓔ
58. Ⓐ Ⓑ Ⓒ Ⓓ Ⓔ
59. Ⓐ Ⓑ Ⓒ Ⓓ Ⓔ
60. Ⓐ Ⓑ Ⓒ Ⓓ Ⓔ
61. Ⓐ Ⓑ Ⓒ Ⓓ Ⓔ
62. Ⓐ Ⓑ Ⓒ Ⓓ Ⓔ
63. Ⓐ Ⓑ Ⓒ Ⓓ Ⓔ
64. Ⓐ Ⓑ Ⓒ Ⓓ Ⓔ
65. Ⓐ Ⓑ Ⓒ Ⓓ Ⓔ
66. Ⓐ Ⓑ Ⓒ Ⓓ Ⓔ

67. Ⓐ Ⓑ Ⓒ Ⓓ Ⓔ
68. Ⓐ Ⓑ Ⓒ Ⓓ Ⓔ
69. Ⓐ Ⓑ Ⓒ Ⓓ Ⓔ
70. Ⓐ Ⓑ Ⓒ Ⓓ Ⓔ
71. Ⓐ Ⓑ Ⓒ Ⓓ Ⓔ
72. Ⓐ Ⓑ Ⓒ Ⓓ Ⓔ
73. Ⓐ Ⓑ Ⓒ Ⓓ Ⓔ
74. Ⓐ Ⓑ Ⓒ Ⓓ Ⓔ
75. Ⓐ Ⓑ Ⓒ Ⓓ Ⓔ
76. Ⓐ Ⓑ Ⓒ Ⓓ Ⓔ
77. Ⓐ Ⓑ Ⓒ Ⓓ Ⓔ
78. Ⓐ Ⓑ Ⓒ Ⓓ Ⓔ
79. Ⓐ Ⓑ Ⓒ Ⓓ Ⓔ
80. Ⓐ Ⓑ Ⓒ Ⓓ Ⓔ
81. Ⓐ Ⓑ Ⓒ Ⓓ Ⓔ
82. Ⓐ Ⓑ Ⓒ Ⓓ Ⓔ
83. Ⓐ Ⓑ Ⓒ Ⓓ Ⓔ
84. Ⓐ Ⓑ Ⓒ Ⓓ Ⓔ
85. Ⓐ Ⓑ Ⓒ Ⓓ Ⓔ
86. Ⓐ Ⓑ Ⓒ Ⓓ Ⓔ
87. Ⓐ Ⓑ Ⓒ Ⓓ Ⓔ
88. Ⓐ Ⓑ Ⓒ Ⓓ Ⓔ
89. Ⓐ Ⓑ Ⓒ Ⓓ Ⓔ
90. Ⓐ Ⓑ Ⓒ Ⓓ Ⓔ
91. Ⓐ Ⓑ Ⓒ Ⓓ Ⓔ
92. Ⓐ Ⓑ Ⓒ Ⓓ Ⓔ
93. Ⓐ Ⓑ Ⓒ Ⓓ Ⓔ
94. Ⓐ Ⓑ Ⓒ Ⓓ Ⓔ
95. Ⓐ Ⓑ Ⓒ Ⓓ Ⓔ
96. Ⓐ Ⓑ Ⓒ Ⓓ Ⓔ
97. Ⓐ Ⓑ Ⓒ Ⓓ Ⓔ
98. Ⓐ Ⓑ Ⓒ Ⓓ Ⓔ

POSTAL EXAM
Test 6
ANSWER SHEET
Address Checking

1. Ⓐ Ⓓ
2. Ⓐ Ⓓ
3. Ⓐ Ⓓ
4. Ⓐ Ⓓ
5. Ⓐ Ⓓ
6. Ⓐ Ⓓ
7. Ⓐ Ⓓ
8. Ⓐ Ⓓ
9. Ⓐ Ⓓ
10. Ⓐ Ⓓ
11. Ⓐ Ⓓ
12. Ⓐ Ⓓ
13. Ⓐ Ⓓ
14. Ⓐ Ⓓ
15. Ⓐ Ⓓ
16. Ⓐ Ⓓ
17. Ⓐ Ⓓ
18. Ⓐ Ⓓ
19. Ⓐ Ⓓ
20. Ⓐ Ⓓ
21. Ⓐ Ⓓ
22. Ⓐ Ⓓ
23. Ⓐ Ⓓ
24. Ⓐ Ⓓ
25. Ⓐ Ⓓ
26. Ⓐ Ⓓ
27. Ⓐ Ⓓ
28. Ⓐ Ⓓ
29. Ⓐ Ⓓ
30. Ⓐ Ⓓ
31. Ⓐ Ⓓ
32. Ⓐ Ⓓ
33. Ⓐ Ⓓ

34. Ⓐ Ⓓ
35. Ⓐ Ⓓ
36. Ⓐ Ⓓ
37. Ⓐ Ⓓ
38. Ⓐ Ⓓ
39. Ⓐ Ⓓ
40. Ⓐ Ⓓ
41. Ⓐ Ⓓ
42. Ⓐ Ⓓ
43. Ⓐ Ⓓ
44. Ⓐ Ⓓ
45. Ⓐ Ⓓ
46. Ⓐ Ⓓ
47. Ⓐ Ⓓ
48. Ⓐ Ⓓ
49. Ⓐ Ⓓ
50. Ⓐ Ⓓ
51. Ⓐ Ⓓ
52. Ⓐ Ⓓ
53. Ⓐ Ⓓ
54. Ⓐ Ⓓ
55. Ⓐ Ⓓ
56. Ⓐ Ⓓ
57. Ⓐ Ⓓ
58. Ⓐ Ⓓ
59. Ⓐ Ⓓ
60. Ⓐ Ⓓ
61. Ⓐ Ⓓ
62. Ⓐ Ⓓ
63. Ⓐ Ⓓ
64. Ⓐ Ⓓ
65. Ⓐ Ⓓ
66. Ⓐ Ⓓ

67. Ⓐ Ⓓ
68. Ⓐ Ⓓ
69. Ⓐ Ⓓ
70. Ⓐ Ⓓ
71. Ⓐ Ⓓ
72. Ⓐ Ⓓ
73. Ⓐ Ⓓ
74. Ⓐ Ⓓ
75. Ⓐ Ⓓ
76. Ⓐ Ⓓ
77. Ⓐ Ⓓ
78. Ⓐ Ⓓ
79. Ⓐ Ⓓ
80. Ⓐ Ⓓ
81. Ⓐ Ⓓ
82. Ⓐ Ⓓ
83. Ⓐ Ⓓ
84. Ⓐ Ⓓ
85. Ⓐ Ⓓ
86. Ⓐ Ⓓ
87. Ⓐ Ⓓ
88. Ⓐ Ⓓ
89. Ⓐ Ⓓ
90. Ⓐ Ⓓ
91. Ⓐ Ⓓ
92. Ⓐ Ⓓ
93. Ⓐ Ⓓ
94. Ⓐ Ⓓ
95. Ⓐ Ⓓ

POSTAL EXAM
Test 6
ANSWER SHEET
Memory for Addresses

1. Ⓐ Ⓑ Ⓒ Ⓓ Ⓔ
2. Ⓐ Ⓑ Ⓒ Ⓓ Ⓔ
3. Ⓐ Ⓑ Ⓒ Ⓓ Ⓔ
4. Ⓐ Ⓑ Ⓒ Ⓓ Ⓔ
5. Ⓐ Ⓑ Ⓒ Ⓓ Ⓔ
6. Ⓐ Ⓑ Ⓒ Ⓓ Ⓔ
7. Ⓐ Ⓑ Ⓒ Ⓓ Ⓔ
8. Ⓐ Ⓑ Ⓒ Ⓓ Ⓔ
9. Ⓐ Ⓑ Ⓒ Ⓓ Ⓔ
10. Ⓐ Ⓑ Ⓒ Ⓓ Ⓔ
11. Ⓐ Ⓑ Ⓒ Ⓓ Ⓔ
12. Ⓐ Ⓑ Ⓒ Ⓓ Ⓔ
13. Ⓐ Ⓑ Ⓒ Ⓓ Ⓔ
14. Ⓐ Ⓑ Ⓒ Ⓓ Ⓔ
15. Ⓐ Ⓑ Ⓒ Ⓓ Ⓔ
16. Ⓐ Ⓑ Ⓒ Ⓓ Ⓔ
17. Ⓐ Ⓑ Ⓒ Ⓓ Ⓔ
18. Ⓐ Ⓑ Ⓒ Ⓓ Ⓔ
19. Ⓐ Ⓑ Ⓒ Ⓓ Ⓔ
20. Ⓐ Ⓑ Ⓒ Ⓓ Ⓔ
21. Ⓐ Ⓑ Ⓒ Ⓓ Ⓔ
22. Ⓐ Ⓑ Ⓒ Ⓓ Ⓔ
23. Ⓐ Ⓑ Ⓒ Ⓓ Ⓔ
24. Ⓐ Ⓑ Ⓒ Ⓓ Ⓔ
25. Ⓐ Ⓑ Ⓒ Ⓓ Ⓔ
26. Ⓐ Ⓑ Ⓒ Ⓓ Ⓔ
27. Ⓐ Ⓑ Ⓒ Ⓓ Ⓔ
28. Ⓐ Ⓑ Ⓒ Ⓓ Ⓔ
29. Ⓐ Ⓑ Ⓒ Ⓓ Ⓔ
30. Ⓐ Ⓑ Ⓒ Ⓓ Ⓔ
31. Ⓐ Ⓑ Ⓒ Ⓓ Ⓔ
32. Ⓐ Ⓑ Ⓒ Ⓓ Ⓔ
33. Ⓐ Ⓑ Ⓒ Ⓓ Ⓔ

34. Ⓐ Ⓑ Ⓒ Ⓓ Ⓔ
35. Ⓐ Ⓑ Ⓒ Ⓓ Ⓔ
36. Ⓐ Ⓑ Ⓒ Ⓓ Ⓔ
37. Ⓐ Ⓑ Ⓒ Ⓓ Ⓔ
38. Ⓐ Ⓑ Ⓒ Ⓓ Ⓔ
39. Ⓐ Ⓑ Ⓒ Ⓓ Ⓔ
40. Ⓐ Ⓑ Ⓒ Ⓓ Ⓔ
41. Ⓐ Ⓑ Ⓒ Ⓓ Ⓔ
42. Ⓐ Ⓑ Ⓒ Ⓓ Ⓔ
43. Ⓐ Ⓑ Ⓒ Ⓓ Ⓔ
44. Ⓐ Ⓑ Ⓒ Ⓓ Ⓔ
45. Ⓐ Ⓑ Ⓒ Ⓓ Ⓔ
46. Ⓐ Ⓑ Ⓒ Ⓓ Ⓔ
47. Ⓐ Ⓑ Ⓒ Ⓓ Ⓔ
48. Ⓐ Ⓑ Ⓒ Ⓓ Ⓔ
49. Ⓐ Ⓑ Ⓒ Ⓓ Ⓔ
50. Ⓐ Ⓑ Ⓒ Ⓓ Ⓔ
51. Ⓐ Ⓑ Ⓒ Ⓓ Ⓔ
52. Ⓐ Ⓑ Ⓒ Ⓓ Ⓔ
53. Ⓐ Ⓑ Ⓒ Ⓓ Ⓔ
54. Ⓐ Ⓑ Ⓒ Ⓓ Ⓔ
55. Ⓐ Ⓑ Ⓒ Ⓓ Ⓔ
56. Ⓐ Ⓑ Ⓒ Ⓓ Ⓔ
57. Ⓐ Ⓑ Ⓒ Ⓓ Ⓔ
58. Ⓐ Ⓑ Ⓒ Ⓓ Ⓔ
59. Ⓐ Ⓑ Ⓒ Ⓓ Ⓔ
60. Ⓐ Ⓑ Ⓒ Ⓓ Ⓔ
61. Ⓐ Ⓑ Ⓒ Ⓓ Ⓔ
62. Ⓐ Ⓑ Ⓒ Ⓓ Ⓔ
63. Ⓐ Ⓑ Ⓒ Ⓓ Ⓔ
64. Ⓐ Ⓑ Ⓒ Ⓓ Ⓔ
65. Ⓐ Ⓑ Ⓒ Ⓓ Ⓔ
66. Ⓐ Ⓑ Ⓒ Ⓓ Ⓔ

67. Ⓐ Ⓑ Ⓒ Ⓓ Ⓔ
68. Ⓐ Ⓑ Ⓒ Ⓓ Ⓔ
69. Ⓐ Ⓑ Ⓒ Ⓓ Ⓔ
70. Ⓐ Ⓑ Ⓒ Ⓓ Ⓔ
71. Ⓐ Ⓑ Ⓒ Ⓓ Ⓔ
72. Ⓐ Ⓑ Ⓒ Ⓓ Ⓔ
73. Ⓐ Ⓑ Ⓒ Ⓓ Ⓔ
74. Ⓐ Ⓑ Ⓒ Ⓓ Ⓔ
75. Ⓐ Ⓑ Ⓒ Ⓓ Ⓔ
76. Ⓐ Ⓑ Ⓒ Ⓓ Ⓔ
77. Ⓐ Ⓑ Ⓒ Ⓓ Ⓔ
78. Ⓐ Ⓑ Ⓒ Ⓓ Ⓔ
79. Ⓐ Ⓑ Ⓒ Ⓓ Ⓔ
80. Ⓐ Ⓑ Ⓒ Ⓓ Ⓔ
81. Ⓐ Ⓑ Ⓒ Ⓓ Ⓔ
82. Ⓐ Ⓑ Ⓒ Ⓓ Ⓔ
83. Ⓐ Ⓑ Ⓒ Ⓓ Ⓔ
84. Ⓐ Ⓑ Ⓒ Ⓓ Ⓔ
85. Ⓐ Ⓑ Ⓒ Ⓓ Ⓔ
86. Ⓐ Ⓑ Ⓒ Ⓓ Ⓔ
87. Ⓐ Ⓑ Ⓒ Ⓓ Ⓔ
88. Ⓐ Ⓑ Ⓒ Ⓓ Ⓔ

POSTAL EXAM
Test 6
ANSWER SHEET
Number Series

1. Ⓐ Ⓑ Ⓒ Ⓓ Ⓔ
2. Ⓐ Ⓑ Ⓒ Ⓓ Ⓔ
3. Ⓐ Ⓑ Ⓒ Ⓓ Ⓔ
4. Ⓐ Ⓑ Ⓒ Ⓓ Ⓔ
5. Ⓐ Ⓑ Ⓒ Ⓓ Ⓔ
6. Ⓐ Ⓑ Ⓒ Ⓓ Ⓔ
7. Ⓐ Ⓑ Ⓒ Ⓓ Ⓔ
8. Ⓐ Ⓑ Ⓒ Ⓓ Ⓔ
9. Ⓐ Ⓑ Ⓒ Ⓓ Ⓔ
10. Ⓐ Ⓑ Ⓒ Ⓓ Ⓔ
11. Ⓐ Ⓑ Ⓒ Ⓓ Ⓔ
12. Ⓐ Ⓑ Ⓒ Ⓓ Ⓔ

13. Ⓐ Ⓑ Ⓒ Ⓓ Ⓔ
14. Ⓐ Ⓑ Ⓒ Ⓓ Ⓔ
15. Ⓐ Ⓑ Ⓒ Ⓓ Ⓔ
16. Ⓐ Ⓑ Ⓒ Ⓓ Ⓔ
17. Ⓐ Ⓑ Ⓒ Ⓓ Ⓔ
18. Ⓐ Ⓑ Ⓒ Ⓓ Ⓔ
19. Ⓐ Ⓑ Ⓒ Ⓓ Ⓔ
20. Ⓐ Ⓑ Ⓒ Ⓓ Ⓔ
21. Ⓐ Ⓑ Ⓒ Ⓓ Ⓔ
22. Ⓐ Ⓑ Ⓒ Ⓓ Ⓔ
23. Ⓐ Ⓑ Ⓒ Ⓓ Ⓔ
24. Ⓐ Ⓑ Ⓒ Ⓓ Ⓔ

POSTAL EXAM
Test 6
ANSWER SHEET
Following Oral Directions

1. Ⓐ Ⓑ Ⓒ Ⓓ Ⓔ
2. Ⓐ Ⓑ Ⓒ Ⓓ Ⓔ
3. Ⓐ Ⓑ Ⓒ Ⓓ Ⓔ
4. Ⓐ Ⓑ Ⓒ Ⓓ Ⓔ
5. Ⓐ Ⓑ Ⓒ Ⓓ Ⓔ
6. Ⓐ Ⓑ Ⓒ Ⓓ Ⓔ
7. Ⓐ Ⓑ Ⓒ Ⓓ Ⓔ
8. Ⓐ Ⓑ Ⓒ Ⓓ Ⓔ
9. Ⓐ Ⓑ Ⓒ Ⓓ Ⓕ
10. Ⓐ Ⓑ Ⓒ Ⓓ Ⓔ
11. Ⓐ Ⓑ Ⓒ Ⓓ Ⓔ
12. Ⓐ Ⓑ Ⓒ Ⓓ Ⓔ
13. Ⓐ Ⓑ Ⓒ Ⓓ Ⓔ
14. Ⓐ Ⓑ Ⓒ Ⓓ Ⓔ
15. Ⓐ Ⓑ Ⓒ Ⓓ Ⓔ
16. Ⓐ Ⓑ Ⓒ Ⓓ Ⓔ
17. Ⓐ Ⓑ Ⓒ Ⓓ Ⓔ
18. Ⓐ Ⓑ Ⓒ Ⓓ Ⓔ
19. Ⓐ Ⓑ Ⓒ Ⓓ Ⓔ
20. Ⓐ Ⓑ Ⓒ Ⓓ Ⓔ
21. Ⓐ Ⓑ Ⓒ Ⓓ Ⓔ
22. Ⓐ Ⓑ Ⓒ Ⓓ Ⓔ
23. Ⓐ Ⓑ Ⓒ Ⓓ Ⓔ
24. Ⓐ Ⓑ Ⓒ Ⓓ Ⓔ
25. Ⓐ Ⓑ Ⓒ Ⓓ Ⓔ
26. Ⓐ Ⓑ Ⓒ Ⓓ Ⓔ
27. Ⓐ Ⓑ Ⓒ Ⓓ Ⓔ
28. Ⓐ Ⓑ Ⓒ Ⓓ Ⓔ
29. Ⓐ Ⓑ Ⓒ Ⓓ Ⓔ
30. Ⓐ Ⓑ Ⓒ Ⓓ Ⓔ
31. Ⓐ Ⓑ Ⓒ Ⓓ Ⓔ
32. Ⓐ Ⓑ Ⓒ Ⓓ Ⓔ
33. Ⓐ Ⓑ Ⓒ Ⓓ Ⓔ

34. Ⓐ Ⓑ Ⓒ Ⓓ Ⓔ
35. Ⓐ Ⓑ Ⓒ Ⓓ Ⓔ
36. Ⓐ Ⓑ Ⓒ Ⓓ Ⓔ
37. Ⓐ Ⓑ Ⓒ Ⓓ Ⓔ
38. Ⓐ Ⓑ Ⓒ Ⓓ Ⓔ
39. Ⓐ Ⓑ Ⓒ Ⓓ Ⓔ
40. Ⓐ Ⓑ Ⓒ Ⓓ Ⓔ
41. Ⓐ Ⓑ Ⓒ Ⓓ Ⓔ
42. Ⓐ Ⓑ Ⓒ Ⓓ Ⓔ
43. Ⓐ Ⓑ Ⓒ Ⓓ Ⓔ
44. Ⓐ Ⓑ Ⓒ Ⓓ Ⓔ
45. Ⓐ Ⓑ Ⓒ Ⓓ Ⓔ
46. Ⓐ Ⓑ Ⓒ Ⓓ Ⓔ
47. Ⓐ Ⓑ Ⓒ Ⓓ Ⓔ
48. Ⓐ Ⓑ Ⓒ Ⓓ Ⓔ
49. Ⓐ Ⓑ Ⓒ Ⓓ Ⓔ
50. Ⓐ Ⓑ Ⓒ Ⓓ Ⓔ
51. Ⓐ Ⓑ Ⓒ Ⓓ Ⓔ
52. Ⓐ Ⓑ Ⓒ Ⓓ Ⓔ
53. Ⓐ Ⓑ Ⓒ Ⓓ Ⓔ
54. Ⓐ Ⓑ Ⓒ Ⓓ Ⓔ
55. Ⓐ Ⓑ Ⓒ Ⓓ Ⓔ
56. Ⓐ Ⓑ Ⓒ Ⓓ Ⓔ
57. Ⓐ Ⓑ Ⓒ Ⓓ Ⓔ
58. Ⓐ Ⓑ Ⓒ Ⓓ Ⓔ
59. Ⓐ Ⓑ Ⓒ Ⓓ Ⓔ
60. Ⓐ Ⓑ Ⓒ Ⓓ Ⓔ
61. Ⓐ Ⓑ Ⓒ Ⓓ Ⓔ
62. Ⓐ Ⓑ Ⓒ Ⓓ Ⓔ
63. Ⓐ Ⓑ Ⓒ Ⓓ Ⓔ
64. Ⓐ Ⓑ Ⓒ Ⓓ Ⓔ
65. Ⓐ Ⓑ Ⓒ Ⓓ Ⓔ
66. Ⓐ Ⓑ Ⓒ Ⓓ Ⓔ

67. Ⓐ Ⓑ Ⓒ Ⓓ Ⓔ
68. Ⓐ Ⓑ Ⓒ Ⓓ Ⓔ
69. Ⓐ Ⓑ Ⓒ Ⓓ Ⓔ
70. Ⓐ Ⓑ Ⓒ Ⓓ Ⓔ
71. Ⓐ Ⓑ Ⓒ Ⓓ Ⓔ
72. Ⓐ Ⓑ Ⓒ Ⓓ Ⓔ
73. Ⓐ Ⓑ Ⓒ Ⓓ Ⓔ
74. Ⓐ Ⓑ Ⓒ Ⓓ Ⓔ
75. Ⓐ Ⓑ Ⓒ Ⓓ Ⓔ
76. Ⓐ Ⓑ Ⓒ Ⓓ Ⓔ
77. Ⓐ Ⓑ Ⓒ Ⓓ Ⓔ
78. Ⓐ Ⓑ Ⓒ Ⓓ Ⓔ
79. Ⓐ Ⓑ Ⓒ Ⓓ Ⓔ
80. Ⓐ Ⓑ Ⓒ Ⓓ Ⓔ
81. Ⓐ Ⓑ Ⓒ Ⓓ Ⓔ
82. Ⓐ Ⓑ Ⓒ Ⓓ Ⓔ
83. Ⓐ Ⓑ Ⓒ Ⓓ Ⓔ
84. Ⓐ Ⓑ Ⓒ Ⓓ Ⓔ
85. Ⓐ Ⓑ Ⓒ Ⓓ Ⓔ
86. Ⓐ Ⓑ Ⓒ Ⓓ Ⓔ
87. Ⓐ Ⓑ Ⓒ Ⓓ Ⓔ
88. Ⓐ Ⓑ Ⓒ Ⓓ Ⓔ
89. Ⓐ Ⓑ Ⓒ Ⓓ Ⓔ
90. Ⓐ Ⓑ Ⓒ Ⓓ Ⓔ
91. Ⓐ Ⓑ Ⓒ Ⓓ Ⓔ
92. Ⓐ Ⓑ Ⓒ Ⓓ Ⓔ
93. Ⓐ Ⓑ Ⓒ Ⓓ Ⓔ
94. Ⓐ Ⓑ Ⓒ Ⓓ Ⓔ
95. Ⓐ Ⓑ Ⓒ Ⓓ Ⓔ
96. Ⓐ Ⓑ Ⓒ Ⓓ Ⓔ
97. Ⓐ Ⓑ Ⓒ Ⓓ Ⓔ
98. Ⓐ Ⓑ Ⓒ Ⓓ Ⓔ

REA's Test Preps
The Best in Test Preparation

- REA "Test Preps" are **far more** comprehensive than any other test preparation series
- Each book contains up to **eight** full-length practice tests based on the most recent exams
- **Every** type of question likely to be given on the exams is included
- Answers are accompanied by **full** and **detailed** explanations

REA publishes over 60 Test Preparation volumes in several series. They include:

Advanced Placement Exams (APs)
Biology
Calculus AB & Calculus BC
Chemistry
Computer Science
English Language & Composition
English Literature & Composition
European History
Government & Politics
Physics
Psychology
Spanish Language
Statistics
United States History

College-Level Examination Program (CLEP)
Analyzing and Interpreting Literature
College Algebra
Freshman College Composition
General Examinations
General Examinations Review
History of the United States I
Human Growth and Development
Introductory Sociology
Principles of Marketing
Spanish

SAT II: Subject Tests
Biology E/M
Chemistry
English Language Proficiency Test
French
German
Literature

SAT II: Subject Tests (cont'd)
Mathematics Level IC, IIC
Physics
Spanish
United States History
Writing

Graduate Record Exams (GREs)
Biology
Chemistry
Computer Science
General
Literature in English
Mathematics
Physics
Psychology

ACT - ACT Assessment

ASVAB - Armed Services Vocational Aptitude Battery

CBEST - California Basic Educational Skills Test

CDL - Commercial Driver License Exam

CLAST - College-Level Academic Skills Test

ELM - Entry Level Mathematics

ExCET - Exam for the Certification of Educators in Texas

FE (EIT) - Fundamentals of Engineering Exam

FE Review - Fundamentals of Engineering Review

GED - High School Equivalency Diploma Exam (U.S. & Canadian editions)

GMAT - Graduate Management Admission Test

LSAT - Law School Admission Test

MAT - Miller Analogies Test

MCAT - Medical College Admission Test

MTEL - Massachusetts Tests for Educational Licensure

MSAT - Multiple Subjects Assessment for Teachers

NJ HSPA - New Jersey High School Proficiency Assessment

PLT - Principles of Learning & Teaching Test

PPST - Pre-Professional Skills Tests

PSAT - Preliminary Scholastic Assessment Test

SAT I - Reasoning Test

SAT I - Quick Study & Review

TASP - Texas Academic Skills Program

TOEFL - Test of English as a Foreign Language

TOEIC - Test of English for International Communication

RESEARCH & EDUCATION ASSOCIATION
61 Ethel Road W. • Piscataway, New Jersey 08854
Phone: (732) 819-8880   **website: www.rea.com**

Please send me more information about your Test Prep books

Name _____

Address _____

City _____ State _____ Zip _____

REA's Test Prep Books Are The Best!

(a sample of the <u>hundreds of letters</u> REA receives each year)

" I am writing to congratulate you on preparing an exceptional study guide. In five years of teaching this course I have never encountered a more thorough, comprehensive, concise and realistic preparation for this examination. "
Teacher, Davie, FL

" I have found your publications, *The Best Test Preparation...* to be exactly that. "
Teacher, Aptos, CA

" I am writing to thank you for your test preparation... your book helped me immeasurably and I have nothing but praise for your GRE preparation."
Student, Benton Harbor, MI

" Your GMAT book greatly helped me on the test. Thank you. "
Student, Oxford, OH

" I recently got the French SAT II Exam book from REA. I congratulate you on first-rate French practice tests."
Instructor, Los Angeles, CA

" The REA LSAT Test Preparation guide is a winner! "
Instructor, Spartanburg, SC

" This book is great. Most of my friends that used the REA AP book and took the exam received 4's or 5's (mostly 5's which is the highest score!!) "
Student, San Jose, CA

(more on front page)